# THE MOWBRAY LEGACY

*The story of one of England's great medieval families.*
*With genealogical tables of famous descendants including Anne Boleyn,*
*Elizabeth I, Sir Winston Churchill, Diana, Princess of Wales, Audrey Hepburn,*
*George Washington, Thomas Jefferson and George W. Bush.*

## MARILYN ROBERTS

Queens-Haven

First published in the United Kingdom
by Queens-Haven Publications
44 Scotter Road
Scunthorpe
North Lincolnshire
DN15 8DR

First published in the United Kingdom
by Queens-Haven Publications
www.queens-haven.co.uk

ISBN 1-904706-11-8

Marilyn Roberts was born in North Lincolnshire and has lived there for the greater part of her life. She was educated at Didsbury College, Manchester, and the University of Hull, from where she was awarded a master's degree in the History and Politics of the Administration of Education in England and Wales.

By the same author:
*The Bare Bones of English History – The Romans to Elizabeth I*
*The Bare Bones of British Royal Family Trees*
*The High and Excellent Princess*
*Trouble in Paradise*
*The Bare Bones of Queen Victoria's Family Tree*

Typeset & Printed by
Fisk Printers
Gemini House, Lee Smith Street
Hull, HU9 4TL

*Dedicated to the people of the
Isle of Axholme, past, present and future*

*And yet time hath his revolution; there must be a period and an end*
*of all temporal things…*
*An end of names and dignities...*
*For where is Bohun? where is Mowbray? where is Mortimer?*
*Nay, which is more and most of all, where is Plantagenet?*
*They are entombed in the arms and sepulchres of mortality.*

Sir Ranulphe Crewe, Judge at the Oxford Peerage Case of 1626

# CONTENTS

# Maps and Charts

## Maps

## Charts

# Author's Introduction

LITTLE COULD I HAVE FORESEEN that a chance conversation about one of England's great medieval families would set me on a course that would reveal local connections with great British leaders, American Presidents and a sprinkling of Hollywood's greatest-ever stars, as well as our present Queen, two wives of Henry VIII, and a host of other famous people. Nor could I have anticipated stumbling upon Pocahontas, the Princes in the Tower, an early American pirate, Diana, Princess of Wales or the Duchess from *Alice in Wonderland* during my subsequent three years of wandering, sometimes aimlessly it seemed, through mountains of books, papers and old documents.

In that conversation, the then Curator at Epworth Old Rectory, once the home of John and Charles Wesley, told me he was interested in finding out more about the Mowbray family, who for centuries had controlled the whole of the low-lying area of Lincolnshire known as the Isle of Axholme, and was fascinated by a floor tile bearing a lion rampant design excavated from where their medieval mansion had once stood close to St Andrew's Church. He knew that a William de Mowbray had been a signatory to Magna Carta in 1215, and that one of the Princes in the Tower was involved somewhere in the family's history. I knew that in the dim and very distant past a certain Lady Mowbray had lost her hood when out riding in the area and that the fun and games associated with its retrieval by local villagers is re-enacted annually on 6th January. That was just about the sum total of our knowledge, except that I remembered a certain John de Mowbray, Lord of Axholme, had appeared in the family tree of Henry VIII's second wife, Anne Boleyn, which I had just finished researching for a book.

When compiling that *Bare Bones of British Royal Family Trees* I had also worked out as a sideline for the interest of American readers, some of the more straightforward lines of Presidents Franklin Delano Roosevelt, George Bush and George W. Bush, whose common ancestors included a certain Elizabeth Fitzalan and her third husband, Sir Robert Goushill. It was only when I was looking through papers at home a few days after the Mowbray conversation that I realised this same Elizabeth's second husband had been Thomas Mowbray, 1st Duke of Norfolk.

The fact that a Mowbray widow, who must surely have had some sort of connections with Epworth, was a forebear of three United States Presidents, albeit by a later husband, created a lot of local interest, but I still wished for a 'proper' link to the true blood of the great Mowbray family that had dominated our part of Lincolnshire for so long, and happily it was not long in coming to light. Elizabeth Fitzalan and Thomas Mowbray were the forebears of the Howard Dukes of Norfolk through their daughter Margaret, and once I knew that, then the Mowbray links to presidents, politicians and film stars started to reveal themselves. Likewise, once I had worked out the Mowbray ancestry from King Edward I to the 1st Duke of Norfolk, other noble names and connections soon emerged.

This book is not attempting to present itself as a definitive or academic account. Its aim is to act as a resource for the local community by clarifying who the Mowbrays were, what they contributed to the nation as a whole and what their position was in that part of Lincolnshire known as the Isle of Axholme, and for this reason I have decided not to swamp the pages with footnotes and references; major sources can be found in the bibliography. Compiling this information, and in particular the family trees, has been rather like putting together several small jigsaw puzzles from pieces that also fit into hundreds of others, a task made more confusing by the fact that it was common practice for families to use the same forenames for generation upon generation. It has been rather like having many pieces of puzzle apparently all identical, but in reality all quite different. The task became easier when certain seemingly ordinary surnames such as Randolph, Ludlow and Welles had established themselves in the memory, because if one spots these, then a Mowbray link is probably just a few generations behind.

Several tangible links with the Mowbrays can still be found in Lincolnshire, Yorkshire, Nottinghamshire, Leicestershire, Norfolk, Suffolk, and other counties in the North and Midlands, as well as in the South and in Wales, but there is little remaining to show what members of the early family might have looked like. Most were buried in monasteries and abbeys and their tomb effigies were lost with the Dissolution of the Monasteries or in the Civil War. John, 3rd Lord Mowbray, who succumbed to the plague in 1361, was celebrated in his own lifetime for his chivalrous conduct and concern for his tenants, and is still remembered in the Isle of Axholme for concessions he made to ease the burden of their harsh existence – but what was he like in appearance? Sadly we shall probably never know, although there is a likeness of his mother in Swansea Museum.

Of the more recent Mowbray descendants the name Edda Kathleen van Heemstra Hepburn-Ruston may conjure-up an image of a well-upholstered elderly European dowager, when, in fact, she was the delicately beautiful Hollywood star better known to the world as Audrey Hepburn. For the most part though, using our imagination will have to be the order of the day. Try to picture the hairy and haughty Norman baron Robert de Mowbray in chains before the walls of Bamburgh Castle on the brink of having his eyes put out, or the dreadful plight of eleven-year-old John locked in the Tower of London with his terrified mother, the Lady Alina, after his father was hanged at York.

Give a thought to the little Lady Anne Mowbray taking her wedding vows as a five-year-old bride at the Palace of Westminster, with her four-year-old royal bridegroom beside her. And never forget the indomitable Katherine Neville, the Mowbray dowager who resided at Epworth and married a twenty-year-old as her fourth husband when she was nearly seventy!

I have tried to place the Mowbrays and their contemporaries in the context of national events and situations, hoping that this will breathe a little life into them and bring them closer to the reader than would mere lists of prominent nobles who were born, entered into arranged marriages, had children and died, and for this reason each chapter is comprised of a general background to the times followed by details of the lives of the heads of the family up to 1481. Like many a prominent northern family, some of them also had lands in Scotland, but the Scottish branch is not dealt with in this book.

Every care has been taken to ensure that the information within these pages is correct, but there will be errors, for which I apologise; this is inevitable when dealing with the lives of people so far removed from us and from times before official records of births, marriages and deaths were kept. Research on the family is continuing and I expect there to be revisions from time to time. I recently heard a speaker on a medieval subject begin by saying that historical evidence for this period can be vague, incomplete and frequently contradictory, and this has certainly proved to be the case with the Mowbrays.

As always, my researches have taken me to places in this lovely country of ours that I had no idea existed and have brought me into contact with some wonderfully friendly, interesting and helpful people whom it has been my great privilege to meet, and whom I cannot thank enough for their contributions, encouragement and support.


Marilyn Roberts
29th May 2004
Revised February 2012

*A note on family names*

MOWBRAY

The Norman family name Montbrai gradually evolved into Mowbray but was also written Montbray, Molbray, Moubray, Mobray and Mowberry in the past. By the end of the fourteenth century it was increasingly 'Mowbray' rather than 'de Mowbray', the French *de* originally simply meaning *of*: for example, Geoffrey of Montbrai.

D'AUBIGNY

This is the correct original spelling of the name of the family who assumed the Mowbray name in 1129, but some of the medieval chroniclers introduced the Latinised spelling, De Albini or d'Albini. Over the centuries it evolved into Daubeney, Daubney, Dabeney and Dabney. D'Albini (or De Albini) was the form used by the d'Aubigny earls of Arundel.

*Terms relating to status*

SIR AND DAME

Many of the people mentioned in the text and Tables were knights and their wives and these titles have been omitted. Among the few exceptions are Sir Robert Goushill and Sir Robert Howard, both of whose wives, being daughters of higher nobility, bore the title 'lady' in their own right. The husbands' titles are retained here as a reminder that they were the social inferiors of their wives who, presumably, had married for love.

BARON

The term 'baron' as in King John and the Magna Carta Barons, was not a title originally but referred to any man who held his land directly from the King, that is, he was on the top rung of the land sub-letting ladder which was the feudal system, a tenant-in chief who then sub-let the land to others. In time there became a natural division into Greater and Lesser Barons as some became more powerful than others; it was the former who were summoned by letter, or Writ, to the first Parliaments established in the reign of Edward I, and addressed as Lords, but the word 'baron' itself was not used as a title until the 14th century. Thus, Roger de Mowbray, the first Lord Mowbray, summoned to Parliament in 1295, was of the lowest rank of the peerage, and in status higher than a knight, but lower than an earl.

Today the peerage is in five ranks: duke, marquess, earl, viscount and baron. As acting premier Baron of England, the grandfather of the present Lord Mowbray, Segrave and Stourton (see Chapter VIII) represented his rank of the peerage at the 1953 coronation when he did homage to Queen Elizabeth II on their behalf. The word 'baron' should not be confused with 'baronet', a rank higher than knight but not included in the peerage dignities; these were originally created by James I after 1611, largely as a way of making money by selling titles, and baronets do not sit in the House of Lords.

DOWAGER DUCHESSES

Although not the conventional forms of address, the redoubtable Mowbray dowagers have been styled as follows for ease of understanding: Elizabeth Fitzalan, Duchess Katherine (Neville), Duchess Eleanor (Bourchier), Duchess Elizabeth (Talbot).

*A note about dates*

Both 'Middle Ages' and 'late medieval' are used in the text, the Middle Ages being the period from 1000 AD to the mid 15th century, and the medieval period in its entirety from the 5th –15th century. 1752 was the first year in England to begin on 1st January and end on 31st December. When researching the period covered in this book it was common to find dates written thus: *John 2nd Lord Mowbray was executed on 23rd March 1321/2*, this is because, until changes were made from the Julian to the Gregorian calendar in 1752, the old year ended on 24th March and the new began on the 25th. Therefore, if we look at the date using the modern interpretation we would say that John was executed on 23rd March 1322, whereas in his time the year 1322 would not begin for another two days; the 'modern' usage has been employed throughout the text and Tables.

   The years between 1066 and 1481 are the main focus of this book, that is, from the time the first Mowbray, Geoffrey of Coutances, settled in England to the death of Anne Mowbray, daughter of the fourth, and last, Mowbray Duke of Norfolk. Therefore, the genealogical tables of the American Presidents are rather sparse in details and dates of some of the more recent generations, but further information is readily available from the Society of American Genealogists, the records and publications of the Church of Jesus Christ of Latter Day Saints (LDS) and the New England Historical and Genealogical Register (NEHGR) amongst others.

*For abbreviations used on the tables see Table II.*

# ACKNOWLEDGEMENTS

*Grateful thanks are due to the following:*

Helen and Arthur Beaumont of Epworth, for the enormous amount of help they have given me in and around the Isle of Axholme.

Matthew Blackbourn of the Royal Armouries, Leeds, for information on medieval warfare and on the Mowbray family.

Stan Boor, former Lord of the Haxey Hood, for information about the Haxey Hood game and on Haxey Church.

Adam Brace of York Minster Library.

Jennifer Carr, who has encouraged my endeavours for so many years.

Steven Catherall, Head of Visitor Services, Westminster Abbey, for making arrangements for me to see Anne Mowbray's final resting place.

John Clark, Curator of Medieval History at the Museum of London.

John Blythe Dobson of Winnipeg, for guiding me to the American genealogy books.

Rev'd Ian M.G. Friars, Rector, Long Melford Church, Suffolk, for permission to photograph the stained glass window depicting Elizabeth Talbot and Elizabeth Tilney.

Joanne Griffith, custodian, Mount Grace Priory.

Pauline Harvey of Epworth, for information on the Mowbray tiles.

The Lord of the Haxey Hood (Philip Coggan) and his team for 2003.

Robert Helmerichs, for information leading to articles on Geoffrey of Coutances.

Professor Richard Holmes of Cranfield University (Royal Military College of Science), for help in locating information on the Battle of Neville's Cross.

Christine Hopwood of the Friends of York Minster, for her kind hospitality and help with the York connections.

Stanley Johnson of Epworth, for the pedigree of H.M. Queen Elizabeth the Queen Mother.

Chris Keating, for his invaluable computer skills.

Cath Maloney of the Museum of London's Archaeological Archive and Research Centre (LAARC).

Staff at the Mechanics' Institute Library in Epworth.

The late Andrew Milson, formerly Curator of the Old Rectory in Epworth, for introducing me to the subject of the Mowbray family.

The late Miss Elizabeth J. Nall of Hoveringham, for her information on the Goushill tomb.

Staff at North Lincolnshire Libraries.

Stephen O'Connor of the National Archive (formerly Public Record Office), for his attempts to locate the Mowbray Deed.

Derek Palgrave of the Palgrave Society, for information on the pirate

Palgrave Williams.
Sara Rodger, Assistant Librarian to the Duke of Norfolk, Arundel Castle.
Dr. Mike Rogers of Lincolnshire Archives, for locating and translating the Thomas Mowbray document of 1392, and to the Archives for permission to reproduce the document here.
St Mary's Church, Warwick, for permission to photograph the Beauchamp tomb.
Tony Scupham-Bilton, for most of the Molesworth/De Havilland family links.
Gordon Simpson of *Gordon Video Services*, Scunthorpe.
Staff of The Society of Genealogists, London.
Wendy Sterry for assistance with the Norfolk connections.
The City and County of Swansea for the photograph of Alina de Mowbray.
Ron Thornton of Owston Ferry, for access to the Carthusian Monastery at Low Melwood.
Tower of London – former assistant curator Jeremy Ashbee, now of English Heritage.
Eileen Wallace, Castle Secretary, Arundel.
Leigh Wetherall Dickson of the Churches' Conservation Trust, for information on the Mowbray stained glass in the Holy Trinity Church in York and for permission to photograph the same.
Thanks also to the staff at the York City Archives, the Borthwick Institute in York and the North Yorkshire Archives at Northallerton for making searches of their indexes, and to William Hodges of the Bodleian Library, Oxford, who tried to locate the original information on Lady Anne Mowbray's wedding.

# Picture Credits

Mr. Stan Boor: 63
Durham County Council: 71
Harrogate International Centre: 48
Lincolnshire Archives: 145
Society of Genealogists, London: 210, 212
City & County of Swansea: 60

Photographs by Marilyn Roberts with kind permission of:
Churches Conservation Trust: 36
Rev'd Ian M.G. Friars, Long Melford Church, Suffolk: cover, 112, 127, 142
Hampshire County Council: 58
St. Mary's Church, Warwick: 101, 114, 118-22, 128
Mr. Ron Thornton: 79

Marilyn Roberts: back cover: 15, 24, 30, 33, 35, 39, 45, 59, 62, 66, 68, 80, 91, 93, 104, 153, 154

# FOREWORD

I first met Marilyn Roberts when I was Curator at Epworth Old Rectory, and during one of her visits there showed her a copy of the Sarum Magna Carta, which was on display. I was aware that the Mowbray family had at one time lived on the land at the rear of the Old Rectory – we had an ancient floor tile bearing the Mowbray lion on display in one of the rooms – and I was also aware that there was a connection between the Mowbrays and Magna Carta.

This was the start of Marilyn's extraordinary and enthusiastic research into the Mowbray family, which has resulted in the publication of this magnificent book. She has travelled many miles and spent endless hours researching and confirming the information and I am amazed at her stamina and tenacity that have at last paid off with the revelation of hitherto little-known facts, including references to royalty, and important American connections.

The Mowbrays, who had control of the Isle of Axholme for nearly four hundred years, have proved to be one of the most notable and interesting families in the history of this country and I strongly recommend this book, which will, I believe, add considerably to the fund of local knowledge.

Andrew Milson
Former Curator of the Old Rectory, Epworth
May 2004

| | |
|---|---|
| | **THE NORMANS 1066-1154:** |
| 1066 | Death of Edward the Confessor; Harold Godwinsson becomes King Harold.<br>**Geoffrey de Montbrai (Mowbray), Bishop of Coutances, accompanies William Duke of Normandy and his invasion fleet to England.**<br>October 14th, Normans victorious at Hastings.<br>The bishop's nephew **20-year-old Robert de Mowbray is thought also to have been on the battlefield.**<br>**Geoffrey de Mowbray is a prominent figure at William's coronation on Christmas Day.** |
| 1067- | The Saxons' revolt put down and their lands given to the Normans.<br>The feudal system is soon introduced. |
| 1069 | **Bishop Geoffrey involved in quashing Saxon rebellion in the West Country.** |
| 1070 | The Church brought into the feudal system<br>The 'Harrying of the North'; lands north of the Humber laid to waste. |
| 1074 | **Geoffrey de Mowbray and Bishop Odo of Bayeux cruelly suppress rebellion of the earls of Hereford and Norfolk.** |
| 1086 | The Domesday Book compiled. **Bishop Geoffrey de Mowbray is one of the ten richest men in the kingdom.** |
| 1087 | The White Tower of London completed.<br>Death of William the Conqueror. **Geoffrey de Mowbray is present at the funeral in Caen.**<br>William II (Rufus) becomes king. |
| 1080's | **Geoffrey de Mowbray and his nephew Robert, Earl of Northumberland join the rebellion against Rufus.** |
| 1093 | **Death of Geoffrey de Mowbray in Coutances.**<br>King Malcolm of Scotland and his son killed at Alnwick. **Robert de Mowbray buries them at Tynemouth Priory, which lies within the precincts of his castle.** |
| 1095 | **Imprisonment of Robert de Mowbray, for rebellion; he will die in prison 34 years later.** |
| 1100 | Murder of William Rufus in the New Forest. Henry I, William's younger brother, becomes king.<br>Advancement of the d'Aubigny (d'Albini) family under Henry I |
| 1129 | **Death of Robert de Mowbray.**<br>**Henry I decrees that Roger d'Aubigny, younger son of Nigel (Nele) d'Aubigny, change his name to Mowbray** |
| 1135 | Death of Henry I.<br>Beginning of the civil war between the cousins Stephen and Matilda; **Roger de Mowbray supports Stephen.** |
| 1154 | Death of King Stephen. |
| | **THE PLANTAGENETS 1154 – 1399:**<br>(Sometimes called the *Angevins*, meaning 'Men of Anjou') |
| 1154 | Henry II, son of Matilda, begins to restore order after the chaotic reign of Stephen. |
| 1166 | England's first involvement in Ireland. |

| | |
|---|---|
| 1167 | Oxford University founded. |
| 1170 | Murder of Thomas Becket, Archbishop of Canterbury. |
| 1173 | Becket canonised<br>**Roger de Mowbray rebels against Henry II** so his castles at Thirsk and Kirby Malzeard in Yorkshire, and Kinard Ferry (Owston Ferry) in Lincolnshire are destroyed. |
| 1188 | **Death of Roger de Mowbray in Tyre, on crusade; succeeded by his son Nigel.** |
| 1189 | Death of Henry II.<br>Accession of Richard I.<br>Extensive money-raising to finance the Crusades.<br>Persecution of Jews begins. |
| 1191 | **Death of Nigel de Mowbray in Acre; succeeded by his son, William.** |
| 1199 | Death of Richard I<br>John becomes king. |
| 1204 | Most of the French territories lost by now. |
| 1209 | Cambridge University founded. |
| 1215 | Protracted disputes between King John and the barons results in the **Magna Carta; William de Mowbray is one of the twenty-five leading barons** charged with overseeing its implementation |
| 1216 | Death of King John.<br>Accession of Henry III, aged 9. |
| 1223 | **Birth of Roger de Mowbray, younger son of William.** |
| 1224 | **Death of William de Mowbray; succeeded by his elder son, Nigel.** |
| 1230 | **Death of Nigel de Mowbray without issue; succeeded by his brother, Roger** |
| 1258 | Barons' rebellion against Henry III led by Simon de Montfort. |
| 1264 | Civil war; Battle of Lewes. |
| 1265 | De Montfort's famous Parliament called. De Montfort killed at the Battle of Evesham. |
| 1266 | **Death of Roger de Mowbray; succeeded by his son, also named Roger.** |
| 1272 | Death of Henry III.<br>Accession of Edward I. |
| 1277- | The conquest of Wales by Edward I; followed by construction of massive border castles. |
| 1286 | **Birth of John de Mowbray, son of Roger.** |
| 1290 | A new persecution of Jews begins. |
| 1295 | The Model Parliament of Edward I; the first real attempt at democracy.<br>**Roger de Mowbray is one of the first to be summoned to Parliament by letter and is created Baron by Writ (24th June 1295); becomes 1st Lord Mowbray.** |
| 1296 | In Scotland Robert Bruce is defeated by the English. |

| | |
|---|---|
| 1297 | Roger, 1$^{st}$ Lord Mowbray, dies in Ghent; succeeded by his son John, 2$^{nd}$ Lord Mowbray. |
| 1305 | William Wallace executed for leading the Scots in rebellion against English rule. |
| 1307 | Death of Edward I.<br>Accession of Edward II. Immediate clashes with the nobility because of his relationship with Piers Gaveston, Earl of Cornwall. |
| 1310 | Birth of John de Mowbray; later 3$^{rd}$ Lord Mowbray. |
| 1312 | Murder of Piers Gaveston, the King's favourite. |
| 1314 | The forces of Edward II defeated by Robert Bruce at Bannockburn. |
| 1322 | John, 2$^{nd}$ Lord Mowbray hanged at York for rebellion against Edward II; his wife and 11-year-old son are confined to the Tower. |
| 1327 | Queen Isabella and her lover Roger Mortimer depose Edward II.<br>Mortimer and Isabella rule in the name of her 14-year-old son, Edward III.<br>The Mowbrays are released from the Tower. John is contracted to marry Joan Plantagenet, a great-granddaughter of Henry III.<br>Murder of Edward II at Berkeley Castle. |
| 1330 | Edward III, aged eighteen, takes power; Mortimer hanged at Tyburn. |
| 1333 | The first House of Commons. |
| 1337 | Beginning of the Hundred Years' War with France because Edward III claims the French throne through right of his mother Isabella. |
| 1340 | Birth of John, later 4$^{th}$ Lord Mowbray. |
| 1346 | Battle of Crécy.<br>John, 3$^{rd}$ Lord Mowbray distinguishes himself at the Battle of Neville's Cross |
| 1349 | The Black Death kills more than a third of the population of England, including Joan Plantagenet, Lady Mowbray. |
| 1356 | Battle of Poitiers. |
| 1359 | John de Mowbray, 3$^{rd}$ Lord Mowbray, now styling himself Lord of Axholme and Bramber, gives the Mowbray Deed to his tenants in the Isle of Axholme, Lincolnshire. |
| 1361 | Black Death epidemic.<br>John, 3$^{rd}$ Lord Mowbray is a victim of the plague and dies in York. Succeeded by his son John, 4$^{th}$ Lord Mowbray. |
| 1361? | Birth of John de Mowbray, later Earl of Nottingham, son of John, 4$^{th}$ Lord Mowbray and Elizabeth Segrave; Elizabeth is a great-granddaughter of King Edward I. |
| 1366 | Birth of Thomas de Mowbray, later Earl of Nottingham and 1$^{st}$ Duke of Norfolk. |
| 1368 | Death of Elizabeth Segrave, Lady Mowbray.<br>John, 4$^{th}$ Lord Mowbray killed near Constantinople. Succeeded by his young son, also John. |
| 1369 | Black Death strikes again. |
| 1376 | Sir Peter de la Mare is the first Speaker of the Commons.<br>Death of the Black Prince, son and heir of Edward III. |

| | |
|---|---|
| 1377 | Death of Edward III.<br>Accession of 10-year-old Richard II, son of the Black Prince.<br>**John de Mowbray is created Earl of Nottingham.** |
| 1381 | Fourteen-year-old Richard II faces the mob during the Peasants' Revolt against the poll-tax. |
| 1383 | **Death of John de Mowbray, Earl of Nottingham; succeeded by his brother Thomas (de) Mowbray, who becomes Earl of Nottingham.** |
| 1384 | **Thomas Mowbray marries Elizabeth Fitzalan**, daughter of Richard Fitzalan, 11th Earl of Arundel. |
| 1385 | **Birth of Thomas Mowbray's son, also named Thomas, later Earl of Nottingham.** |
| 1388 | **King Richard's supporters and friends impeached, banished or executed at the instigation of the Lords Appellant, who include Thomas Mowbray and his father-in-law and also Richard's cousin, Henry Bolingbroke, son of John of Gaunt.**<br>**Mowbray is apparently forgiven and appears to be rising in the King's favour.** |
| 1392? | **Birth of a second son, John, to Thomas Mowbray and Elizabeth Fitzalan, in Calais.** |
| 1397 | **Mowbray betrays his father-in-law, who is beheaded for treason, and is rewarded with the dukedom of Norfolk.**<br>**Mowbray implicated in the murder of the Duke of Gloucester, but goes unpunished.**<br>**Henry Bolingbroke reveals that Thomas Mowbray does not trust the King.** |
| 1398 | **Mowbray and Bolingbroke banished from the realm; he leaves behind his wife Elizabeth Fitzalan, sons Thomas, who keeps his title Earl of Nottingham, and John and daughters Isabel, Margaret and Elizabeth Mowbray.** |
| 1399 | Richard II deposed by his cousin Henry Bolingbroke.<br>**Thomas Mowbray, Duke of Norfolk, dies of the plague in Venice.** |
| | **THE HOUSES OF LANCASTER AND YORK 1399 – 1485** |
| 1399 | Henry Bolingbroke becomes King Henry IV.<br>**The young Earl of Nottingham is taken into the household of the King's mother-in-law.** |
| 1400 | King Richard dies a prisoner in Pontefract Castle, possibly starved to death. |
| 1401 | **Elizabeth Fitzalan, widow of the Duke of Norfolk, marries Sir Robert Goushill. Two daughters, Joan and Elizabeth, are born in quick succession.**<br>A priest burned at the stake, under new heresy laws, for preaching Lollard doctrines. The Lollards are followers of Wycliffe and question the teachings of the Roman Catholic Church. |
| 1403 | **Sir Robert Goushill killed at the Battle of Shrewsbury.**<br>First Percy (Earl of Northumberland) Rebellion. |
| 1404 | **Thomas Mowbray, dissatisfied that his late father's dukedom of Norfolk has not been restored to him, becomes involved with the Percy family in the Second Rebellion against Henry IV.** |
| 1405 | **Thomas Mowbray, still only 19, is beheaded with the Archbishop of York; succeeded by his brother John.** |
| 1408 | Third Percy rebellion; Northumberland killed. |
| 1412 | **John Mowbray marries Katherine Neville,** daughter of the Earl of Westmorland. |
| 1413 | Death of Henry IV. Accession of Henry V. Hundred Years' War resumed. |

| | |
|---|---|
| 1415 | **John Mowbray passes judgement at the trial of Richard Earl of Cambridge.** <br> **Battle of Agincourt; Mowbray, suffering from dysentery, is not at the battle.** <br> **Birth of a son, John, to John Mowbray and Katherine Neville.** |
| 1422 | Death of Henry V. <br> **John Mowbray, Earl of Nottingham, is one of the guardians of the late King's ten-month-old son, Henry VI.** |
| 1425 | **The dukedom of Norfolk is restored to the Mowbrays.** <br> **Death of Elizabeth Fitzalan, Dowager Duchess (Countess) of Norfolk.** |
| 1428 | **John Mowbray, 2$^{nd}$ Duke of Norfolk, nearly drowned in the Thames when his barge** <br> **is in collision with London Bridge.** |
| 1430 | Joan of Arc burnt at the stake by the English. |
| ? | Katherine de Valois, widow of Henry V, gives birth to her first child by his former squire, Owen Tudor |
| 1432 | **Death of John 2$^{nd}$ Duke of Norfolk at Epworth; succeeded by his son John, 3$^{rd}$ Duke of Norfolk.** |
| 1437 | Queen Katherine de Valois and Owen Tudor forced to part; he is imprisoned but escapes, and she dies within the year. |
| 1444 | **Birth of John Mowbray, later 4$^{th}$ Duke of Norfolk.** |
| 1445 | Henry VI marries Margaret of Anjou. |
| 1452 | King Henry takes a kindly interest in his Tudor half-brothers; Edmund is made Earl of Richmond, and Jasper is given the earldom of Pembroke the following year. |
| 1453 | The end of the Hundred Years' War. Only Calais remains in English hands. <br> Richard, Duke of York, appointed Protector of the Realm during Henry's bout of mental illness, tries to curb the power of royal favourites. The King's only child born. |
| 1454 | The King recovers and immediately restores York's enemies to favour . |
| 1455 | **Beginning of the Wars of the Roses. In the early stages the Mowbrays support the Yorkists. The Duke of Norfolk arrives late for the first Battle of St Albans.** <br> **Mowbray is then reconciled to the Lancastrians; he travels Europe in search of a cure for the King's madness.** |
| 1457 | 13-year-old lady Margaret Beaufort, Countess of Richmond, gives birth to Henry Tudor; her husband, Edmund Tudor, has died in Yorkist custody. |
| 1458 | **The Duke of Norfolk and his wife are in the service of Margaret of Anjou.** |
| 1460 | **Mowbray espouses theYorkist cause once more.** <br> Richard of York and one of his sons are killed at the Battle of Wakefield. |
| 1461 | After the second Battle of St Albans the Earl of Warwick, the 'Kingmaker', proclaims York's eighteen-year-old son King Edward IV. <br> Palm Sunday, the Battle of Towton, Yorkshire, the most vicious of the war, over 20,000 killed; **John Mowbray, Duke of Norfolk, arrives late but is instrumental in the Yorkist victory. Throughout this period he is intent on taking Caister Castle from the Paston family** <br> **Mowbray dies in the autumn and is succeeded by his son John, 4$^{th}$ Duke of Norfolk.** |
| 1469 | **The 4$^{th}$ duke takes Caister Castle from Margaret Paston by force.** |

| | |
|---|---|
| 1471 | Warwick the Kingmaker killed at the Battle of Barnet.<br>The Prince of Wales, only child of Henry VI, killed at the Battle of Tewkesbury.<br>**Lancastrians seeking sanctuary in the abbey there are dragged out to face 'trial' before the Duke of Gloucester (later Richard III) and the Duke of Norfolk.** A week later King Henry VI is murdered in the Tower of London. |
| 1472 | **Birth of Lady Anne, only child of John Mowbray, 4th Duke of Norfolk.** |
| 1476 | **Death of the 4th Duke of Norfolk; the end of the male line, so the dukedom becomes extinct. Lady Anne Mowbray becomes Countess of Norfolk.** |
| 1478 | **Anne Mowbray, Countess of Norfolk is married to Prince Richard of York, younger son of Edward IV, who has been created Duke of Norfolk; he is 4 and she is 5 years of age. Lady Anne is now Duchess of York and Norfolk.** |
| 1481 | **Death of Anne Mowbray at Greenwich Palace; she is buried in Westminster Abbey. Acts of Parliament ensure that Prince Richard keeps the Mowbray inheritance.** |
| 1483 | Death of Edward IV. His young sons, Edward V and Prince Richard are brought to London but are declared to be illegitimate, disinherited and then disappear, believed murdered in the Tower on the orders of their uncle the Duke of Gloucester, who then becomes Richard III. **King Richard has great hopes of Lord John Howard, son of Margaret Mowbray and Sir Robert Howard, and makes him Earl Marshal and Duke of Norfolk in a new creation. Howard's cousin William Berkeley, son of Margaret's sister Isabel Mowbray, is a rather less enthusiastic Richard supporter but still becomes Earl of Nottingham. The men share the Mowbray fortune. Eventually the Berkeleys will sell the Isle of Axholme to the Stanley family who are descended from Elizabeth Fitzalan and Sir Robert Goushill.** |
| 1485 | Invasion by the Earl of Richmond (Henry Tudor) who defeats Richard III, killed at Bosworth Field. Henry Tudor becomes King Henry VII.<br>Tudor has been greatly assisted by the fact that **Thomas and William Stanley failed to come to Richard's aid on Bosworth battlefield, even though they had sworn allegiance to him. The Stanley brothers are the sons of Joan Goushill, daughter of Elizabeth Fitzalan and Sir Robert Goushill. Lord Thomas Stanley, being the husband of Lady Margaret Beaufort, is the stepfather of Henry Tudor; in the following decade William will be executed for treason against Henry.**<br>**John Howard, Duke of Norfolk, another grandson of Elizabeth Fitzalan, dies in the early stages of the battle.**<br><br>*Over the following centuries the Howard family has its ups and downs and its fair share of beheadings, but manages to hold on to the dukedom of Norfolk.* |
| 1749 | Winifred Howard marries William, Lord Stourton |
| 1877 | Winifred's descendant **Alfred Joseph Stourton (b. 1829) successfully appeals to the House of Lords for the barony of Mowbray to be brought out of abeyance in his favour.** |
| 1906 | **The then Lord Mowbray, Segrave and Stourton, Charles Joseph Botolph Stourton, fails to convince the House of Lords Committee for Privileges that he has a claim to the earldom of Norfolk.** His petition is vigorously opposed by Henry Fitzalan-Howard, 15th Duke of Norfolk and Earl Marshal, and their Lordships unanimously reject it. |
| 1923 | **Birth of Charles Edward Stourton, Lord Mowbray Segrave and Stourton.** |
| 1953 | **The acting premier baron, William Marmaduke Stourton, Lord Mowbray Segrave and Stourton, as the representative of his rank of the peerage, is called-upon to pay homage to Queen Elizabeth II at her coronation.**<br><br>**Birth of the present Lord Mowbray, Segrave and Stourton, Edward William Stephen Stourton, who succeeded his father in 2006.** |

## Chart 1: *The Mowbray Family 1066-1481*

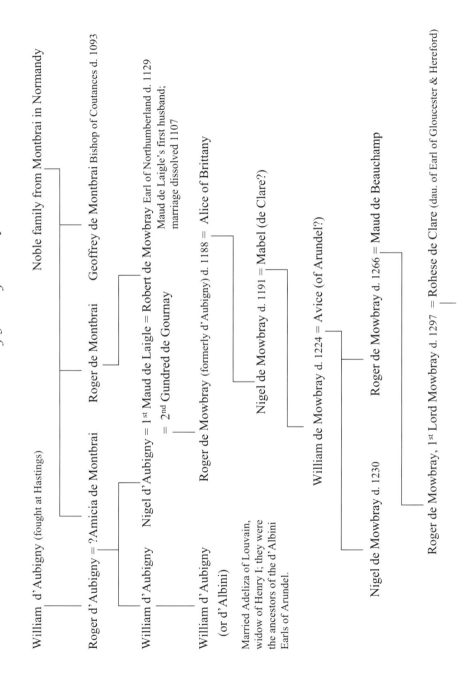

William d'Aubigny (fought at Hastings)    Noble family from Montbrai in Normandy

Roger d'Aubigny = ?Amicia de Montbrai    Roger de Montbrai    Geoffrey de Montbrai Bishop of Coutances d. 1093

William d'Aubigny    Nigel d'Aubigny = 1ˢᵗ Maud de Laigle = Robert de Mowbray Earl of Northumberland d. 1129
                                                                                  Maud de Laigle's first husband;
                                      = 2ⁿᵈ Gundred de Gournay                     marriage dissolved 1107

William d'Aubigny    Roger de Mowbray (formerly d'Aubigny) d. 1188 = Alice of Brittany
(or d'Albini)

Married Adeliza of Louvain,
widow of Henry I; they were        Nigel de Mowbray d. 1191 = Mabel (de Clare?)
the ancestors of the d'Albini
Earls of Arundel.

                          William de Mowbray d. 1224 = Avice (of Arundel?)

Nigel de Mowbray d. 1230    Roger de Mowbray d. 1266 = Maud de Beauchamp

Roger de Mowbray, 1ˢᵗ Lord Mowbray d. 1297 = Rohese de Clare (dau. of Earl of Gloucester & Hereford)

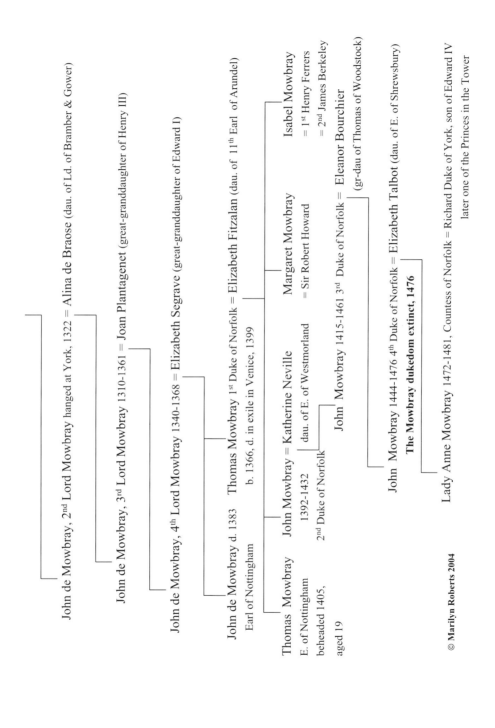

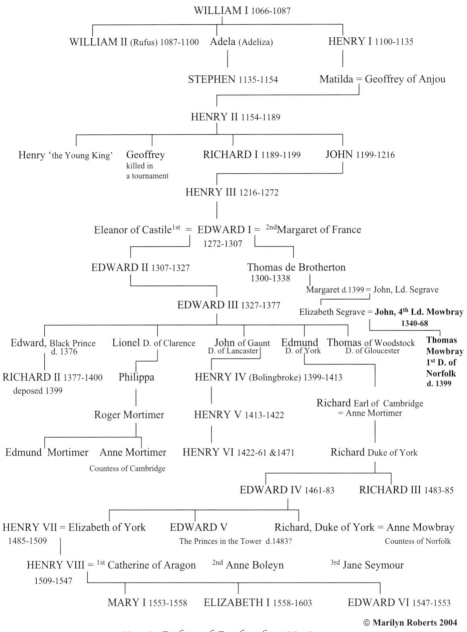

Chart 2: *Rulers of England 1066-1603*

# CHAPTER I

## 1066-1100: THE CONQUEST AND ITS AFTERMATH

*William had much to bestow and was soon surrounded by needy and greedy courtiers.*
Leslie G. Pine *They came With the Conqueror*

ILLIAM, DUKE OF NORMANDY, was a tough and generally uncompromising man, which is hardly surprising, for even in times when treachery and bloodshed were commonplace, he had seen more than his fair share, and from a very young age too.

He was descended from Rollo the Norwegian Viking, a glorified pirate. Charles the Simple, King of France, granted lands to Rollo and his Norsemen in the hope that a place to call their own would put a stop to their marauding activities. They were expected to pay homage for their new land of Normandy but, as was the case in some of the other French duchies and counties, they became a law unto themselves and too strong to be effectively challenged by the King.

William's grandfather, Richard the Good, was the brother of Emma of Normandy, Edward the Confessor's mother. Richard's son, Robert the Devil, took as his mistress Arlette, Fulbert the Tanner's daughter, a local woman of Falaise, whom he is supposed to have first noticed as she washed linen in the river. There would be no marriage for Robert and Arlette, although she lived the life of a great lady, but the Duke recognised William as his son, and upon his father's death the eight-year-old found himself Duke of Normandy. Being a leader in the Middle Ages was a dangerous occupation, but being a leader while still a child was frequently fatal, so as his duchy descended into anarchy, the little boy, whose guardian was murdered before his very eyes, had to learn how to be a survivor, and had to grow up fast. His active military career began at about the age of fourteen, and by the time he was twenty William was a highly experienced statesman and soldier, and although he was nicknamed *the Bastard*, only an incredibly foolhardy man with a death wish would have uttered such words to his face, especially after he had had men mutilated or flayed alive and their skins hung from the walls of their town for daring to cast aspersions on his humble tanner blood.

Edward the Confessor, William's close kinsman, was brought up in his mother Emma's Norman homeland from the time when his father, the rather nasty and politically inept Aethelred the Unready, had lost the kingdom of England to the Danes. Emma was a resourceful woman who not only stayed on in England after her husband's death in exile, but also married his successor Canute, or Knut, of Denmark. Canute was a very competent ruler who saw to it that the conquerors and conquered lived and worked together in peace and mutual respect for the common good, and the country became so stable that he was able to go on pilgrimage and leave his kingdom in the hands of the great Saxon earls, including Godwin, Earl of Wessex, and Leofric of Mercia, husband of the never-to-be-forgotten Lady Godiva. Sadly, Canute's sons had but few of his leadership qualities and his death opened up the power struggles between Hardicanute and his half-brother Harold Harefoot. Matters were further complicated by the return of Alfred, Emma's elder son by Aethelred the Unready, who was brutally murdered, with the connivance of Earl Godwin, before he could make his claim to the throne.

Fortunately for all concerned, Canute's unworthy sons died young, reigning for only six years in total, and in 1042 Emma and Aethelred's second son, Edward, returned from Normandy, where he had spent all his adult years, and was crowned with the backing of the Witan, the Wise Council. Relationships with Godwin were never going to be easy; Edward knew all about his part in the death of his dear brother Alfred, and although he entered into a marriage with the Earl's daughter, his vow of celibacy would rob Godwin of the glory of being the grandfather of a future King. Edward was striking in appearance, tall and pale, a man with an air of otherworldliness about him, but it was his excessive piety that set him apart. Before he was King he had promised the Pope he would make a pilgrimage to Rome, but England was not as stable as it had been in his step-father Canute's time, and he was unable to be absent from his kingdom, even though after his death he was canonised and became the most venerated of all the saints in medieval England. The Pope excused the pilgrimage on condition that Edward build a great abbey in England for St Peter, and this he did, together with a new palace for himself, two miles west of London on Thorney Island, an uninviting area of tangled bramble on slightly higher ground in the Thames marshes. He was too ill in the early days of 1066 to attend the consecration service, but, dying soon afterwards, had the distinction of being the first monarch to be buried in his imposing new West Minster.

In spite of there being several other claimants, William, Duke of Normandy, aged thirty-nine in 1066, fully expected to become King of England when his kinsman the childless Confessor died, so when news arrived that the Witan had not only chosen Harold Godwinsson, son of the late Earl of Wessex, but had already crowned him, William was momentarily lost for words, furious that he had been duped, as he saw it, by the very man who had once sworn an oath on holy relics to be his loyal supporter. William himself was said to have also sworn an oath when he recovered from the initial shock, but not of the sort that could be repeated in polite company. It was not long before preparations for an invasion of England were set in motion, William convincing himself, and the Pope, that it was God's will, and in the autumn of 1066 he named his eldest son, Robert, as his successor should he not return from his expedition.

The Duke of Normandy's invading army landed at Pevensey on the south coast of England towards the end of September. The English put up a magnificent fight when they finally faced them near Hastings on 14th October, but the luck of the House of Godwin had finally run out. King Harold was killed, leaving his subjects at the mercy of William and the band of assorted retainers, opportunists and adventurers who had crossed the water with him in search of wealth and who, in most cases, were not too particular as to how they acquired it. The historian and genealogist Leslie G. Pine, writing in the 1950's, observed.

> *"William had much to bestow and was soon surrounded by needy and greedy courtiers. Every bloodthirsty swashbuckler, every penniless or landless younger son flocked to William at London or Winchester. Every saintly palm-droner between Rome and Coutances who saw his chance to cash in on the forfeiture of English sees and abbeys found his way to England."*

We know the names of just a few of the Conqueror's original companions from the accounts of Norman chroniclers, and amongst these we can see that there were two great bishops, Odo of Bayeux and Geoffrey de Montbrai (Mowbray), Bishop of Coutances. (see Appendix A).

The early years following the Conquest saw rebellion and brutal suppression; there would be no long-term concerted attempt after 1066 to follow the example of King Canute's policy of integration. Nor would the Norman invaders make any distinction in their treatment of the vanquished between the English of Saxon blood and those of Danish extraction, even though the latter, like themselves, were the descendants of Scandinavian Vikings. The stunned natives were mesmerised and terrified as the newcomers swept through their countryside, rapidly constructing Norman-style castles, the like of which they had never seen before, and were astounded at the almost total reallocation of Saxon lands to William's supporters. Technically, according to the workings of the feudal system as he intended to use it, William the Conqueror owned England. Beneath him were about 200 tenants-in-chief, who had been given land in reward for their services and were bound to provide men-at-arms to the King for the defence of the realm. This group then sub-let some of their lands to under-tenants, their knights, who in turn sub-let again.

The tenants-in-chief, holding land directly from the King, we call the 'feudal barons'. At this time the term 'baron' meant no more than a tenant-in-chief of the King and was not an indicator of rank such as the title of 'earl' would be, and the word was not used as such until the late thirteenth and early fourteenth centuries. Eventually, the group would divide naturally into the Greater and Lesser Barons, with many of the former being called to the Councils as advisors to the ruler and then to the first Parliaments at the end of the thirteenth century. These barons would, almost always, be military men and would have been knighted. Knighthood was a military rank and honour independent of land tenure and for the purposes of this book it has been assumed that all the Mowbrays mentioned were trained knights, with the possible exception of the Bishop of Coutances who, nevertheless, was an experienced military man. These 200 barons, who together with their 5,000 or 6,000 knights formed the new aristocracy, had not only the duty to protect the Conquest for their master, but also the incentive to protect the status quo for themselves.

By the time of his death twenty-one years after the conquest, William had achieved two of the goals for which he is best remembered today, namely the building of the great keep of the Tower of London to protect the approach from the Thames, and the compiling of the Domesday Book, the latter achieved by quizzing people about what they owned to the point that they thought such exhaustive questions would be matched only at the Last Judgement, or 'Domesday'. But there was so much more to William the Conqueror than simply working the feudal system for his own ends. His great strength of purpose demanded complete loyalty to the Crown, and the severe punishment of any who stood in the way of his achieving his goals for the ultimate good of the country meant that medieval England would eventually develop into a united nation with more patriotic fervour than either Normandy or any of the other semi-independent French territories probably ever had.

There was also fundamental change in England's social development through the new manners and fashions brought by the invaders; Norman French became the language of the ruling and administrative strata of society and was, with Latin, the language in which the nation recorded its political and legal matters until the late Middle Ages. Good old Anglo-Saxon names such as Ethelbald, Alfred, Eadwig and

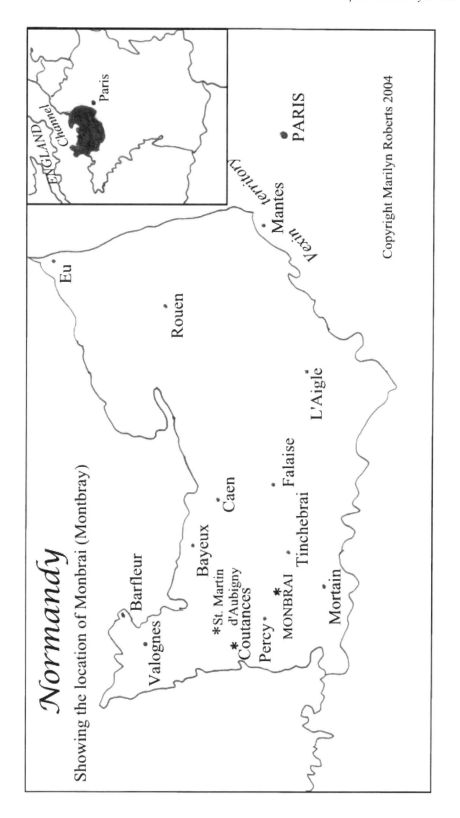

*Normandy*

Showing the location of Monbrai (Montbray)

Copyright Marilyn Roberts 2004

Ealhswith were slowly but surely replaced by the likes of Guillaume (William), Henri, Robert and Mathilde.

The Conqueror's death brought power struggles between his sons Robert, who became Duke of Normandy, and William Rufus, the new King of England, that would continue for their lifetimes and bring a huge downturn in fortunes for some of the original great Anglo-Norman barons, including the earliest Mowbrays. As long as England and Normandy were under the rule of one man, the barons' lands held in both territories were comparatively safe, but suddenly they found themselves torn between the two feuding brothers. Then there was William Rufus himself to consider; the powerful and tough military men had forced themselves to tolerate the constraints that the iron grip of the first William imposed upon their lofty ambitions, but some could not stomach the personality and style of leadership of the second.

*⸱⸱⸱⸱⸱*

*GEOFFREY DE MONTBRAI*, DIED FEBRUARY 1093.
Bishop of Coutances.

Bishop Geoffrey, possibly then in his late thirties, was at the forefront of the subjugation of the English after 1066, which was brutal and, more often than not, unfair. Writing a generation later, the chronicler Orderic Vitalis, himself half Norman, describes the great Bishop thus,

> *"This Geoffrey, being of noble Norman extraction, and more skilful in arms than divinity, did good service at the Battle of Hastings."*

Geoffrey's noble family hailed from Montbrai in Normandy (*Montbray* is a more modern spelling), a village on the Cotentin peninsula some twenty miles southeast of Coutances. In the fullness of time the family name would evolve into *Moubray*, and eventually *Mowbray*, and be proudly borne by one of the greatest houses of medieval England. Geoffrey, a younger son, who could expect little by way of an inheritance, would have entered the Church with a view to making a lucrative career for himself, the done thing in those days, although in his case it was with some reluctance initially. His career was long and eventful and falls roughly into two halves, the first coming before the Conquest, when his main concern was to establish the Christian Church once and for all in an area which was still prone to lapses into heathenism and when he set about building and beautifying his great cathedral at Coutances, where his good friend Duke William was present at the consecration of the nave in 1056. The second, and even more lucrative part of his career, came after 1066, when he was closely involved in the administration and subjugation of England.

At Hastings, Geoffrey de Montbrai and his fellow bishop, the over-mighty Odo of Bayeux, Duke William's half-brother, were called-upon to give benedictions and impose penances. They are thought to have led the other priests who kept watch the night before the battle and to have sung the Mass on the morning of 14th October. Unlike Odo, whose image looms large on the great embroidery commissioned for Bayeux Cathedral, there is no concrete evidence that Geoffrey himself actually bore arms on that fateful day, but both his brother Roger and nephew Robert are believed to have been involved in the fighting, although are not always included on the lists of the 'known' original companions of the Conqueror.

William of Normandy was crowned King of England in Edward the Confessor's brand new West Minster on Christmas Day 1066, and it was Bishop Geoffrey's task to demand of the assembled Normans whether they consented to having the Conqueror for their King. Unfortunately, the English present, who actually had no choice in the matter, and whose positions as men of importance would shortly be denied them, were being asked the same thing at the same time by the Archbishop of Canterbury. The Norman guards outside, hearing their loud responses but not understanding the language, feared some sort of treachery was taking place within, and in their confusion set fire to the surrounding houses. Those inside the Abbey panicked as the smell of burning permeated the church, and upon hearing the desperate cries of the terrified citizens outside, most made an undignified rush for the doors, leaving the bewildered clergy, including Geoffrey de Montbrai in all his finery, and the newly-crowned monarch, to draw the ceremony to a close with as much haste as was decent on so solemn an occasion. The new King himself was said to be trembling with fear, although in the case of this seasoned fighter it was probably with rage at the inconvenience, anger at the thought of the unrest that could result from such an unthinking act on the part of the soldiers, and perhaps the loss of his royal dignity also had something to do with it.

In 1069 Bishop Geoffrey of Coutances was a leader of the men who defeated the rebellious West Saxons of Dorset and Somerset. In 1071, when Bishop Odo was in disgrace for helping himself to much of the property of the see of Canterbury, his half-brother was represented by Geoffrey at the ensuing trial, but by 1074 the two bishops were working together as military leaders engaged in suppressing the rebellion of the Earls of Hereford and Norfolk, and many they took prisoner were slaughtered or punished by having the right foot cut off.

For his efforts on behalf of the Conqueror, Geoffrey de Montbrai was rewarded with over 250 manors spread over a large area. A manor was a piece of landed property with tenants over whom the landlord exercised rights of jurisdiction in a private manor court, and it might consist of one village, several, or only a part of a village. The problem with the feudal system, whereby the King owned everything, was that the ruler could repossess his lands almost as easily as he had allocated them, and a wise tenant throughout the sub-letting chain sought not to displease his landlord. The Domesday Book reveals Geoffrey de Montbrai, one of the Domesday Commissioners for East Anglia, as being one of the top ten wealthiest men in the kingdom. He is recorded as having 265 manors in all in 1086, in Somerset, Devon, Gloucestershire, Wiltshire, Dorset, Northamptonshire, Buckinghamshire, Bedfordshire, Oxfordshire, Huntingdonshire, Leicestershire, Warwickshire, Berkshire and Lincolnshire. Spreading out a man's lands and making it difficult for him to mobilise a large force in secret from amongst his far-flung tenants was a clever move by King William that would save him from a predicament like that of the Kings of France; William, having the luxury of starting with a clean slate, would tolerate no kingdoms-within-kingdoms for England.

In 1087 William was at the end of his tether over French raids into his Norman lands by the captains of the castle at Mantes and sent a message to the King of France demanding they cease; he also took the opportunity to mention that it was about time the Vexin area was restored to him. When William was a boy on the run from his enemies and anarchy ruled in Normandy, the French King had occupied the border areas in the east called the Vexin; the Normans had always maintained that this was part of the lands given to Rollo by Charles the Simple, but there had never been an opportunity to recover the territory. Philip I, although called King of France, actually had control over only a relatively small area and had no intention of letting go of the Vexin. Not only did he scoff at the demands of the Duke of Normandy, but joked in front of his horrified envoys, whose unenviable task it would be to relay the message back to their leader, that William, known to be heeding advice on diet and periodically taking bed rest, was actually 'lying in', a reference to his corpulent figure resembling that of a heavily pregnant woman. Already sensitive about his appearance, this was just too much for the Conqueror, and the punitive expedition began almost at once. At nearly sixty William might have been considered quite old for the times and was rather overweight, but he was still very active and maintained his sharp mind.

Mantes, on Normandy's southern border, a typical town of its times constructed of timber and thatch, was soon ablaze. Nothing was spared, and the inevitable looting had already begun when disaster struck the Conqueror as he rode through the devastation surveying his handiwork, magnificent and terrifying on his warhorse. Neither conquerors nor flames were selective in their victims and churches and abbeys went up in smoke like the rest. A flaming timber falling from the church could have startled the horse or it might have stepped on a burning ember; whatever the cause, the animal reared and William's ample abdomen was hurled against the iron peak of the pommel of the saddle. He was not thrown off but was so badly injured internally that he had to be helped to dismount. He was taken to his castle at Rouen on a litter drawn by slow oxen, but without hope of recovery and in need of peace and quiet, and perhaps in order to atone for his sins, he ended his days at the Priory of St Gervais outside the city walls. Those sins, he believed, were many, and according to the chronicler Orderic Vitalis he was particularly disturbed about his behaviour in England, though we do have to remember that Orderic himself was not a witness to the Conqueror's last days,

*"I have persecuted its native inhabitants beyond all reason. Whether gentle or simple I have cruelly oppressed them; many I unjustly disinherited; innumerable multitudes, especially in the county of York, perished through me by famine or the sword."*

He lived for five weeks, conscious and in terrible pain, but lucid enough to give instructions for the future of England, Normandy and Maine.

William had designated his eldest son Robert his successor as Duke of Normandy on the eve of his departure for England over twenty years earlier. Robert, whom he nicknamed *Curthose* ('short pants') because of his short legs, or perhaps for his preference for wearing brief leggings, was a boy of twelve in 1066, but the years between had made great enemies of the father and son. Robert, impatient for his inheritance, was still in exile as his father's life was coming to its close; nevertheless, William kept his vow. In Normandy it would have been expected that the eldest son follow the father, but this law of primogeniture had not been the norm in England. True enough, the successor was often a son of the late ruler, but the father could only recommend his candidate, it was up to the Witan, that wise council, to have the final say. What would happen after the death of the first Norman ruler of England was by no means certain, especially if he were to die abroad. So William furnished his favourite son, William Rufus, with a written recommendation to the Archbishop of Canterbury, the much respected Lanfranc, who was acting as regent, and the young man set out for England, knowing that his father had very little time left. The youngest son, Henry, who stayed with his dying father, complained of his exclusion from power, whereupon the Conqueror granted him silver to the weight of five thousand pounds from the royal treasury. This prudent young man asked that he might receive it right away and get it safely stowed – he would do something similar at Winchester thirteen years later when his circumstances were very different. His father died peacefully on 9th September 1087.

The Conqueror had built Caen's Abbey Church of St Stephen as a penance because he and his wife were related within the permitted boundaries; now it was the scene of the great man's funeral, with his good friend Bishop Geoffrey de Montbrai in attendance. But no matter how solemn the occasion might have been, the fact remains that after death the King's body had been stripped all but naked, robbed of its finery and left for some time on the bare floor. According to Orderic Vitalis,

> *"... the inferior attendants, observing that their masters had disappeared,* [presumably to secure their castles before the change of power] *laid hands on the arms, the plate, the robes, the linen, and all the royal furniture, and leaving the corpse almost naked on the floor of the house, they hastened away."*

William, however, had his revenge from beyond when his bloated and putrefying corpse would not fit into the too-small sarcophagus, no matter how hard Bishop Geoffrey and the others tried to force it, and in a scene worthy of a Hammer Horror film, inflated with gas and pus and the putrefaction of gangrene, the huge abdomen burst open. As the bespattered clergymen fought to maintain their dignity and composure in the face of such an unusual challenge, the indescribably awful smell sent the mourners scurrying for the doors, a scene reminiscent of the great man's coronation at Westminster Abbey some twenty years earlier.

It is easy to forget that many of the Norman barons busily acquiring huge riches in England viewed it as a second home, their true roots being in Normandy. When William the Conqueror died there was consternation amongst some of them over Normandy and England being under different rule. The division suited the King of France well, but the red-haired and ruddy-complexioned William II, known as *Rufus* ('red'), a blasphemer and possibly an atheist, was a shock for some of the Anglo-Norman barons. His father had been quite a pious man and, a rare specimen amongst kings, was faithful to his wife, the

Chart 3: *The Family of William the Conqueror*
*Duke of Normandy and King of England.*
(Although William's ancestor Rollo was a Norwegian Viking,
he led Danish raiders who settled in northern France)
The Normans ruled England from 1066 - 1154

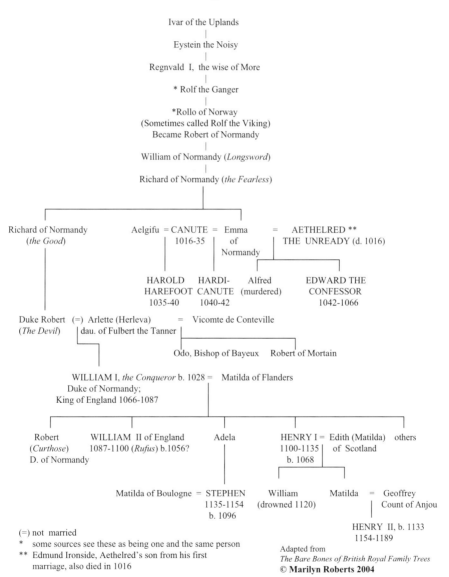

(=) not married
* some sources see these as being one and the same person
** Edmund Ironside, Aethelred's son from his first
marriage, also died in 1016

Adapted from
*The Bare Bones of British Royal Family Trees*
© **Marilyn Roberts 2004**

diminutive Matilda of Flanders, whom he had kicked and beaten when she rejected his first proposal of marriage, but with whom, by the standards of the times, he seems to have made a successful union. Rufus, however, appears to have showed little interest in women, which led to speculative gossip and was a great cause for concern.

Neither Rufus in England nor Curthose in Normandy had quite the qualities of leadership their late father possessed, nor did they have his ability to keep their respective barons in check. The Conqueror had had Bishop Odo, self-styled *Tamer of the English*, under lock and key in Normandy and on his deathbed wondered if he was doing the right thing in releasing him. He was not. Within months Odo and his old partner in terrorising the vanquished, Geoffrey de Montbrai, were campaigning for the unification of England and Normandy under Robert Curthose. It is interesting that Curthose himself sent no aid and could not be bothered to show up, although it could be argued that he had enough troubles to deal with at home. Bishop Geoffrey had a castle in Bristol and set out from there on a mission to cause an uprising against William II, but despite burning Bath and causing destruction and devastation in Wiltshire, the plan failed. The King's supporters wanted to see the two bishops hang, but it would appear that either Rufus was not yet sufficiently confident in his own power to mete out the ultimate punishment, or saw the death penalty as unnecessarily harsh, because the great Geoffrey de Montbrai was to be allowed to live out what remained of his life quietly, and so retired to his French diocese in 1091, not long before his precious cathedral at Coutances was rocked by an earthquake and struck by lightning.

When the gleaming new gilded weathercock on the cathedral tower was struck down it was seen as a portent of Geoffrey's impending death, and indeed, his health did begin to fail shortly afterwards. The dying bishop lived long enough to see the repairs completed and had his bed moved to a position where he could see the weathercock, by then restored to its former glory by a plumber named Brismet, who had been sent over from England especially for the purpose. Barely conscious for the last few days of his life, Geoffrey continually promised blessings upon all who helped his cathedral and curses upon any who harmed it. Five days before he died on 2nd February 1093, a monk had a vision of his being received into Heaven. Despite his disloyalty to his king, Geoffrey's lands and wealth were allowed to pass to his brother Roger's son, Robert de Montbrai (Mowbray). After a fire in 1218, what was left of the foundations, nave and towers of Geoffrey's cathedral was incorporated into the rebuilding.

{Over a period of time the name *de* (of) *Montbrai* evolved into *de Mowbray*, which will be used in the text from this point on. This is the familiar spelling of our own times but the alternative spelling *Moubray* was much in use throughout medieval times.}

### ROBERT DE MOWBRAY, DIED 1129.
Earl of Northumberland.

The north of England was extremely difficult for the Normans to subdue and the Scots were making the most of the instability. The formidable Hastings veteran Robert de Mowbray was made Earl of Northumberland, effectively Governor of the North, in 1080 but the chronicler Simeon of Durham accuses him of governing badly and with great cruelty, while Orderic Vitalis says of him,

> *"Powerful, rich, bold, fierce in war, haughty, he despised his equals, and, swollen with vanity, disdained to obey his superiors. He was of great stature, strong, swarthy and hairy. Daring and crafty, stern and grim of mien, he was more given to meditation than speech, and in conversation scarce ever smiled."*

Hairy and haughty Robert de Mowbray, the grim-faced crafty baron, had frequently been the companion-in-arms of his powerful uncle and had been involved with him in the rebellion against William II, but he too had managed to escape severe punishment. He had a castle at Thirsk in that part of Yorkshire still called the Vale of Mowbray today; the impact of its coming is described by Edmund Hogg in *The Golden Vale of Mowbray* published in 1909,

> *"The condition of the town began to change when the Mowbrays appeared upon the scene towards the close of the eleventh century, and their great stronghold of timber, typical of feudalism, arose to the southwest of the river, and some three hundred paces from the older settlement. Artificially, it was rendered as impregnable as its low situation would permit, this being strikingly evident from the depth of the moat and height of the banks. New Thirsk owes its existence to the Norman Castle. During its erection a throng of craftsmen would congregate, merchants naturally anxious to create a trade were attracted hither, a population of serfs and retainers of the potent Mowbray settled within or near the castle, a market became a necessity: this came about early in the twelfth century."*

The temporary reconciliation between Rufus and Malcolm III of Scotland came to an end after a meeting in England in 1093. On the way home Malcolm Canmore (whose surname means 'big head') stopped off to attack Alnwick but met his match in Robert de Mowbray and his unsavoury nephew, Morel. King Malcolm, son of the Duncan killed and succeeded by Macbeth in 1040, had been attacking the northern counties since 1070 and had carried off hundreds of captured English into slavery, women and children included. Malcolm and his son were killed on 13th November 1093, St Brice's Day, by Robert de Mowbray and his followers, who then buried them in the spectacularly sited cliff top priory he, Robert, had founded at Tynemouth on the Northumbrian coast, which, to protect it from the Scots, lay within the precincts of his castle there. In his book *Sons of the Conqueror*, George Slocombe has this to say of Robert and his nephew Morel,

> *"The assailants were two of the worst ruffians in England and a few years later they provoked a sanguinary revolt against Rufus himself… Robert was a typically violent and unruly baron of the period, but he surpassed all the Normans, save only Robert of Bellême, in his cruelty and arrogance."*

The priory where Malcolm III and his son were laid to rest had been founded after Robert had quarrelled with the Bishop of Durham over ownership of lands and had retaliated by expelling the monks from the church of St Oswine within his castle walls. He then gave the church to the Benedictines of St Albans Abbey, much to the chagrin of the see of Durham.

In 1095 Robert, Earl of Northumberland led the barons' new revolt against William Rufus, an attempt to depose him in favour of his cousin Stephen of Aumale, Count of Champagne, but the catalyst for Robert's downfall was his greed and inability to resist easy pickings. Four Norwegian trading vessels had anchored off the Northumbrian coast and Robert and Morel promptly stole their cargoes. The merchants appealed to the King for assistance and he ordered Mowbray to restore the stolen goods;

THE ARMS OF THE BISHOP OF DURHAM

14

Robert refused, so Rufus paid off the merchants himself and then ordered Mowbray to appear before him. The Earl ignored a summons to be at the Easter Court at Winchester in March, and, when denied hostages or promise of safe conduct, refused to attend the King's Whitsuntide feast at Windsor, even though threatened with outlawry if he failed to appear.

These were the special occasions when the monarch appeared in full royal regalia before the barons, as a reminder to them of where their loyalties lay, and their attendance was expected. Rufus decided Robert was pushing him too far and set off up north to get him. Mowbray's frontier fortress, the New Castle on the Tyne, where he had most of his manpower, was attacked and taken, as was Tynemouth Castle after a siege of two months, and Rufus finally cornered him at Bamburgh and laid siege to the great castle on the coast. Rufus knew he would never be able to take him quickly and was called away to fight the Welsh, but at his nearby hastily constructed castle nicknamed *Malvoisin* ('bad neighbour'), he left a garrison that was prepared to sit it out for as long as was necessary.

Robert was lured away from safety by a secret message from the Newcastle garrison promising to surrender to him. He slipped out of Bamburgh at dead of night, but when he arrived at Newcastle discovered he had been tricked. He somehow managed to escape and make for his castle at Tynemouth, seeking sanctuary in the priory, but six days later, having been wounded in the leg, he was unceremoniously dragged from the house of God and taken back to Bamburgh, where his bride of only a few weeks was still holding out and refusing to surrender the castle. William II's commander ordered that Robert de Mowbray be paraded in chains before the castle walls

BAMBURGH CASTLE, NORTHUMBERLAND.
*A stronghold of Robert de Mowbray, whose wife was forced to surrender it.*

while his wife wrestled with the stark choice of surrendering the great fortress or condemning her husband to having his eyes seared out there and then. Local chroniclers, no doubt scribbling for all they were worth, saw Robert's misfortune as a punishment for having peevishly taken St Oswine's church from the Bishop of Durham. The young Countess had little choice but to surrender Bamburgh Castle and Robert's life was spared, but he was kept a prisoner for most, perhaps all, of the rest of his days. This seems a severe penalty, but, in fact, he might have thought he got off somewhat lightly. Many of the rebels captured at about the same time were from the same stable that had revolted in 1088, but this time Rufus would take no more chances and some suffered the cruellest of punishments. His own kinsman, William de Alderi, who always protested his innocence, was whipped at every church in Salisbury before being hanged, and William of Eu was blinded and castrated. The dreaded Morel managed to escape and died in exile. All Robert's properties, lands and titles were confiscated, but for Maud (Matilda) de Laigle, his new wife, the challenges of life's rich tapestry were far from over.

The chroniclers are divided as to the date of Robert de Mowbray's death, the earliest put forward being 1106 and the latest 1129. However, his wife was granted an annulment in 1107 on the grounds that she was a widow in all but name, which would not have been necessary if Robert had died the year previous. It seems unlikely that young Maud was his first wife. If he had fought at Hastings with his father and Uncle Geoffrey in 1066, Robert could have been around fifty at the time of his marriage and imprisonment, and if he died as late as 1129 he would have been an octogenarian. There is a tradition that in his later years, frail and probably blind, Robert de Mowbray was allowed to become a monk at St Albans Abbey, but this view is not entirely substantiated. Here, with the death of Robert, former mighty Earl of Northumberland, too arrogant and violent for his own good, the Mowbray story should end, and would have done so but for a special command of King Henry I which brought to prominence a penniless younger son of their old neighbours in St Martin d'Aubigny.

# CHAPTER II

## 1100-1216: RULED BY THE DEVIL'S BROOD

*...unlawful and unjust as it is base and shameful!*
Pope Innocent III on Magna Carta 1215.

ILLIAM II, RUFUS, came to a sticky end in the New Forest one fine August day in 1100, accidentally killed when out hunting with a small group of companions. His younger brother Henry, he who had once so prudently stowed away the fortune in silver, rushed into his new role as King of England with such gusto that many thought he had seen his elder brother's 'accident' coming for quite some time. His first act upon hearing of the death was to ride to Winchester and demand the keys to the royal treasury: obviously with him old habits died hard. He who held the treasury held the power, but Henry's action presented a very delicate situation because he had never figured in his late father's plans for the succession. Robert Curthose, however, a much-admired crusader, was far away when their brother Rufus was killed, and so the youngest son was able to seize the reins of power initially almost unhindered. King Henry I was pious like his father but had none of his conjugal fidelity, fathering at least twenty illegitimate children. He was the only one of the Conqueror's sons to be born in England, spoke some English and was well educated for the times.

His wife Edith, who upon her marriage changed her name to become yet another Matilda, was a daughter of Malcolm III of Scotland, and after his assassination by Robert de Mowbray had been sent to the safety of Romsey Abbey in Hampshire. Henry continued the struggle against his brother Robert in Normandy, whom many believed really should now be accepted as King of England, but with Robert's prolonged absence on crusade Normandy was in a bad way and some barons there actually began to think they would be better off under the rule of the King of England. Henry finally defeated his brother at the Battle of Tinchebrai on 28th September 1106, the fortieth anniversary of their father's landing at Pevensey. Thereafter Henry I took control of Normandy and kept his brother prisoner in various English and Welsh castles, particularly Cardiff, for the last twenty-eight years of his life.

At his coronation, Henry I presented his Charter of Liberties, and we shall find associations with its provisions throughout the Mowbray family's history. The feudal system made the King dependent on his barons' loyalty, as they supplied the forces to ensure the country's security in exchange for lands, but as time went on, rather than call-up their tenants, whose labour they needed in their fields, many barons chose to pay the King *scutage* or 'shield money' to enable him to engage mercenaries; but there were other changes less advantageous to the great men. Henry's Charter confirmed that he could claim a relief on lands of a deceased baron, a sort of inheritance tax paid by the successor, usually the very large sum of £100. The King could also administer the lands of a minor, or allow them to be administered by his nominee, and an example of this we shall see in later times when John de Mowbray, Earl of Nottingham, tries to prove his age in order to recover his lands from the second wife of Henry IV.

The monarch could give the hand in marriage of his vassals' widows, daughters or sisters wherever he wished, another aspect of life we see throughout the Mowbray story. By his Charter of Liberties Henry I promised he would not force a woman to marry against her will, a promise he failed to keep, and in reality these medieval women of high rank were given in marriage to the highest bidder, although a few were able escape by paying a huge fine if they wished to remain unmarried or to marry a husband of their own choice – the latter being the option taken by some the wealthy Mowbray dowagers of the fifteenth century.

If King Henry I really had been a party to the death of his brother William Rufus in the New Forest, he was certainly punished for the sin on the night of 25th November 1120, and his English subjects would still be suffering long after his death from the repercussions of what happened that night. Henry had decided to return to England after four years in Normandy, and as the day of the long-planned voyage approached, one Thomas Fitzstephen sought permission to speak to the King, and it turned out that his father had been the pilot of *La Mora*, the ship that had borne Duke William across the Channel in 1066. Thomas spoke proudly of a great new vessel, *The White Ship* (*Blanche Nef*), of which he was the master, and begged for the honour of conveying the Conqueror's son across the water. Henry was satisfied with the arrangements he had already made but had no objection to his son William and his entourage sailing with Thomas if they so wished. The King had many children, possibly as many as twenty-nine, but only two were legitimate, seventeen-year-old William and his full sister Matilda, and now that the law of primogeniture and the requirement that the heir be a legitimate child were established, it was assumed that William would succeed his father. Most of the King's motley brood were on reasonably good terms, and also on this trip were Richard and another Matilda, half-siblings of the heir.

The Prince and the noisy and wealthy bright young things of his acquaintance thought it was a wonderful idea to travel on *The White Ship* and sent casks of complimentary wine to the excited crew, which was gratefully accepted and consumed in no time at all. The young people were in loutish spirits that dark November evening and, to the disgust of some of the more staid courtiers, who decided to disembark as a result, jeered at the priests who came aboard to bless the ship as she lay at anchor in the port of Barfleur. She was a very large vessel for the times, with fifty oarsmen as well as the mariners dealing with the rudder and sails, but the addition of up to three hundred passengers with their luggage and food and drink, as well as heavy caskets containing royal treasure, meant she was overloaded. Even so, she ought to have made it across the Channel.

King Henry departed first. Perhaps the Prince wanted to impress his entourage and overtake his father as they hit the open sea, maybe the sailors wanted to show what their great, but largely untried, ship could do. Perhaps the pilot was drunk. We shall never know the cause of the disaster, nor did the royal father and his companions realise that the noises they heard behind them in the dark were their drowning relatives' and children's desperate cries for help. *The White Ship* had hit rocks, was holed below the waterline, and sank immediately; this was the *Titanic* disaster of its day. Thomas Fitzstephen was a good swimmer but when he surfaced he saw nothing in the blackness. Eventually he managed to locate what little wreckage there was, but finding only two men clinging to the mast, one a butcher, the other Maud de Laigle's nephew, but no sign of the three royal children, or of anyone else, Fitzstephen gave himself up to the freezing November sea rather than face the King's wrath. Godfey de Laigle died of exposure, and of the three hundred and more aboard *The White Ship,* only the humble butcher lived to tell the tale.

Having lost his male heir, King Henry, a widower, decided he must marry again, but his union with the young Adeliza of Louvain brought him no other children. The next in line, therefore, was his haughty daughter Matilda, widow of the Holy Roman Emperor, who used the grand title 'the Empress' for the rest of her days. It has often been said that the Empire was not holy, not Roman and not an empire. What it was, in fact, was a loose alliance of Germany and other European territories (northern Italy, Austria, Bohemia, Belgium and Burgundy) with the common ideal of recreating the old Roman Empire of the West. (The 'Emperor' was elected by the German princes and the word 'Elector' was used as a title for centuries. The German who came to the English throne as George I when the Stuart line died out in 1714 was the Elector of Hanover. The Holy Roman Empire was finally brought to an end by Napoleon Bonaparte in 1806.)

In 1127 Henry I exacted a vow from the barons that they would recognise Matilda as his successor, a proposition they accepted on condition that she would seek their consent before remarrying, but only six months later, with her father's connivance, she was secretly betrothed to Geoffrey Martel, eleven years her junior and the son of the Count of Anjou. This alliance would be most advantageous for her father, but the barons in both England and Normandy were far from impressed when the news became public. Some were already having doubts about the prospect of a woman ruler, especially a woman as unpleasant as Matilda and married to a man like Geoffrey, so their thoughts turned to her cousin, Stephen of Blois, the son of the Conqueror's daughter Adela.

When Henry I died in 1135 many transferred their allegiance to Stephen, who unfortunately turned out to be a weak ruler, and there followed a prolonged civil war that drained the country's manpower and resources. The hapless population of England, already dispossessed of land and property by the Norman invaders, now found themselves called-up by their feudal lords for military purposes. Fear of starvation, the barons fighting each other with the inevitable suffering it caused their minions, and the threat of gangs of roaming armed bandits added to their woes, and it seemed that God had abandoned them. The century following the Norman Conquest was very rough as a whole for the vanquished, but the civil war years, some of the worst times English people have ever had to endure, were especially terrible and people wept at the thought that 'Christ and His saints slept'.

The situation was worsened by the continuing struggles against the Scots who, naturally, took every advantage of the King of England's predicament and were able to venture deep into English territory, pillaging, raping, murdering, and rustling both cattle and people. Eventually Matilda had to concede defeat and Stephen ruled until 1154, but the finger of fate had already intervened in 1153 with the death of Prince Eustace, his son and heir, so it was agreed that the throne of England and the dukedom of Normandy would eventually go to Matilda's son, Henry of Anjou, a tough individual cast in the same mould as William the Conqueror, his great-grandfather.

The stocky, red-headed Henry II, known as *Curtmantle* ('short cloak') or Henry *FitzEmpress* ('son of the Empress'), was a conscientious, incredibly energetic and innovative ruler, and it is a great pity that today his many excellent points are overshadowed by his prodigious appetite as a womaniser that alienated his wife and helped split his family, for the unfortunate episode that culminated in the murder of

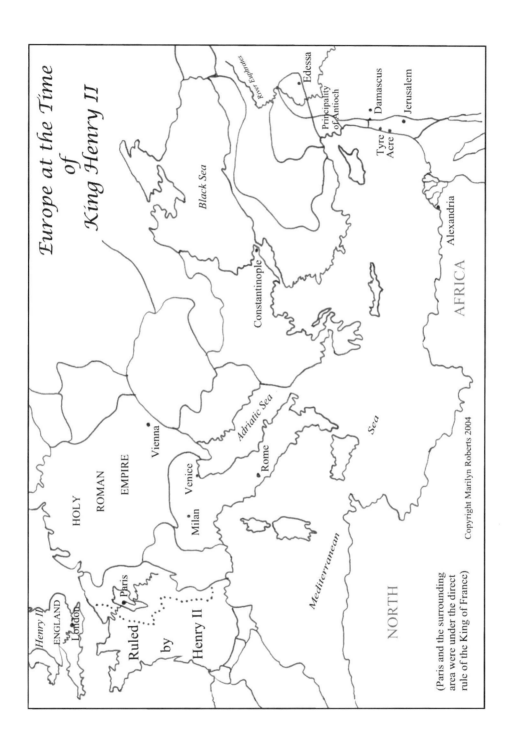

*Europe at the Time of King Henry II*

River Euphrates

Edessa

Principality of Antioch

Damascus

Jerusalem

Tyre
Acre

Black Sea

Alexandria

AFRICA

Constantinople

Adriatic Sea

Sea

Vienna

ROMAN

EMPIRE

HOLY

Venice

Rome

Milan

Mediterranean

NORTH

Henry II

ENGLAND

London

Paris

Ruled

by

Henry II

Copyright Marilyn Roberts 2004

(Paris and the surrounding
area were under the direct
rule of the King of France)

21

Thomas Becket, and for the troubles brought upon him by his inability to control his own self-seeking and reckless sons. His father, Geoffrey of Anjou, wore a sprig of broom, or *planta genista*, in his helmet, hence the name 'Plantagenet', used by the family themselves only from the fifteenth century onwards. In their own time Henry's family, who fought each other like cat and dog, were aptly nicknamed the *Devil's Brood*. Henry was the second husband of the beautiful and all-too-often outrageous Eleanor of Aquitaine, sometime Queen of France, who, at about twenty-nine years of age when they married, was ten years Henry's senior. Eleanor was phenomenally wealthy and powerful in her own right and was already a woman with a past every bit as colourful as her young husband's future would prove to be.

In 1137, at about sixteen and just before her father's death made her the great Duchess of Aquitaine, Eleanor had married her first husband, Louis, also sixteen, who adored her but nevertheless was something of a dull and pious cold fish of a man. However, within a few months of the marriage Louis became King of France. In 1145 Queen Eleanor at long last had her first child, a daughter she named Marie, from whom was descended the twentieth century actress Audrey Hepburn (Edda Kathleen van Heemstra Hepburn-Ruston); Miss Hepburn was also descended from the Mowbrays, see Table XI. Eleanor's performance as a producer of babies was a great disappointment to King Louis, but, as her subsequent large brood to her second husband would prove, this was hardly her fault. She was something of a good time girl who loved having political power in her own right, revelled in her own legendary beauty, was a fashion icon, enjoyed the pop music of the day, and the company of the musicians, and who delighted in the idea of being the object of many a young man's protestations of undying love, which frequently, she was.

This was the time of the Crusades, and in 1147 St. Bernard of Clairvaux preached the Second Crusade in the presence of the King and Queen of France. Inspired by the monk's oration, they went to the Holy Land together, but the whole episode was a dismal failure. In the first place, Eleanor had with her numerous retainers all expecting good food, fine clothes, reliable transport and suitable accommodation. In the second place were the cumbersome cartloads of the trappings of grandeur to which she was accustomed, all of which not only slowed down their travelling arrangements, but also laid the party even more wide open than usual to attacks by bandits. But Eleanor's pièce de resistance on this journey, that wrecked her first marriage and changed her life, was the brief affair it was widely believed she had with Raymond of Poitou, Prince of Antioch, her own young, rich and very handsome uncle. The Anglo-Norman knight Sir Roger de

Mowbray (died 1188) had been in France on business in 1146-47, and inspired by St Bernard, he too was in the Holy Land at the same time as Eleanor and Louis and, although it is unlikely he would have been known to Eleanor at this stage in his life, he would surely have had first-hand experience of the juicy gossip currently doing the rounds of the crusader encampments.

The Pope tried to effect a reconciliation between the royal couple, but in the end they were divorced on the convenient grounds of consanguinity, that is, they were too closely related for comfort. Once Eleanor of Aquitaine had acquired a reputation as a woman of doubtful virtue it became difficult to separate fact from fiction. What is not in doubt is that with her feisty personality, seemingly endless supply of money, extensive territories, and her stunning good looks Eleanor, now in her prime, would be a wonderful catch for either an already great prince or an aspiring one, and there was a very real danger of her being kidnapped by some bold noble and forced into marriage. Scandal raised its ugly head again when it was rumoured she had once had an affair with Geoffrey, Count of Anjou, and eyebrows were raised even further when it was his and Matilda's athletic young son Henry that she chose to marry in 1152, the year before he became King of England. Eleanor's Uncle Raymond had fared less well: he was killed in battle shortly after her departure from the Holy Land and his once-handsome head was packed into a silver box and sent as a present to the Caliph of Baghdad.

King Henry II of England ruled an area stretching from the Scottish borders to the Pyrenees. He and Eleanor had eight children. Their surviving sons, the Princes Henry, Geoffrey, Richard and John, were constantly in armed dispute with each other, but on occasion they would join forces against their father, encouraged by their mother who at times was embittered by Henry's celebrated womanising and jealous of the power he wielded in her French territories. Henry thought that having his heir crowned as Henry the Young King might defuse the situation, but he was sadly disappointed and Roger de Mowbray was amongst those who rebelled in the son's favour. Henry II died in 1189, predeceased by his sons Henry the Young King and Geoffrey. Eleanor of Aquitaine died in 1204 at the grand old age of eighty-two, plotting to the last.

Their son Richard, *Lionheart*, reigned for ten years, but totally smitten by the excitement, glamour and challenge of being a crusader, he spent only six months in England, a place he hated. On his way back through Europe in December 1190 he was apprehended by Leopold, Duke of Austria, whom he had previously offended in the Holy Land, and was handed over to the Holy Roman Emperor and held hostage with some of his barons, including William de Mowbray, Roger's grandson, until March 1194, while the King's ransom of 150,000 marks (£100,000 – a mark was £²/₃, that is, thirteen shillings and fourpence) that nearly ruined the kingdom was being raised. The ransom was a terrible blow for a country already nearly bled dry to finance the crusaders' expeditions, but upon his return Richard treated himself to a second lavish coronation, managed to raise yet more money from somewhere – he admitted that he would even have sold London to the highest bidder if he could – and then went away again, never to return.

Richard I was killed in France in 1199 and, having no child, was succeeded by his brother John, the youngest of the Devil's Brood. It could be said that the rightful heir was Arthur, son of the late Prince Geoffrey, and when he was murdered the finger pointed at John. The King of France was expecting John at Court to go through the motions of doing homage for the French lands and took the extremely bold step of confiscating them when, knowing that he would be called upon to prove his innocence of Arthur's murder, he failed to turn up.

King John's reputation, rightly or wrongly, is one of being a wicked and incompetent tyrant in conflict with some of his most powerful barons, the latter understandably seething at the loss of their historic homeland of Normandy, a conflict that would culminate in the signing of Magna Carta in 1215. Magna Carta is really a series of concessions wrung from King John by those rebellious barons, including William de Mowbray (died 1224), tired of his extortionate and often illegal demands for taxes and his vicious reprisals against defaulters. However, it established for the first time that the power of a king could be limited by a written

*PUBLIC HOUSE SIGN IN LINCOLN.*
*One of only four remaining Magna Carta copies of 1215 can be seen at Lincoln Castle a few yards away.*

grant, although by the time of his death the following year, John had already gone back on his word and Magna Carta barons had been excommunicated by the Pope.

~∰∿

*Nigel (or Nele) d'Aubigny*, died 1129.
Often called Nigel d'Albini or De Albini by the chroniclers; the father of Roger de Mowbray.

Nigel was one of Henry I's strongest supporters. His grandfather, William d'Aubigny, Seigneur, or feudal lord, of St Martin d'Aubigny in Normandy, was very likely at Hastings. The family was already well-established in the Norfolk area, and had been  bow-bearers to William Rufus. William, the elder son, and heir, held the royal manor of Kenninghall in Norfolk, which required him to perform the duties of King's Chief Butler, or *Pincerna Regis*, at the coronation banquet. Nigel's father was Roger d'Aubigny and his mother, Amicia (or Avicia), is said by some sources to be the sister of Bishop Geoffrey and his brother Roger de Mowbray, making Nigel the cousin of Robert, Earl of Northumberland, imprisoned in 1095. This is not confirmed, although if he were Robert de Mowbray's nearest male relative it would go some way to explaining later events. Nigel was instrumental in the capture of Henry I's brother, Robert of Normandy, and in 1106 after the Battle of Tinchebrai was rewarded with the lands of Duke Robert's supporter Robert de Stuteville in Yorkshire, Northamptonshire, Leicestershire, Nottinghamshire, Warwickshire and Lincolnshire; the Lincolnshire lands included the whole of the Isle of Axholme. These are not the old Mowbray lands as held by Bishop Geoffrey and Robert, Earl of Northumberland before 1095, and at the time of the Domesday Survey those in Lincolnshire were held by one Geoffrey de Wirce (or Guerche). Nigel's prosperity, then, came to him not from his family, from whom as a younger son he could expect little, but from his king to whom he remained a loyal and very important servant throughout his life.

It was certain that Robert de Mowbray, although imprisoned by William Rufus, would never be set free by Henry I, so in 1107, after his first twelve years of incarceration, Pope Paschal II annulled his marriage to Maud de Laigle on the grounds of consanguinity. It is quite possible that they were related, but their familial relationship is not known; in reality, however, it was a convenient way of getting her out of a marriage with an elderly man destined to spend the rest of his life in custody. *The Oxford History of England* says that Maud, Robert's 'gallant wife, thus deprived of conjugal felicity,' obtained a licence from Pope Paschal to contract a second marriage. Alas, that marriage, to Nigel d'Aubigny, brought to him status and the Norman manor of Montbrai and others, but to her there would be little joy and no children so he was able to repudiate her on those ever-reliable and very convenient grounds of consanguinity. If Amicia de Mowbray were Nigel's mother, then he would have been able to get the separation because Maud had previously been married to his cousin Robert. Nigel was far from gallant and was crafty enough to wait till her brother Gilbert de Laigle died, and, to add insult to injury, he was rewarded for his services to the King with the Norman lands of Maud's former husband, Robert de Mowbray, still languishing in prison at Windsor. Nigel d'Aubigny took as his second wife Gundred de Gournay, granddaughter of the Conqueror's best friend William de Warenne, 1ˢᵗ Earl of Surrey. Gundred was the mother of Nigel's son Roger and was a benefactress of Byland, Rievaulx and Whitby Abbeys in Yorkshire, and of St Peter's Hospital in York. (Early in the year 2000 the *Sunday Times* newspaper published a list of the 200 richest Britons of the last millennium, monarchs excluded, and Gundred's grandfather took first place with a fortune estimated at £57.6 billion in today's terms.) Nigel d'Aubigny founded Hurst (Hirst) Priory in the Isle of Axholme, now a golf course, as a cell of Nostell Priory in Yorkshire, and died in 1129. At about the same time his son Roger took the name of Mowbray by royal command, not necessarily because the families were related, but because at the time his Montbrai manor in Normandy would have had higher status in the eyes of the Normans than any of his English holdings. In medieval times a great collection of feudal holdings such as Roger's was known as an *honour,* and the manor which gave it its name was the *caput,* or head.

### Sɪʀ Rᴏɢᴇʀ ᴅᴇ Mᴏᴡʙʀᴀʏ (ғᴏʀᴍᴇʀʟʏ ᴅ'Aᴜʙɪɢɴʏ), ᴅɪᴇᴅ 1188.

Roger, who had a long and active life, was a minor at the death of his father Nigel d'Aubigny in 1129, six years before King Henry I died and his nephew, Stephen of Blois, seized the throne. It would only be a matter of time until Matilda, living in Normandy and alienating the barons there through her arrogance and her open encouragement of her husband's interests at the expense of her own people, took steps to claim the English throne. Meanwhile, there were fresh threats from the Scots, and Roger de Mowbray was still very young to be involved in war when he took part in the Battle of the Standard near Northallerton in North Yorkshire in 1138, although Ailredus the abbot of Rievaulx tells us that because of his tender years Roger was not unduly exposed to danger.

As part of a truce, King David I of Scotland's son had been granted Carlisle, Doncaster and the Honour of Huntingdon, but what he really wanted was the earldom of Northumberland. It is also likely that David was making a nuisance of himself on the borders because he knew Matilda's appearance on the south coast was imminent. The chronicler Richard of Hexham wrote of the events of 1138,

*"But God's mercy, being moved by the tears of innumerable widows, orphans, and victims, no longer permitted such wickedness to remain unchastised. For whilst he [King David] and his men were engaged in this course of outrage, information of his crimes, his proceedings, and his designs was conveyed to the men of Yorkshire, both by common report and by sure intelligence; whereupon the barons of that province, to wit, archbishop Turstin [Thurston], William de Albemarle, Walter de Gant, Robert de Bruce, Roger de Mowbray, Walter Espec, Ilbert de Lacy, William de Percy, Richard de Courcy, William Fossard, Robert de Stuteville, and other powerful and sagacious men, assembled at York, and anxiously deliberated as to what course should be pursued at this crisis."*

The Norman-English barons were near Northallerton when their scouts warned that the Scots were close, so they fixed-up a ship's mast they had brought with them to a heavy wagon and from it hung the banners of St Peter the Apostle, St John of Beverley and St Wilfrid of Ripon. There was also a vessel of silver containing communion bread to act as a reminder to the men that their efforts were going to save the Holy Church from despoliation by the enemy, and also to be a clearly visible rallying point: hence the exchange became known as the 'Battle of the Standard'. What the Scots thought was happening as a ship's mast was raised miles inland is not recorded.

Thurston organised his men into one large division, not three as was more usual, and kept the horses well back in case the noisy war cries of the Scots unnerved them. The knights were to fight on foot and the strategy was to mix-up knights and archers so as to be attacking and defending at the same time. The Scottish King at first put his best-equipped troops up front, which offended the terrifying and brave men of Galloway, who insisted on being in David's front line claiming they had 'sides of iron and a breast of bronze'. They also had a blood-curdling battle cry but were no match for the English archers, although Richard of Hexham says they were still brandishing their swords even though their lightly clad bodies bristled with arrows. Then an English archer had the bright idea of holding up an anonymous severed head, shouting at the top of his voice that it was that of King David; Scottish morale collapsed and for them the day was lost.

King Stephen was a gallant man and was both brave and merciful. That he lacked good judgement relevant to his circumstances he demonstrated after the Battle of the Standard by making a truce with

David of Scotland and giving his son the earldom of Northumberland in exchange for their promise of loyalty, and he would soon demonstrate this weakness again by a chivalrous act towards his cousin Matilda, shortly to arrive on English soil. By now Matilda and her husband were firmly established in Normandy, and although Stephen had attempted to dislodge them, he had found his Flemish mercenaries were distrusted and disliked by the Normans almost as much as the *Angevins*, Geoffrey's men of Anjou, and had to withdraw. Unfortunately for Stephen, in his absence certain barons in England whose loyalties tended towards Matilda, had organised themselves and taken the opportunity to construct castles without seeking royal approval.

Matilda landed at Portsmouth in September 1139 and was met by her stepmother Adeliza of Louvain, the Queen Dowager, recently married to Roger de Mowbray's cousin, William d'Aubigny. Matilda took refuge with the couple at Arundel Castle and then made preparations to join her half-brother, Robert of Gloucester, at his castle in Bristol; some barons thought it a pity that the circumstances of Robert of Gloucester's birth ruled him out of the succession. There can have been absolutely no doubt about the purpose of Matilda's arrival on English soil, yet, in a characteristic but ill-judged act, Stephen gave her safe conduct to travel.

(Although it is through Roger d'Aubigny that the Mowbray name was preserved, we should not forget his cousin William d'Aubigny, known as *Stronghand*, ancestor of the d'Aubigny, (d'Albini) Earls of Arundel. When Henry I died in 1135 he left Arundel Castle and much land to his widow, Queen Adeliza, and three years later she married William d'Aubigny, who in later life was made Earl of Arundel by Henry II. William must have been a dashing, charismatic sort of fellow whose exploits lent themselves to the stuff of legend, for he had already captured the heart of another Adeliza, also a Queen Dowager, but this time of France, who had fallen in love with him at a tournament. Folklore has it that when William d'Aubigny spurned her proposal of marriage, Queen Adeliza of France sent him out to take a stroll alone in her palace gardens where, as she knew only too well, a very hungry lion was lurking in a cave. As the beast set itself to pounce, William d'Aubigny, quick as a flash, wrapped his cloak around his arm, thrust his strong hand into the animal's terrifying great mouth and ripped out its tongue, which he then calmly handed to a lady-in-waiting who just happened to be passing, telling her to deliver it to the woman scorned. One wonders if the lion matured into the gentle old beast that legend has it followed his cousin Roger home to Thirsk many years later.)

Much of the action in the Stephen and Matilda conflict took place in the West Country, but the horrors that befell the citizens of Lincoln deserve mention here. In December 1140 Stephen was in Lincolnshire when some of his main supporters revolted and seized Lincoln Castle, but the city and shire remained loyal to the King. The way the castle was taken was childlike in its simplicity: the wives of the barons concerned decided to pay a social visit to the castellan's wife and their dutiful husbands accompanied them, carrying the ladies' voluminous cloaks over their arms. A lady's voluminous cloak is just the thing to disguise a drawn sword, and the defenders of the castle were overcome before they knew what had hit them. The citizens and the bishop sent to King Stephen for help but Robert of Gloucester and 10,000 Welshmen were quickly on the scene. Before the two sides met, Stephen attended Mass in Lincoln Cathedral at dawn on 1st February 1141 when there came the omen of impending doom: the King's candle went out and then broke into pieces.

The battle between Stephen's paid Flemish mercenaries and Matilda's Welshmen looking for anything they could lay their hands on was fierce and bloody. The chronicler Henry of Huntingdon gives an insight into what happened the day Roger de Mowbray found himself on the losing side, and how Stephen bravely fought on, after being brought down when someone threw a stone at him, reminiscent of his biblical namesake,

> *"He* [Stephen] *drew out his sword, worthy of a king, and performed wonders with his right hand, until the sword, too, was shattered. Seeing this, William of Cahagnes, a most puissant knight, rushed upon the King, and seizing his helmet, cried out in a loud voice, "Here, everyone, here! I have the King!" Everyone flew up, and the King was captured…. After the King's capture the royal force, unable to escape through the encirclement, continued fighting until they were all either captured or slain. Consequently the city was sacked according to the law that governs hostilities, and the King was brought into it in misery."*

The *'law that governs hostilities'* was the acceptance of the inevitable pillage, rape and murder the victors would perpetrate on their own countrymen, and the brutality and misery that was about to be visited on hundreds of innocent people in Lincoln, rich and poor alike. King Stephen was taken before Matilda at Gloucester and from there to captivity in Bristol Castle, where he remained for nearly a year. Matilda had the title *Lady of the English* conferred upon her, which she would exchange for that of Queen on her coronation day, but that day never came, for she so upset the citizens of London with her disdainful manner and demands for money that they drove her away and attacked her army before she could get anywhere near either the Abbey or the royal palace at Westminster. Even Stephen's brother, Henry de Blois, the Bishop of Winchester, a Matilda supporter, changed his mind once he got to know her better and, after having negotiated the terms for his brother's release, changed sides and joined him.

Roger de Mowbray too lost his freedom after Lincoln but does not seem to have been in captivity long, his family no doubt paying a large ransom to secure his release. Around about this time he could have been residing in Yorkshire with his mother, Gundred de Gournay, whose generosity to religious establishments appears to have rubbed off on her son. Back in 1134 monks from the Abbey at Furness had set up a new colony at Calder in Coupland, but after four years had to abandon the project because the Scots would not leave them alone. Not wishing to return to Furness, they were on their way to York to seek advice from Archbishop Thurston when they met Gundred who sent them to Hood near Thirsk to her relative, the hermit Robert de Alneto, formerly a Benedictine monk at Whitby, who subsequently joined them. The Mowbray mother and son gave them one-tenth of the victuals of their castle [Thirsk?] but by 1143 the little community had outgrown its site, so Roger gave them his house at Byland-on-the-Moors in Ryedale. However, they were only three miles away from Rievaulx Abbey, founded on the opposite bank of the Rye

BYLAND ABBEY, NORTH YORKSHIRE
*The original was founded a few miles away in 1143 by Roger de Mowbray and his mother Gundred de Gournay; these buildings date from 1177.*

twelve years earlier by Walter L'Espec, and both communities found themselves unable to go about their business properly owing to the intrusive sound of each other's bells, so in 1147, the year he first went on crusade, Roger gave the newcomers a new site eight miles south of Coxwold. The land, however, was of poor quality, so in 1177 he moved them again and work began on what must have been a most awe-inspiring group of buildings the monks still called Byland Abbey, although they were far from their original site; the remains are still magnificent today even after centuries of abuse and neglect.

In 1145 Roger and his relative Sampson d'Aubigny founded Newburgh Abbey, and he is known to have founded or aided many other religious houses including the abbeys of Fountains and Rievaulx (Yorkshire), St Mary (York), Kenilworth (Warwickshire), Sulby (Northamptonshire), and to have given the Knights Templar lands at Keadby and other places in the Isle of Axholme. The Templars, a military monastic order properly called the Poor Knights of Christ and the Temple of Solomon, held him in great esteem and had a respect for his family that did not diminish with the passage of time, so that even after the Order had been persecuted to extinction and their lands and properties conferred upon the Knights of the Order of St John of Jerusalem, known as the 'Hospitallers', the latter decreed in 1335 that the Mowbrays should be treated as those to whom they were most obliged after the King. In the Isle of Axholme Roger doubled his father's endowment to Hirst Priory a few miles from Epworth, while at Burton, a village near Melton Mowbray in Leicestershire, now known as Burton Lazars, he founded a dependency of the Leper Hospital of St Lazarus Outside the Walls of Jerusalem, which became one of the chief leper hospitals in England.

On 25th December 1144 something happened far away in the mysterious East that changed the situation on the home front: the Christian-controlled city of Edessa was captured by the Turks and there was consternation that Jerusalem itself could be in danger. In some ways this was a turning point in the Stephen and Matilda fiasco, as barons on both sides found the call to defend their faith, the possibility of acquiring exotic goods and the challenge of what they saw as some good old fashioned warfare, to be a much more attractive prospect than the tedious conflict at home that was getting nowhere. Suddenly several of the leading lights were gone, Roger de Mowbray amongst them. In 1146-47 Roger's visit to Normandy to defend Bayeux Castle coincided with St Bernard preaching the Second Crusade and Louis VII and Queen Eleanor of France taking up his call-to-arms against the unbelievers. Roger, no doubt inspired by all this pious activity, is known to have taken up the Cross in 1147 and according to Simeon of Durham soon became renowned

The
Isle of Axholme
At the centre of Mowbray power

Copyright Marilyn Roberts 2004

for having defeated a famous Saracen champion in single combat, an event that unfortunately is not that well documented.

In 1148, instead of sticking to their original plan of recovering Edessa from the ruler of Aleppo, going to the assistance of Raymond of Antioch and then making sure that Jerusalem was secure, some of the leaders of the Second Crusade thought it would be a very fine thing to capture the great Muslim city of Damascus, as it was also very important to Christians. Others were horrified at the idea because Damascus was their ally and also a useful buffer between their Kingdom of Jerusalem in the south and the enemy in Aleppo, to the north, who was also much feared by the Damascenes. Sir Roger de Mowbray would have had little say in the decision-making. In the baking July heat they tried to penetrate the areas of dense orchard enclosed by mud brick walls that lay outside the city's defensive walls, but found them to be criss-crossed by narrow paths and even more walls, making their advance difficult and providing the enemy with ample opportunity for ambush, as William of Tyre tells us,

> *"There were, moreover, men with lances hiding inside the walls. When these men saw our men passing by, they would stab them as they passed, through little peepholes in the walls which were cleverly designed for this purpose, so that those hiding inside could scarcely be seen. Many are said to have perished miserably that day in this way."*

At last it seemed the city would fall to the Christians, but then they moved to an area of the actual city wall they thought would be easy to storm, but the siege had to be abandoned altogether after only four days because of lack of food and water. Roger managed to escape.

Meanwhile, at home in 1147, Henry Plantagenet, Matilda's son, whom she had groomed to be the future King of England, arrived in his would-be kingdom, and again King Stephen was magnanimous to a fault, for when

*KINARD CASTLE MOTTE, OWSTON FERRY.*
*This photograph of the motte (mound) where the keep of Roger de Mowbray's castle stood, was taken from the elevated churchyard; there is a drop over the wall. The moat, or ditch, can still be seen in places, and the soil from there would have been piled up to make the motte. The beautiful church stands in the bailey (courtyard) of the old castle. Locally the motte is known as 'Castle Hill'.*

the young man's attempted revolt failed and he found himself without money, Stephen, instead of holding him hostage, paid for him to get home. Henry repaid the kindness two years later by allying himself with the King of Scotland and attempting to capture the city of York. Henry's father was still openly ruling in Normandy and the King of France recognised him as the duke, but in September 1151 Geoffrey Plantagenet died, so Henry FitzEmpress styled himself Duke of Normandy and of Anjou, and in 1152 married Eleanor of Aquitaine. His fortunes took another turn for the better with the death of King Stephen's son and heir in 1153 when Prince Eustace, not a man of the same moral fibre as his father, was suddenly taken ill and died when on a pillaging spree at the abbey of Bury St Edmunds. Stephen, by now worn out and broken by the years of struggle, had little option but to name Henry Plantagenet as his successor and within a year England had a new King.

Being the ruler of territories stretching from Scotland to the Pyrenees meant that Henry II spent more time away from England than he did in it. We have already seen that his domestic life was a seething cauldron of intrigue as well, and Roger de Mowbray and his sons Nigel and Robert took the side of Henry the Young King in the 1174 rebellion against his father. Roger's defection was especially worrying, since his Axholme and Yorkshire castles were ideally placed to block loyal troops advancing northward and to provide refuge for rebellious English barons from the Midlands moving north to rendezvous with William the Lion, King of Scotland. Roger's castle at Kinard Ferry, now the village of Owston Ferry in the Isle of Axholme, was captured, although supposedly impregnable because of the nature of the marshy terrain, and later Henry II sent his natural son, Geoffrey Plantagenet, bishop-elect of Lincoln to destroy it. Ironically, in an area of marsh and bog noted for its excess of water, it was the lack of something safe to drink that forced the castle garrison, under the direction of Roger's younger son Robert, to surrender. Robert escaped but was captured on his way to seek help from the Mowbray Leicestershire manors. Of the castle nothing now remains except the earthworks, the motte and ditch clearly discernible beside the lovely church at Owston Ferry.

Roger de Mowbray, meanwhile, besieged by Henry II's men at his castle at Kirkby Malzeard six miles northeast of Ripon, escaped and fled north to join the King of Scotland, who offered him shelter as long as he helped him invade Yorkshire, believed to be rallying behind Robert de Stuteville, who was loyal to the King. It was during this conflict that the chronicler Jordan Fantosme described Roger de Mowbray and his fellow rebel Adam de Port as 'the best warriors known to men'. Mowbray was captured by Stuteville in July at Alnwick but escaped again to Scotland and stayed three weeks, but when the uprising in the Midlands and North collapsed he surrendered himself and Thirsk Castle, and with the other rebels came before Henry II at Northampton at the end of the month. Some sources

St. Andrew's Church Epworth and the Site of the Mowbray Manor House.
*The church is known worldwide for its association with the Wesley family and it was here that John Wesley stood on his father's tomb to preach when denied access to the building. The trees conceal the area known as the* Vinegarth, *the site of a great Mowbray residence and the place where William de Mowbray, the Magna Carta baron, died in 1224.*

believe that he had actually been working with the King of Scots for some time, leaving his sons and retainers to defend the Mowbray castles, and was involved on the Scottish side in the siege of Carlisle and the capture and sacking of other border towns. Although Henry appeared to forgive Roger, the wily Plantagenet was no fool, and the Mowbray castles at Thirsk and Kirby Malzeard were ordered to be destroyed by the Archbishop of York in 1176, after which time the family's main residence appears to have become the place nowadays called the *Vinegarth*, their castle or fortified mansion situated beside St Andrew's Parish Church at Epworth (see Appendix C). Their lands in the North and Midlands swept north to south in a great crescent shape between Yorkshire and Warwickshire, placing the Isle of Axholme in northern Lincolnshire, lying about halfway between, at the very centre of Mowbray power.

At the Parish Church of St Oswald in the North Lincolnshire village of Luddington, an annual ceremony on the Feast of the Purification of the Blessed Virgin Mary in early February reminds us that some of Roger's lands were confiscated and he had to make payments to the Church by way of penance for his disloyalty to his king. Robert de Stuteville, seeing that Mowbray's power and authority were considerably weakened, tried to recover lands that had been in his own family's possession before Henry I gave them to the d'Aubigny/Mowbray family in 1106, but he had to settle for Roger making Kirkbymoorside over to him.

35

*Mowbray Lion.*
*Holy Trinity Church, Goodramgate, York.*

His power bases demolished, Roger de Mowbray appears to have been allowed to make his lasting peace with Henry II and the last reliable documentary evidence we have of his movements is as a crusader yet again. Roger of Howden records him as arriving in Jerusalem at Easter 1186 during a period of truce; unlike some others who went home, Roger and Hugh de Beauchamp stayed on. The following year came the dreadful encounter on the shores of the Sea of Galilee known as the battle of Hittîn, named after the nearby mountain,

> "The nephew of Saladin, took....the wood of the Cross of our Lord, after slaying Rufinus, bishop of Acre, who was carrying it. Nearly all the others, being utterly routed, were taken prisoners and either slain or loaded with chains."

Roger de Mowbray was among those taken but ransomed by the Knights Templar, to whom he had given the land between the Ouse and Fosse rivers in York now known as St George's Fields. According to ancient chronicles of Byland he died and was buried at Tyre in 1188, aged seventy or more.

There is, however, an alternative and much more romantic account emanating from Newburgh Abbey chronicles in which the elderly Roger did get back to England but en route came upon an exhausted old lion losing a fight against an exceptionally vicious dragon in a valley called

Sarranel. His bravery and strength apparently undiminished by his advancing years, Roger fought the dragon and, after a hard struggle, killed it, whereupon the poor lion was so grateful that it followed him back to one of his Yorkshire manors near Thirsk, and lived there with him until he died fifteen years later. The Mowbray coat-of-arms was a silver lion on a red background, so there could be some truth in it! By the late 13th century the notion fostered by the canons of Newburgh that their mutual benefactor was buried in Byland chapter house close to his mother Gundred de Gournay had become an established tradition and was recorded as fact by a 1535 Royal commission of Henry VIII. Roger had married Alice de Gant, a great-granddaughter of Stephen, Count of Brittany and Lord of Richmond, and by her had his sons Nigel and Robert.

### Sir Nigel (Nele) de Mowbray, died 1191.

Nigel was already in possession of the Norman lands in 1172, although his father Roger was still alive, and shortly afterwards joined him in the rebellion against Henry II. In September 1189 he attended the coronation of Richard I and went on crusade with him, dying at Acre in 1191. In 1170 he had married Mabel, whose parentage is not definitely known, and by her had William, who was his successor, Philip, founder of the Scottish Mowbrays, and Robert, founder of the Mowbrays of Kirklington in Yorkshire.

### Sir William de Mowbray, died 1224.
Magna Carta Baron.

It is possible that William went on crusade with Richard I, for whom he was held hostage in Germany for nearly four years while the King's ransom was being raised in England. William is known to have paid at least £100 as his share of the King's ransom money, not long after he had paid the same amount for the relief, or transfer, of his late father's lands. There must have been some enlightening conversations amongst that band of captive brothers around the fire of an evening, including, no doubt, gossip about the somewhat unorthodox behaviour of the Devil's Brood, for as a younger man King Richard had seen his vision of young love blighted by his own father's legendary sexual appetite when Henry II was rumoured to have seduced his future daughter-in-law, whom Richard then refused to marry. Upon Richard's death in 1199 William de Mowbray, with the other barons, Greater and Lesser, swore fealty to his brother John, but only on the assurance that each would have his rights, and he, like many others, fortified his strongholds in case of trouble; he was abroad in the King's service in 1202 and again in 1203. When John lost the French possessions in 1204 William's Montbrai lands in Normandy were gone forever. He went with John on expedition to Ireland in 1210, but soon afterwards was sufficiently concerned about the way things were going to strengthen his properties yet again.

William de Mowbray sided with those barons who revolted against King John in 1215. He had a long-standing grudge against the King that went back almost to the beginning of the reign and had come about when the question of rights to certain of the former Stuteville lands was brought up again by William de Stuteville, despite the arrangements made between the previous generation only twenty-five years earlier. King John was notorious for extortion and the accepting of bribes, so Mowbray hoped a 'gift' to him of 2000 marks (about £1,333) would help win his case, this at a time when the income of even the most affluent baron would not exceed £800 a year. Mowbray met Stuteville, who apparently had made a similar 'gift' to the King, at the Bishop of Lincoln's country house at Louth in January 1201 and, in spite of being forced into an expensive compromise that King John could possibly have overruled, William never saw the refund of so much as a penny of the bribery money. We can appreciate that insult was added to injury by virtue of the fact that he had spent precious years on the Continent as a hostage against John's late brother's ransom.

At the Magna Carta negotiations at Runnymede in June 1215, William demanded his right to the custody of the forests in Yorkshire and the castle in York, the latter being granted impending an inquiry into his rights. He was one of the twenty-five leading barons appointed to enforce the provisions of Magna Carta and subsequently had all his lands confiscated by John, and was one of those excommunicated at the King's behest by Pope Innocent III, who most obligingly denounced Magna Carta as being '...unlawful and unjust as it is base and shameful'. One of only four survivors of the original copies of Magna Carta can be found in Lincoln Castle; there are two in the British Library and another in Salisbury. (For the names of the barons involved on both sides in the negotiations see Appendix B.)

The barons were not universally opposed to John and some were prepared to fight for him. His opponents responded by securing the backing of the Dauphin of France, to whom they were prepared to offer the crown. When King John died in 1216 the reason for the unrest should have died with him, but William de Mowbray and like-minded barons continued to give their support to Louis of France in preference to the child Henry III, John's nine-year-old son. The unfortunate inhabitants of Lincoln once again suffered terribly, this time as a consequence of the two sides doing battle there in May 1217, and yet again we are indebted to a chronicler of the day, this time Roger of Wendover, for an account of the hardships, including the state of the French soldiers,

*M*OWBRAY *L*ION *F*LOOR *T*ILE *E*XCAVATED FROM THE *V*INEGARTH *S*ITE.

> *"They therefore marched through the valley of Belvoir, and there everything fell into the hands of these robbers, because the soldiers of the French kingdom, being as it were the refuse and scum of that country, left nothing at all untouched, and their poverty and wretchedness was so great that they had not enough bodily clothing to cover their nakedness."*

William de Mowbray was amongst the combined English and French soldiers who besieged the King's forces at Lincoln Castle, but when royal reinforcements arrived they scoffed at the English scouts' estimates of their numbers,

> *"The barons who were in the city and the French felt such great confidence of success in their cause, that when their messengers told them of the approach of their adversaries they only laughed at them, and continued to hurl missiles from their mangonels, [giant catapults] to destroy the walls of the castle."*

They were deceived, and the relieving troops were able to enter the city fairly easily and engage those attacking the castle,

> *"Then sparks of fire were seen to dart, and sounds of dreadful thunder were heard to burst forth from the blows of swords against helmeted heads; but at length, by means of the crossbowmen, by whose skill the horses of the barons were mown down and killed like pigs, the party of the barons was greatly weakened, for, when the horses fell to the earth slain, their riders were taken prisoners, as there was no one to rescue them.*
>
> *Had it not been for the effect of relationship and blood, not a single one of all of them would have escaped. ...There were also made prisoners, the barons Robert Fitzwalter, Richard de Montfitchet, William de Mowbray, William de Beauchamp..."*

Then the horrors began for the people of Lincoln, most of whom would have had absolutely no say in what had gone on but who were to be punished by their own boy-King and his regents for harbouring the traitors,

> *"Having then plundered the whole city to the last farthing, they* [the King's soldiers] *next pillaged the churches throughout the city, and broke open the chests and storerooms with axes and hammers, seizing on the gold and silver in them, clothes of all colours, women's ornaments, gold rings, goblets, and jewels. Nor did the cathedral church escape this destruction, but underwent the same punishment as the rest, for the legate* [the Pope's representative] *had given orders to the knights to treat all the clergy as excommunicated men, inasmuch as they had been enemies to the church of Rome and to the King of England from the commencement of the war...*
>
> *Many of the women of the city were drowned in the river, for, to avoid insult, they took to small boats with their children, female servants, and household property, and perished on their journey; but there were afterwards found in the river by the searchers, goblets of silver, and many other articles of great benefit to the finders ...*
>
> *It must be believed that this defeat happened to Louis and the barons of England by a just dispensation of God, for as they had now continued nearly two years under sentence of excommunication, unless they were corrected by divine punishment, men would say, 'There is no God,' and so there would be none who acted rightly, no, not one."*

Louis and his men limped home to France realising the cause was lost. The Norman English appear to have decided it was better to patch up their differences and Mowbray's lands were restored to him after he surrendered his manor of Banstead in Surrey by way of ransom, possibly before the winter. In 1223 the King again took away his lands when he defaulted in his service against the Welsh, but they were restored before the end of the year. William de Mowbray was a very powerful and wealthy baron able to deal in vast sums of money, whose households at Epworth and elsewhere would be run along the same lines as that of the King, with officers such as stewards, constables of the stables, a chancellor, perhaps, to deal with the paperwork, butlers, and a multitude of lesser servants to tend to his every whim and need. William had married a noble lady named Avice, possibly a relative from the Arundel branch of the d'Aubigny family, and died in the Isle of Axholme in March 1224 at his home in Epworth. He was succeeded by his sons Nigel (Nele), who left no heir, and Roger.

The Honour of Mowbray as passed from Nigel d'Aubigny to the young Roger had been one of the greatest feudal holdings of all. Nigel was a high-profile king's man through-and-through, often in his ruler's company and in consequence a man of not inconsiderable power and influence. Not so his son, who seems to have been something of an outsider with an unfortunate tendency to back the losing side, and consequently suffering all the penalties that incurred. At his death, although the holdings were still very substantial and conveniently compact, they had, nevertheless, been significantly reduced.

THE HONOUR OF MOWBRAY c.1170

NORMANDY

Twenty manors and the castles of:
**Montbray** †×, Bazoches-en-Houlme ×, Château-Gontier ×

ENGLAND

*LINCOLNSHIRE*

*Isle of Axholme:* Amcotts, Crowle, Keadby, Hirst, Althorpe, Mosswood, Sandtoft, Wroot, Ellers, **Belton\***, **Belwood\***, **Beltoft\***, **Butterwick\***, **Epworth\***, **Melwood\***, **Burnham\***, **Haxey\***, **Owston/ Kinard\*** ×; *other:* Gainsborough, Somerby, Blyborough, Yawthorpe, South Ferriby. (The Isle of Axholme demesnes were the most important and valuable of the whole honour. Diane Greenway, *The Honour of Mowbray*.)

*NOTTINGHAMSHIRE*

Finningley, Serlby, Torworth, Tuxford, Egmanton, Weston, Winkburn, Kelham, Averham, Staythorpe, Longford

*LEICESTERSHIRE*

Melton Mowbray, Stathern, Eastwell, GoadbyMarwood, Sysonby, Welby,

**Thorpe Arnold\***, The Spinney, Freeby, Wyfordby, Burton Lazars, Little Dalby, Pickwell, Leesthorpe, Somerby, Cold Newton, East Norton, Queniborough, KirkbyBellars, Eye Kettleby, Thrussington, Burton on the Wolds

*WARWICKSHIRE/NORTHAMPTONSHIRE*

Bentley, Lindley, Shustoke, Copston Magna, Ullesthorpe, Walton, Bitteswell, Withybrook, Hopsford, Monks Kirkby, Newnham Paddox, Brockhurst, Cestersover, Smyte, Newbold Revel, Combe Abbey, **Brinklow ×**, Cosford, Binley, Little Lawford, Long Lawford, Newbold on Avon,Wappenbury, Sulby,Welford, Elkington, Cold Ashby, Crick, Hampton in Arden, Temple Balsall, Chadwick, Baddesley Clinton

*YORKSHIRE*

Adlingfleet, Ousefleet, Wressell, Loftsome, Broomfleet, North Cave, **South Cave\***, West Ella, Willerby, Kirk Ella, Anlaby, Tranby, Hessle

*Burton in Lonsdale vicinity*: **Burton in Lonsdale ×**, Thornton in Lonsdale, Ingleton, Newby, Clapham, Austwick, Bentham, Horton in Ribblesdale, Winterburn, Flasby, Elslack, Hebden, Appletreewick

*Kirby Malzeard and outlying areas:* **Kirby Malzeard ×**, Ellington, Burton, Masham, Aldburgh, Nutwith, Roomer, Sleningford, Mickley, Azerley, Sutton Grange, Studley Roger, Kilinghall, Birstwith, Dacre, Brimham, Bewerley, Pateley Bridge, Yeadon, Skeldene, **Grewelthorpe\***, **Winksley\***, **Laverton\***, **Braithwaite\***, **Galphay\***, Swetton, Lofthouse, Bramley Grange, Ilton, Swinton, Healey, Colsterdale, Theakston, Sand Hutton, Carlton Minott, Thorpfield, Fawdington, Cundall, Thornton Bridge, Brafferton, Humburton, Kirby Hill, Myton on Swale

*York and outlying areas:* Kirby, Whixley, Nun Monkton, Beningborough, Nether Poppleton, Upper Poppleton, Middlethorpe, Copmanthorpe, Appleton, Roebuck, Acaster Selby, Nun Appleton, Tulston, Wothersome, Bardsey, Collingham, Thorp Arch, Easdike, Steeton, Catterton, Wighill, Walton, Healaugh, Askham Richard, Bilton, Long Marston, Rufforth, Tockwith, Cattal, Bickerton, Wilstrop, Kirk Hammerton, Green Hammerton, Stockton on the Forest, North Duffield, Lund, Gunby, Bubwith, Harlthorpe, Laytham, Foggatthorpe, Gribthorpe, Willitoft, Spaldington, Bursea, Holme on Spalding Moor, Houghton, Sancton, Hessleskew, Burnby, Hayton, Thorpe le Street, Goodmanham, Bainton

*Thirsk/Hovingham and outlying areas:* **Thirsk ×**, Norby, Balk, Bagby, Thorpfield, Osgoodby, Kilburn, Thirlby, Islebeck, Over Silton, Kepwich, Arden, Hawnby, Dale Town, Murton, Old Byland, Scawton, Hood, Oldstead, Byland Abbey, Coxwold, Newburgh Priory, Oulston, Thornton Hill, Brandsby, Ampleforth, Gilling, Grimston, Yearsley, Scackleton, Stearsby, Dalby, South Holme, **Hovingham\***, Slingsby, Fryton, Airyholme, Butterwick, Ryton, Broughton, Norton, Sutton, Welham, Sledmere, Sherburn, Gillamoor, Fodmoor, Skiplam, Hutton le Hole, Kirby Moorside, Newton, Welburn, Wombleton, Bowforth, Harome, Normanby, Little Barugh, Great Barugh, Kirby Misperton, Thornton Dale, Brampton

† *caput* – head of the honour
\* *demesne* – retained by the feudal lord for his own private use, the rest sub-let
× Mowbray castle

# CHAPTER III

## 1216-1327: THE GREAT MEDIEVAL MAGNATES

*O day of vengeance and disaster, day of utter loss and shame, evil and accursed day... that blemished the reputation of the English, despoiled them and enriched the Scots.*
The 'Monk of Malmesbury' *The Life of Edward II.*

THE FRENCH THREAT to King John's son, the young Henry III, was countered and he had good advice from his regents for several years, but his troubles began when he was old enough to take matters into his own hands. In 1236, when he was twenty-nine, Henry married Eleanor, daughter of Raymond Berengar, Count of Provence. Although it was an arranged marriage, Henry was anxious to please his wife, but the favouritism and power afforded her huge and expensive entourage of friends and relations, coupled with Henry's often-unpleasant personality, were a certain recipe for discontent. By 1258 the barons were in revolt, led by the French knight Simon de Montfort, Earl of Leicester, the King's brother-in-law. De Montfort, although a relative newcomer to England, saw that there had to be changes in the way the country was governed, and he and his supporters pressed for a system where elected members met in a 'parley ment' (talking place) to advise the King. Simon was killed and his body shamefully dismembered at the Battle of Evesham in 1265, but the seed of the idea that would grow into the British Parliamentary System had been sown.

Henry III reigned for fifty-six years and was succeeded in 1272 by Edward I, a very different sort of ruler from his father, and known variously as *Lawgiver* and *Longshanks* (at six feet he was unusually tall for the times), but most notably as *The Hammer of the Scots*, inscribed on his tomb in Westminster Abbey. Throughout the period with which we are concerned in this book, the English and Scots were involved in cross-border raids and frequently in open warfare (see Appendix D). Having lands in Lincolnshire and Yorkshire, the Mowbrays were naturally heavily involved in the defence of the northern part of the realm for generation upon generation.

King Edward's attempt to ease the situation between the two countries, to his own advantage of course, by marrying his son and heir to the seven-year-old Queen of Scots, Margaret the *Maid of*

*Norway*, was foiled by her death at sea in 1290 on her way from Bergen to Leith for her coronation and marriage. Little Margaret was the last of the Canmore line, so a new ruler had to be selected from a shortlist of thirteen candidates. In return for being acknowledged as Lord Superior of Scotland, Edward I agreed to choose between the two strongest candidates, Robert Bruce and John Balliol. This is a rather confusing period, since those with lands in both England and Scotland were often flexible with their loyalties, depending on how the situation was going, and the Bruce and Balliol families had fought on both sides. The Chronicle of Lanercost Abbey tells us,

> *"The Scots were so divided among themselves that sometimes the father was on the Scottish side and the son on the English, and vice versa... yea even the same individual be first with one party then with the other."*

Edward chose Balliol, the one he thought would be easier to manipulate, and subsequently treated him with such open contempt that he had no chance of making a success of his 'reign' that lasted only four years, leaving the situation between the two countries as bad as ever. The Scots rebelled against the attempted English take-over, and Sir William Wallace, one of their more colourful leaders, was captured and executed, and great English families like the Mowbrays found themselves fighting their Scottish relations. The Welsh conflict saw the building of a magnificent chain of border castles and the killing of the last native Prince of Wales, Llewelyn ap Gryuffyd, with King Edward then creating his own son Prince of Wales.

It is true that Edward I's reign was a violent era of crusading and fighting the Scots, the Welsh and the French, but it also brought overdue legal and political reform, and it was in his time that the first real Parliament met. Edward had been summoning certain of his Greater Barons to various Parliaments, Councils and Assemblies for a number of years, but in 1295 came the Barony by Writ whereby some of the most influential and wealthy men in the land were summoned to Parliament by letter from the King and addressed as Lords; amongst them was Roger de Mowbray (died 1297). From now on Parliament would consist of the Lords, both Spiritual and Temporal, and the Commons in the shape of the elected Knights of the Shires. Up to this point it was common for a man to refer to his superior as lord, thus Sir Roger would have been 'my lord' to his underlings, but after 1295 the word written with a capital letter signified a rank higher than a knight but lower than an earl. If a father had been summoned it very often meant that his successor would be called to Parliament as well, but this was not always the case, and it would be some years

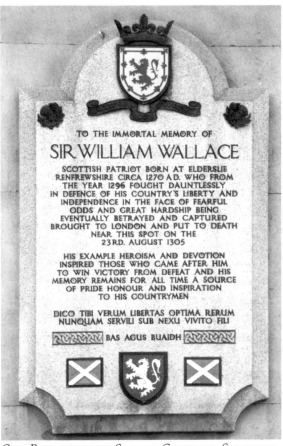

TO THE IMMORTAL MEMORY OF

# SIR WILLIAM WALLACE

SCOTTISH PATRIOT BORN AT ELDERSLIE
RENFREWSHIRE CIRCA 1270 A.D. WHO FROM
THE YEAR 1296 FOUGHT DAUNTLESSLY
IN DEFENCE OF HIS COUNTRY'S LIBERTY AND
INDEPENDENCE IN THE FACE OF FEARFUL
ODDS AND GREAT HARDSHIP BEING
EVENTUALLY BETRAYED AND CAPTURED
BROUGHT TO LONDON AND PUT TO DEATH
NEAR THIS SPOT ON THE
23RD. AUGUST 1305

HIS EXAMPLE HEROISM AND DEVOTION
INSPIRED THOSE WHO CAME AFTER HIM
TO WIN VICTORY FROM DEFEAT AND HIS
MEMORY REMAINS FOR ALL TIME A SOURCE
OF PRIDE HONOUR AND INSPIRATION
TO HIS COUNTRYMEN

DICO TIBI VERUM LIBERTAS OPTIMA RERUM
NUNQUAM SERVILI SUB NEXU VIVITO FILI

BAS AGUS BUAIDH

*Grim Reminder of the Scottish Campaigns, Smithfield, London*
*Monument To William Wallace who was hanged, drawn and quartered in an area between St Bartholomew's Hospital (Bart's) and the church of St Bartholomew the Great, both of which remain.*

before this level of the peerage became hereditary. From this time onward the English Mowbrays were prominent at Court and some would marry women of the royal Plantagenet blood.

The military conflicts continued into the reign of Edward II who, although tall, blond and handsome like his father and not afraid of going into battle, was just about as different from him in personality and political ability as it is possible for a son to be. He was a late baby for Eleanor of Castile, and his birth was followed a few months later by the death of ten-year-old Alfonso, Edward I's heir and only other surviving son at the time, a catastrophe from which the grieving parents seem never to have fully recovered.

Queen Eleanor died when Edward was only five, and although he had a large number of sisters, nobody seems to have cared much about the boy's welfare and development, and to some extent it is hardly surprising that he turned out the way he did. He was terrified of his father and found friendship where he could, amongst servants, craftsmen and Court entertainers, hence his love of gardening, swimming, singing and acting in preference to what were seen as the more manly pursuits of the times.

The magnates, used to a tough 'man's man' like Edward I, must have been dreading the day when his effeminate son would succeed him. Married shortly before his coronation, because duty compelled him to be, and eventually the father of four children, Edward II's heart

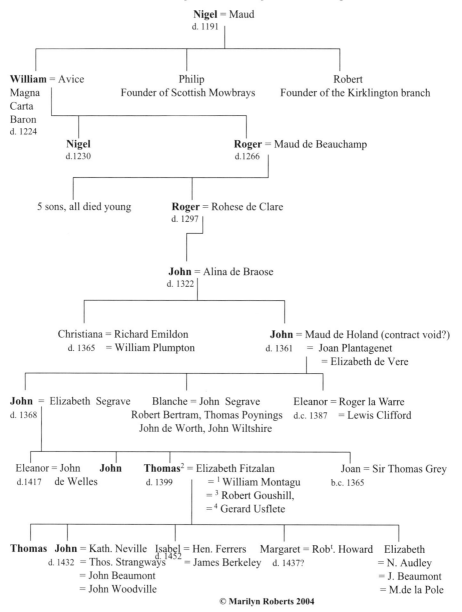

Chart 4: *The Mowbrays - Marriages Made by the Heads of the Family and Some of Their Siblings*

**Nigel** = Maud
d. 1191

**William** = Avice
Magna
Carta
Baron
d. 1224

Philip
Founder of Scottish Mowbrays

Robert
Founder of the Kirklington branch

**Nigel**
d.1230

**Roger** = Maud de Beauchamp
d.1266

5 sons, all died young

**Roger** = Rohese de Clare
d. 1297

**John** = Alina de Braose
d. 1322

Christiana = Richard Emildon
d. 1365    = William Plumpton

**John** = Maud de Holand (contract void?)
d. 1361    = Joan Plantagenet
= Elizabeth de Vere

**John** = Elizabeth Segrave
d. 1368

Blanche = John Segrave
Robert Bertram, Thomas Poynings
John de Worth, John Wiltshire

Eleanor = Roger la Warre
d.c. 1387    = Lewis Clifford

Eleanor = John        **John**
d.1417    de Welles    d. 1399

**Thomas**[2] = Elizabeth Fitzalan
= [1] William Montagu
= [3] Robert Goushill,
= [4] Gerard Usflete

Joan = Sir Thomas Grey
b.c. 1365

**Thomas**   John = Kath. Neville
d. 1432  = Thos. Strangways
= John Beaumont
= John Woodville

Isabel = Hen. Ferrers
d. 1452  = James Berkeley

Margaret = Rob$^t$. Howard
d. 1437?

Elizabeth
= N. Audley
= J. Beaumont
= M. de la Pole

© Marilyn Roberts 2004

46

really belonged to his male friends, the most prominent and dangerous of whom were the Gascon knight Piers Gaveston, Earl of Cornwall, and, after Gaveston's murder, the terrifying father and son both named Hugh le Despenser. These two would imprison eleven-year-old John de Mowbray (died 1361) and his mother in the Tower and were the root-cause of his father's execution. The reign lasted twenty long years, until the humiliated Queen Isabella, aided by her lover Roger Mortimer, deposed King Edward, whose son was recognised as Edward III on 25th January 1327. Some months later Edward the father was disembowelled with a red-hot poker at Berkeley Castle in Gloucestershire.

⁓ ⚡ ⌐

## SIR NIGEL (NELE) DE MOWBRAY, DIED 1230

Nigel, the son of Magna Carta Baron William de Mowbray, paid the astronomical sum of £500 to receive his father's lands, married Maud, whose parentage is not definitely known, and died without issue in 1230, to be succeeded by his brother Roger. In the spring he had sailed with the King's invasion expedition to France and it is possible that he died abroad, perhaps at Nantes. Nigel was still alive, then, in the spring, but on 2nd October the King's steward, Ralph FitzNicholas, paid £500 for the right to marry the newly widowed Maud to one of his sons. However, dower was granted to her on 10th November and it could be that coming into her widow's entitlement gave Maud the chance to buy herself out of the arrangement and either stay single or marry a man of her own choice, for in July 1232 she had licence not to marry or to marry where she pleased, and in January 1234 married John de Courtnay.

## SIR ROGER DE MOWBRAY, BORN ABOUT 1223, DIED 1266.

A minor when he succeeded his brother Nigel, Roger's affairs, including arrangements for a suitable marriage for him, were put first into the hands of Hubert de Burgh, Earl of Kent, and then transferred to John de Lacy, Earl of Lincoln, until he came of age. He served in the Scottish campaigns in 1258 and against the Welsh in 1260 and was sent to Chester to negotiate a truce with Llewelyn of Wales on behalf of Henry III. Roger was a benefactor to many religious establishments in Lincolnshire and Yorkshire, including Fountains Abbey, although at one stage the Pope had to write to the canons of York Minster ordering them to stop pestering Sir Roger for compensation, apparently already paid, for damage done when he was fighting for Henry III in the early stages of the barons' opposition. Roger died in November 1266 in the Isle of Axholme and is thought to have been buried in the Church of the Friars Preachers at Pontefract. His son was under age so his lands were granted to Richard, King of the Romans, a brother of Henry III, who in turn granted them to Roger's widow, Maud de Beauchamp, in exchange for 400 marks a year.

### Sir Roger de Mowbray, died 1297.
First Lord Mowbray.

*Fountains Abbey, North Yorkshire*
*Burial place of Roger, First Lord Mowbray; family members were benefactors for centuries.*
*Reproduced by kind permission of Harrogate International Centre.*

Barony by Writ; created Lord Mowbray on 24th June 1295, with Summons to the famous 1295 Model Parliament of Edward I. (As a result of a case Lord Stourton brought before the House of Lords Committee for Privileges in 1877 Roger's barony was judged to date from his summons to the Shrewsbury Assembly of 1283, which surprised some of the peerage lawyers of the day because up until this case the Shrewsbury gathering itself had not been regarded as being a true Parliament, whereas the gathering of 1295 was; see Chapter VIII and Appendix E.)

Still a minor at the time of his father's death, Roger did not come into possession of his lands until 1278. He saw service against the Scots and Welsh between 1282 and 1291, and his lion coat of arms on a stone shield is to be found high up in the nave of York Minster, together with those of other veterans of the Scottish campaigns. He was sent on a diplomatic mission to Gascony in 1294, at the time when the King of France cheated Edward I out of his lands there and the latter was beginning his campaign to restore them. Gascony had remained under English control even though King John lost most of the French possessions, and the Gascons themselves were not averse to this, England being one of their major trading partners. In the Hundred Years' War of the fourteenth and fifteenth centuries they did not surrender to the French until 1453, and then only reluctantly.

Raising money for the campaign for the recovery of Gascony in the 1290's was unpopular in England and lacked the enthusiastic support of many of the great magnates who saw little in it for themselves, since it concerned the King's private power and fortune rather than, initially at least, an immediate threat to the defences of the realm of England. King Edward, therefore, summoned a Parliament for the purposes of tackling the Gascony situation, which consisted of both Lords and elected Knights of the Shire (eventually the Commons) who met in the Palace of Westminster. Roger de Mowbray was summoned to this Model Parliament as 'Rogero de Mubray' in June 1295, attended again in 1296, and in January 1297 was summoned to the Parliament at Salisbury.

In 1270 Roger de Mowbray, then still very young, had married Rohese de Clare, daughter of the late Earl of Gloucester and Hertford, a match arranged by their mothers, and it is possible that Rohese was under fifteen at the time. Roger died in Ghent in 1297 and was buried in Fountains Abbey in 1299. A deed in the Public Record Office, now the National Archives, signed and dated at Epworth in February 1299 relates to some of his widow's properties and rights in Melton Mowbray, Leicestershire, while his Inquisitions Post Mortem show her to have retained extensive lands in the Isle of Axholme.

*JOHN DE MOWBRAY*, BORN 4ᵀᴴ SEPTEMBER 1286, HANGED AT YORK 23ᴿᴰ MARCH 1322.
Second Lord Mowbray.

John was aged only eleven when his father died and almost immediately King Edward I granted William de Braose (Brews), Lord of Gower in Wales and Bramber in Sussex, the right to marry him to his daughter Alina, (or Aline), whom John married in Swansea when he was twelve. In May 1306 he and three hundred other young men, including one Edmund Fitzalan and a certain Hugh le Despenser the Younger, were knighted at the same time as Prince Edward, whose coronation as Edward II he witnessed the following year, and whose unsavoury friends would be John's undoing a few years later. The Prince received his honour, long overdue because his father despaired of him, in Westminster Abbey, whereas the others were knighted at the London church of the Knights Templar, off Fleet Street, where such was the excitement that two of them were trampled to death in the crush. John was with Edward I's forces when the magnificent old warrior could fight no more and died at Burgh by Sands almost within sight of Hadrian's Wall, with his last breath exhorting his incompetent son to bury his heart in Jerusalem and then carry his bones before the English army so that, even in death, he could put the fear of God into the Scots.

In August 1307, at only twenty, John de Mowbray was summoned to Edward II's first Parliament and would attend every year up to 1321. Parliaments in those days were held at different venues throughout the country where the King happened to be at the time, and not always in London as is the practice now. John would be no stranger either to the London Court of King Edward and his constant companion Piers Gaveston. Piers was a knight from Gascony whom Edward I had brought to the royal Court in England as a goodwill gesture to his father, his staunch and loyal Gascon supporter. It was a decision he would soon regret, and, angered by his son's infatuation with Piers, he tore out some of the terrified future King's hair during a dreadful argument over him, and sent the knight into exile. Upon becoming King, Edward II immediately brought Piers Gaveston back, created him Earl of Cornwall and, possibly for the sake of appearances, married him to his niece, Margaret.

At the coronation, where he carried the crown and also, somewhat tactlessly in the circumstances, wore some of the choicest pieces of the jewellery the King's bemused twelve-year-old wife of only a few weeks had brought with her from France, Gaveston so enraged the nobility that one lord had to be held back from running him through with his sword. He was made regent when Edward was away in France in 1308 but his arrogance was too much for the long-established nobility to endure and, under pressure, Edward had to agree to his exile to Ireland soon after. Things did not improve when it was discovered that over there, and with the King's blessing, he was embezzling money belonging to the Crown. He returned to England briefly but was exiled again, only to return once more in 1312.

Piers and Edward removed to York when their opposition, some of the greatest of the magnates, started drumming up support, and civil war looked inevitable. Eventually they made their way to Scarborough

Castle where they were separated, Edward managing to escape and make his way back to York, and Gaveston being captured and incarcerated in Scarborough Castle, one of the strongest in the kingdom. He would probably have been safe at Scarborough, but Pembroke, one of his custodians, thought his own castle at Wallingford nearer London would be more suitable. In one way it made sense to move him because Edward was trying to raise support in Yorkshire, but there was an element of risk, and as the party rested overnight, Gaveston was abducted by the earls of Lancaster, Warwick and Hereford who took him to Blacklow Hill outside Warwick and beheaded him. This murder caused a dangerous division amongst those opposed to Edward and significantly weakened their position. John de Mowbray, who appears to have stayed loyal to Edward, would be well-known to the main players in this unfolding drama, and they to him.

The Piers Gaveston fiasco was disastrous on many levels but not least in that precious time, resources and goodwill were being squandered that would have been better employed in dealing with the worsening Scottish situation. Robert Bruce, grandson of the Bruce who was passed-over in favour of Balliol, was a man of quite different calibre and abilities from Edward II of England. Driven by the desire to be rid of the English once and for all, although he had spent part of his formative years at the Court of Edward I, he had had himself crowned King of Scotland at Scone on Palm Sunday 1306 with a golden circlet run up by the local blacksmith, a month after he had murdered his rival aspirant to the throne, John Comyn, in a church in Dumfries.

Throughout 1312-13 Bruce had great success in taking and reducing those great Scottish castles in English hands from the time of Edward I, and the English castellan of Stirling, Sir Philip Mowbray, realising that he could not hold out for much longer, got himself some breathing space by reaching the compromise with Edward Bruce, the King's brother, that if the English had not relieved the castle by the feast of St John the Baptist on 24th June 1314, a year hence, he would surrender it. The inevitable confrontation that would follow this truce did not suit the plans of the leaders of either side at that particular time, but Edward II could not lose face and was determined to relieve the castle and go on to subjugate the whole of Scotland. The story is taken up by the 'Monk of Malmesbury', writer of the *Life of Edward II*, who gives a fine account of the chaos of medieval warfare that could hardly be bettered, and of how a king's arrogance, stupidity and refusal to consider sound advice can lead to ignominious defeat, near ruin and the deaths of good and loyal men.

England, Scotland and Wales*
Some of the Places Associated
With the Mowbrays

Stirling
EDINBURGH
Berwick-upon-Tweed
Bamburgh
Alnwick
Tynemouth
Newcastle
Carlisle
Durham
Scarborough
Northallerton · Thirsk
Boroughbridge · YORK
Towton · Pontefract
Wakefield ·
Doncaster · *Epworth and the*
Tickhill · *Isle of Axholme*
LINCOLN
Nottingham
Melton Mowbray
Leicester NORWICH
Framlingham
Warwick Cambridge
Tewkesbury Ipswich
Gloucester
Chepstow Oxford St. Albans
Swansea Berkeley LONDON
Battle
Winchester
Arundel · Bramber Hastings
Pevensey

*Modern day borders shown

Copyright Marilyn Roberts 2004

52

*"About the beginning of Lent messengers came to the King with news of the destruction of the Scottish cities, the capture of castles, and the breaching of the surrounding walls. The constable of Stirling [Sir Philip Mowbray] came too, and pointed out to the King how he had been compelled by necessity to enter upon the truce. When the King heard the news he was very much grieved, and for the capture of his castles could scarcely restrain his tears."*

When the plans for the call-up were announced, some of the more prudent of the barons, probably John de Mowbray was amongst them, advised the King that according to the Ordinances he must have the consent of Parliament before proceeding further. The Ordinances were regulations drawn up by a group of magnates in 1310 to prevent Edward going to war or leaving the country without Parliament's consent. Others urged him to assert his authority and proceed as he pleased, and, of course, this was the advice he followed. Using money once belonging to the now disbanded Templars, he was able to furnish an army at least four times greater than that of the Scots and appears to have been in no doubt that an easy victory would be his. Bruce, for his part, was far from intimidated: he might have had only a quarter of the manpower, but he was a natural leader and had recruited and trained his soldiers himself. Burdened with all the necessary trappings, the English set out from Wark in Northumberland on 17th June, rather late considering that their very latest deadline for arriving at Stirling, or within a distance of three leagues of it, was only a week away.

*"When all the necessaries had been collected, the King and the other magnates of the land with a great multitude of carts and baggage-wagons set out for Scotland. … Indeed, all who were present agreed that never in our time has such an army gone forth from England. The multitude of wagons, if they had been placed end to end, would have taken up a space of twenty leagues.…Brief were halts for sleep, briefer still for food; hence horses, horsemen and infantry were worn out with toil and hunger, and if they did not bear themselves well it was hardly their fault."*

They reached Falkirk on the evening of 22nd June, having done a hundred miles in six days; a further twenty miles brought them to the boggy wetland of the Bannock Burn within three miles of Stirling the following afternoon. The battle-experienced amongst the leaders begged for a rest period for their men, and Philip Mowbray himself came out of the castle to advise King Edward that by the laws of chivalry a castle was deemed to have been relieved once the relieving army was within three leagues, and therefore an engagement between the forces was unnecessary as far as the future of Stirling Castle was concerned. Sir Philip warned Edward that the Scots were well prepared, had dug pits and set up metal spikes, and would not be an easy adversary; much less would they be intimidated by the large numbers of English and the rich apparel and expensive armour of the great lords. He was ignored.

Things went badly from the start. All were exhausted and it was late in the day to be thinking about engaging the enemy, but Edward was anxious to get on with the job, and his leaders could not believe their men were to fight without having had food and rest. The plan was for the earls of Hereford and Gloucester to drive the Scots into the arms of Clifford and Beaumont and their men, who had crept up from behind. It did not go unnoticed, and was frowned upon by some battle veterans, that Hereford's nephew, Sir Henry de Bohun, was, somewhat unconventionally, riding ahead of the commanders, he and his great steed decked out in the richest, most colourful battledress of the day. Another lone rider was then spotted on the scene, much less flamboyant, mounted on a 'litill and joly' grey palfrey, and making an inspection of the lie of the land at the edge of the woods. Sir Henry would have paid him little heed, until suddenly his heart must have nearly leapt out of his chest as the summer sunlight glanced off the rider's headgear betraying the golden circlet Robert Bruce wore around his helmet. De Bohun, overcome by what he saw as his chance of everlasting fame and glory, rushed at him with his lance. Bruce's pretty little grey horse was easily manoeuvrable and Sir Henry missed, but Robert Bruce's own aim was true, and raising himself in the stirrups, he swung his battleaxe so that instead of becoming the stuff of legend and romantic ballads, the reckless de Bohun was 'cleft to the brisket'.

At the end of the day's engagement between the two armies the English were much the worse for wear and,

> *"The day being spent, the whole army met at the place where it was to bivouac that night. But there was no rest, for they spent it sleepless, expecting the Scots rather to attack by night than to await battle by day. When day came it was abundantly clear that the Scots were prepared for the conflict with a great force of armed men. Wherefore our men, the veterans that is, and the more experienced, advised that we should not fight that day, but rather await the morrow both on account of the importance of the feast* [of St John the Baptist] *and the toil that they had already undergone. This practical and honourable advice was rejected by the younger men as idle and cowardly.*
>
> *Meanwhile, Robert Bruce marshalled and equipped his allies, gave them bread and wine, and cheered them as best he could; when he*

*learned that the English line had occupied the field he led his whole army out from the wood. About forty thousand men he brought with him* [a massive exaggeration], *and split them into three divisions; and not one of them was on horseback, but each was furnished with light armour, not easily penetrable by a sword. They had axes at their sides and carried lances in their hands. They advanced like a thick-set hedge, and such a phalanx could not easily be broken."*

What followed was an unmitigated disaster bemoaned by the writer, with the English running for their lives and many drowning in the marshy land or in trying to cross the Bannock Burn,

*"O famous race unconquered through the ages, why do you, who used to conquer knights, flee from mere footmen?"*

When it was over, Sir Philip Mowbray, wisely perhaps, refused the King entry to Stirling Castle, where he would surely have been taken prisoner, surrendered it, and thereafter sided with the Scots. The Lanercost Chronicle tells us that Edward and his favourite, Hugh le Despenser, 'who after Piers Gaveston was as his right eye', to their perpetual shame fled like miserable wretches to Dunbar Castle, from where they managed to get a ship to England, and left the cream of the English nobility to the vengeance of the Scots. Amongst the five hundred men of substance initially assumed dead but later ransomed was Sir Humphrey de Bohun, Earl of Hereford (see Table III), who was exchanged for Bruce's wife and his daughter, the Princess Marjorie, a young girl who had spent eight years in English custody. Many of lesser importance were killed, but the Scots were more interested in securing the valuable baggage train, and again we allow the writer of the *Life of Edward II* to take up the story,

*"O day of vengeance and disaster, day of utter loss and shame, evil and accursed day, not to be reckoned in our calendar; that blemished the reputation of the English, despoiled them and enriched the Scots, in which our costly belongings were ravished to the value of £200,000! So many fine noblemen and valiant youth, so many horses, so much military equipment, costly garments and gold plate - all lost in one unfortunate day, one fleeting hour."*
From *The Life of Edward the Second (Vita Edwardi Secundi)*

It is not difficult to see that Edward II had little of the military skill or political acumen of his late father, and none of the natural leadership talents of Bruce. Obviously he expected a great, yet virtually effortless, victory at Stirling and throughout Scotland, and had intended to reside there for some time in the great splendour to which he was accustomed, hence the 'costly belongings ravished to the value of £200,000'. Bruce saw to it that his men were well rested and properly fed 'cheering them as best he could', whereas Edward allowed no time for rest, and the English, exhausted and famished before they ever arrived, had to spend the night soaked to the skin on cold boggy ground too afraid to take the sleep they desperately needed in case the Scots came out of the woods in the dark.

Exactly where John de Mowbray was at this time is debatable. Under Edward II he was called-up for service against the northern neighbour every August from 1308 to 1319, was appointed Governor of the City and County of York in 1312, and in 1313 became Warden of the Marches towards Carlisle (the north-west borders), although some authorities believe this last to be the Scottish John de Mowbray who was also lord of Bolton in Cumberland. He was made Captain and Keeper of Newcastle-on-Tyne in March 1314, but whether he stayed there or joined Edward at Bannockburn is not clear. Naturally the Scots were elated by the humiliation of their enemy and only a year later were extorting protection money from the long-suffering northerners and still wreaking havoc. This was at the time when an extremely anxious John de Mowbray, still in charge at Newcastle, would have received news that both Durham and Hartlepool had been attacked at the end of June. July brought the siege of Carlisle and John must have been making preparations in case his turn was at hand; the Lanercost Chronicle describes what he might have been expecting,

> *"... on the feast of S. Mary Magdalene* [22nd July] *the King of Scotland, having mustered all his forces, came to Carlisle, invested the city and besieged it for ten days, trampling down all the crops,* [this in a year of widespread famine] *wasting the suburbs and all within the bounds, burning the whole of that district, and driving in a very great store of cattle for his army…Now on the fifth day of the siege they set up a machine for casting stones… and they cast great stones continually, but they did little or no injury to those within, except that they killed one man. But there were seven or eight similar machines within the city, besides other engines of war, which are called springalds, for discharging long darts, and staves with sockets for casting stones, which caused great fear and damage to those outside.*
>
> *Moreover, the Scots had made many long ladders, which they brought with them for scaling the wall in different places simultaneously; also a sow* [a covered siege engine which was

constructed to contain men who could be wheeled right up to the town wall to undermine the foundations]; *but neither sow nor ladders availed them aught. Also they made great numbers of fascines of corn and herbage to fill the moat outside the wall so as they might pass over dry-shod. Also, they made long bridges of logs running upon wheels, such as being strongly and swiftly drawn with ropes might reach across the width of the moat. But during all the time the Scots were on the ground neither fascines sufficed to fill the moat, nor those wooden bridges to cross the ditch, but sank to the depths by their own weight..."*

In 1317 John, 2<sup>nd</sup> Lord Mowbray was given custody of the castle at Malton and the town and castle of Scarborough, both in Yorkshire. A charming image of him, clad in armour and with his sword girded about him, is to be found in the stained glass of the Peter de Dene Window in the nave of York Minster, given by a Minster canon some time between 1304 and 1320. In April 1317, in the Minster chapter house, John confirmed a grant of land to Fountains Abbey. His seal, bearing a Mowbray lion, is on a document in the National Archives dated York, 4<sup>th</sup> November 1318, when he was probably attending the Parliament that had been convened to meet there on 20<sup>th</sup> October.

John had managed to steer clear of the trouble caused by the Gaveston affair and had remained loyal to the King, but he was powerless against the devastating effects of his next infatuation. Hugh le Despenser the Younger, shameless thug and privateer, who had soon replaced the murdered Piers Gaveston in Edward's affections, was the son of Hugh le Despenser, 3<sup>rd</sup> Earl of Winchester. Both father and son were unscrupulous and became phenomenally wealthy and powerful and were greatly feared. Despenser the Younger, lord of neighbouring Glamorgan, coveted John de Mowbray's lands in Gower that his father-in-law William de Braose had conveyed to him, and persuaded his master that John should have sought royal permission for the transfer and that, he having failed to do so, Gower should be taken from him. In October 1320 the escheator was ordered to take Gower into the King's hand. In 1321 Mowbray joined in rebellion with the Mortimer family, the Earl of Hereford, Humphrey de Bohun, veteran of Bannockburn (see Table III), and the Earl of Lancaster, who had been party to the murder of Gaveston, all of whom feared their West Country lands could fall into the hands of the Despensers. The border, or 'Marcher', lords had already flexed their collective muscle in the reign of Edward I and now their heirs maintained that John did not need the King's permission to take possession of his father-in-law's lands, for in the Marches, a special case since the time of the

*ARMS OF HUGH LE DESPENSER THE ELDER; WINCHESTER GREAT HALL.*
*The Despensers, father and son, were responsible for the death of John, 2ⁿᵈ Lord Mowbray in 1322.*
*Photo M. Roberts, by kind permission of Hampshire County Council.*

Conqueror, it was neither illegal nor unusual for such transfers to occur.

For Edward II his dearest Hugh could do no wrong; he even turned a blind eye for two months as the Despenser father and son turned pirate, preying on shipping in the Channel, and without provocation murdering the crew of a rich vessel from Genoa. In March 1321 the lords opposed to the King and his hateful friends harried Glamorgan and entered London. Both Despensers were banished after the deliberations of Parliament in July and King Edward pardoned those responsible the following month. The King had little choice but to restore Gower to Mowbray, but all knew that it would be only a matter of time before Edward gathered himself together and exacted his revenge upon his errant subjects.

In November, John de Mowbray was amongst those prominent lords ordered by their King not to attend a meeting called by the Earl of Lancaster at Doncaster, but he disobeyed. However, John and his fellow rebels found some of the support they expected had not materialised. By the following January Edward had defeated the Mortimers, and John de Mowbray and the others, with their small force of about 3,000 men, had already encountered the King's side at

Burton-on-Trent and decided to flee north. John was involved in the siege of the royal castle at Tickhill in Yorkshire, when his men were said to have done much damage in the area. For these acts of rebellion his lands were seized and his wife and son conveyed to the Tower in February.

On 11th March 1322, a warrant was issued for the arrest of the second Lord Mowbray, for treason. Meanwhile, Sir Andrew de Harcla came down from the castle at Carlisle with a force of 4,000, and arriving at Boroughbridge after marching through the night, he blocked the rebels' way across the bridge over the River Ure. On 16th March, under a shower of enemy arrows, Hereford and Sir Roger de Clifford set-about taking the bridge, then, in an act reminiscent of the taking of Stamford Bridge, that other great battle of 1066 where the Viking hero defending it single-handed was 'brogged from below', someone crept under the Usk Bridge and thrust his spear so hard into Hereford that, the witnesses reported, his bowels spilled out. Mercifully, the great Humphrey de Bohun, veteran of Bannockburn and 'a worthy knight of renown through all Christendom', died almost at once.

The rebels had no real chance and had already suffered heavy losses. As night fell the two sides called a truce, but many of the rebel forces deserted under cover of darkness, and in the morning some of those left cast aside their armour and took to the roads hoping to pass themselves off as innocent travellers. The Earl of Lancaster was found

CLIFFORD'S TOWER, YORK.
*After the Battle of Boroughbridge Sir Roger de Clifford was hanged and his body suspended from the walls of the keep of York Castle; hence 'Clifford's Tower'.*

praying in a church, from where he was dragged to his trial and execution. Sir Roger de Clifford was hanged and his body hung in chains over the walls of the keep of York Castle – hence 'Clifford's Tower'. John de Mowbray was captured and was hanged at York a week later. The vindictive King refused to allow his body to be removed from the gallows and it was left in chains for more than three years, a sad end at the age of only thirty-five for a man who had given sustained service to King and country since he was little more than a boy. According to William Grainge in his book *The Vale of Mowbray*, published in 1859, a tradition grew up in the Vale that John

had been caught and executed between Thirsk and Upsall at a place known as 'Chophead Loaning', where his armour, rumoured to be hanging on an oak, could be heard creaking at midnight. Knight in his *History of the City of York* says that after being suspended from the scaffold for three years, John's body was interred at the Dominican Friars at Toft Green; others believe he could have been buried at Fountains Abbey.

John de Mowbray's estates were forfeit and in June 1323 his wife Alina was given into the custody of the reinstated Despensers who terrorised her into granting her rights to her father's manor and castle of Bramber and other of her lands to Hugh the Elder the following year. Her father, she claimed later, when he was 'frantiqe and not in good memory', had granted them his manor of Witham in Kent on the promise that his daughter and grandson would be

*LADY ALINA DE MOWBRAY.*
*Photo Courtesy of the City and County of Swansea.*

released, which they were not. However, after the deposition of Edward II in 1326, the Despensers were executed on Queen Isabella's orders, Hugh the Younger being put to death on an extra tall scaffold so that all could witness the suffering of one who had persecuted so many. With Parliament's recognition of Edward III in January 1327 Lady Alina de Mowbray had her lands reinstated, although after her death her son would be involved in litigation over lands and property for many years with her second husband, Sir Richard Peshale. Sir Richard was an escheator, whose job it was to ensure the King was being paid all he was due; this is the origin of the word 'cheat' and there is little doubt that such officials knew all about lining their own pockets.

## CALENDAR OF CLOSE ROLLS EDWARD III 1327-30
### NORTHAMPTON 8TH MAY, 2 EDWARD III[1]

Agreement between John, 3rd Lord Mowbray (1310-1361), his mother Alina de Braose (Lady Mowbray) and his stepfather Sir Richard Peshale.

> *Enrolment of deed of John de Moubray lord of the Isle of Axhiholme, witnessing that whereas the Lady Alina, his mother, has granted to Richard de Pessale, knight, for her life the manor of Wynlynton, Co. Bedford, which she held of John in dower, and a third of the manors of Crich, Northamptonshire, and Shudoke, Co. Warwick, which she likewise held for life of her son's inheritance, the said John accepting the said grant and wishing to show favour by reason of his grateful service to Alina, and to him, grants that if Richard survive Alina[2] he may hold the premises to the end of his life.[3]*

[1] 1328; there is another reference to Alina's transactions with Sir Richard in the Calendar of Patent Rolls for 1327-30.

[2] Alina is known to have died before July 1331, whereas Sir Richard, escheator for the counties of Warwick, Nottingham, Lancaster, Derby, and Leicester and sometime sheriff of Salop and Staffordshire, was still living in November 1342.

[3] This is another of John's generous gestures, but somehow things went wrong and after Alina died he had to sue to get back some of her lands from Sir Richard, but not necessarily those set out in this deed.

# THE HAXEY HOOD GAME

This wonderfully entertaining ritual takes place annually on Twelfth Night around the villages of Haxey and Westwoodside in the Isle of Axholme in North Lincolnshire and in some ways is rather like a glorified hundred-strong rugby scrum, with 'the Sway' taking all in its path. The pushing and shoving sometimes goes on for hours and the aim is to get the Hood, nowadays a leather-bound rope 23½ inches long with a diameter of 2¾ inches and strengthened with bamboo sticks, rushes and reeds, to a favourite pub in one of the two villages – the *Loco Inn*, the *Duke William* or the *King's Arms* in Haxey, or the *Carpenter's Arms* in Westwoodside – where the landlord then keeps it for the next twelve months.

The game is said to commemorate the occasion when Lady Mowbray lost her hood in a gust of wind when out riding and was so amused by the antics of the rustics who chased it across muddy fields and retrieved it for her that she gave them a reward and hoped they would re-enact the event every year. In the spirit of fun she addressed the man who returned the hood to her as 'Lord', and nowadays the Lord of the Hood and the Boggins, his assistants who represent the rest of the men, keep order. The Fool, based on the character who actually retrieved the hood but was supposed to be so shy he could not summon the courage to hand it back to Lady Mowbray, makes a speech outside Haxey Church before the real business of getting the Hood moving begins. The Haxey Hood is not a game for faint-hearted

*The Main Players in the Haxey Hood Game, 2003*
*The Lord (Phil Coggan)*
*The Chief Boggin (Ian Dawes), holding the Hood*
*The Fool (Dale Smith)*

*LIVING PROOF THAT A FOOL CAN BECOME A LORD!*
*Stan Boor (left) was first the Fool, then Lord of the Hood. Fortunately in World War II young lads like Stan and the older men of the villages kept the ancient tradition alive. This photograph from the 1970's shows him with the late Peter Bee (The Fool, centre) and the late Arthur Clark (Chief Boggin).*
*Photo reproduced by kind permission of Mr. S. Boor.*

participants, but neither is it an excuse for bad behaviour, as the Fool is careful to make clear in his speech,

> *"Hoose agin hoose, toon agin toon, if tha' meets a man, knock 'im doon – but doan't ot 'im."* [House against house, town against town, if you meet a man knock him down – but don't hurt him.]

Have we any real idea as to the identity of the noble Lady of the Hood? The answer has to be in the negative because there is no definite known date for the original event. However, the date is sometimes given as 'thirteenth century', a period of time in which the Mowbray wives are shadowy figures. The late twelfth/early thirteenth century would give us Avice, wife of Sir William de Mowbray, the Magna Carta baron, but unfortunately little is known about this lady except that she might have been from the Arundel d'Albini branch of the d'Aubigny family. The first Mowbray wife to take on any sort of personality for us is Alina de Braose, wife of John, 2nd Lord Mowbray. Living right at the end of the thirteenth century, the Lady Alina calls to us from the pages of history because her misfortunes were so well known at the time. John was only twelve when they married in 1298, and Alina was possibly even younger. Nevertheless, she would be addressed as Lady Mowbray, and such an amusing event as the locals chasing after her hat or hood and then arguing amongst themselves for the privilege of returning it to her might well have appealed to a child. In view of the hardships she suffered as a woman, it would be pleasant to think that Alina the child found amusement in the fun and games of a fresh January day as she rode through the Isle.

Alina's son, born in 1310, married Joan Plantagenet, whose eldest son was born in Epworth in 1340, so we can be forgiven for speculating that the headgear could even have belonged to Joan herself, a great-grandchild of Henry III, making the mysterious Lady of the Haxey Hood one of the finest ladies in the land. An article about the Haxey Hood in *The Times* on 4th January 1928 suggests that the Hood tradition and the Mowbray shield fastened to a post in the centre of Haxey village are associated with Elizabeth Fitzalan, wife of Thomas Mowbray, the first Mowbray Duke of Norfolk.

The Haxey Hood Game could have its real foundation in ancient fertility rites and also bears some similarity to Camp-ball, a precursor of modern football, often played between two villages with the goals miles apart. The field of play was called the 'camping-close' and hundreds of players could be involved in a game that was often as much about good-humoured rough-and-tumble as reaching the other team's goal. Initially the ball, about the size of a modern cricket ball, was made of leather but was eventually an inflated pig's bladder filled with dried peas and could be kicked as well as thrown. Sometimes kicking only was permitted and the game was known as 'kicking-camp' and, in the fifteenth century, as 'football'.

Love of football could be said to be posing a threat to national security on both sides of the border. Edward III, hard-pressed by both his Scottish and French commitments, declared that able-bodied men must proceed to archery practice after church on Sundays instead of wasting time playing football, and in 1457 King James II of Scotland, whose naughty subjects were finding practising their military skills rather tedious and were making the most of the little leisure time their harsh lives allowed, decreed that, 'futeball and golfe be utterly cried down'.

# CHAPTER IV

## 1327-1400: War, Plague and Betrayal

*Why, man, I first loosed string in battle when I was but a lad, younger by two years than you, at Neville's Cross, under the Lord Mowbray. Later, I served under the Warden of Berwick, that very John Copeland… the same who held the King of Scots to ransom.*
Sir Arthur Conan Doyle, *The White Company*

DWARD III WAS FOURTEEN when his father was murdered and for a time had no option but to allow his mother Isabella, the *She Wolf*, and her lover Roger Mortimer to rule in his name, a situation he remedied four years later by abducting Mortimer from Nottingham Castle and hanging him at Tyburn, now the site of London's Marble Arch. Through his mother Edward laid claim to the throne of France and started what has become known as The Hundred Years' War. In his reign the House of Commons began meeting separately from the Lords, the former in the chapter house of Westminster Abbey, the latter continuing to meet in the Palace of Westminster, a huge step forward on the road towards democracy. The Scottish problem remained much as before, with the third Lord Mowbray distinguishing himself against the army of King David II at Neville's Cross in 1346.

As if ongoing wars were not bad enough, Europe at large had to suffer the ravages of the bubonic plague, which in its main outbreaks in 1348-9, 1361 and 1369, claimed between a third and a half of the total English population of about four million. Whole villages were deserted because nobody was left, but people who did survive were sometimes able to move from their villages to better paid work in towns, because there was nobody left in authority to stop them. Apart from the misery, despair and devastation it brought, there were some positive outcomes of the Black Death. As we have said, people could now move more freely, and there was unoccupied land to be had, enabling an enterprising and thrifty peasant, such as Clement Paston of Norfolk, to acquire property and land cheaply.

Equally important was the realisation amongst the ordinary people that the plague, assumed to have been sent by God as a punishment for their sins, had afflicted all levels of society from the King's own family down to the most humble in the land. No matter how much

BYLAND ABBEY
*Joan Plantagenet, Lady Mowbray, was buried before the altar here in 1349.*

they spent on trying to buy a smooth pathway to Heaven, it seemed that perhaps God was looking for finer qualities in His people, qualities like charity and compassion, to which anyone, powerful or humble, could aspire. Nevertheless, John, third Lord Mowbray, arguably the greatest gentleman and humanitarian of his dynasty, was taken by the disease in 1361. The ordinary thinking man began to ask questions and make comment about the existing social order. William Langland, a humble chantry chapel clerk wrote the wonderful masterpiece the *Vision of Piers Plowman* in the 1370's containing telling little phrases such as,

> *"And so up came a hundred barristers-at-law wearing silk coifs. They pleaded their case for fees small and large, but wouldn't open their lips for pure charity's sake."*

On his travels Piers comes upon all types of people, the greatest and haughtiest in the land amongst them, but at the end of this marvellous story it is shown that there is none greater in heart and mind than honest Piers the Plowman, a humble farm labourer. Not surprisingly it became a best seller and was soon followed by Geoffrey Chaucer's motley bunch of so-called 'pilgrims' on their way to Becket's shrine at Canterbury. Chaucer was a Court official and the fact that he dared turn out such an amusing, yet in its way revolutionary, piece of writing shows that the social order was slowly changing and a few brave people dared to draw attention to the wrongs and hypocrisies of the day.

In his later years King Edward III, the once-great ruler, suffered ill health and senile dementia and, having lost the steadying influence of his late wife, Queen Philippa, was at the mercy of his unscrupulous courtiers. His ghastly mistress, Alice Perrers, was reputed to have stooped so low as to steal the very jewels from his corpse. His son, the Black Prince, an occasional supporter of the House of Commons, died the year before his father, so in 1377 the throne passed to the Prince's son, a vulnerable child of ten, who became King Richard II.

In 1381, when Richard was still only fourteen years old, rebellion broke out in the shape of the Peasants' Revolt, an energetic and violent protest against the introduction of a poll tax. The boy, facing the insurgents at Mile End Fields just beyond the Tower, and at Smithfield, saved the day, and his life, by making promises he had no intention of keeping, a most brilliant piece of public relations brought about through the cunning youth's deceit. Defusing a dreadful situation that nobody else had been able to handle only further boosted Richard's already over-inflated ego and led the young King to believe he was superhuman and invincible.

In Richard's minority the government was in the hands of a group of advisers led by his uncles Thomas of Woodstock and John of Gaunt, the Dukes of Gloucester and Lancaster respectively, but a group of friends formed itself around him, powerful, expensive to maintain and, in some cases, a bad and dangerous influence. The *Merciless Parliament* of 1388 removed many of these after a group of lords made appeals of treason against them. The Lords Appellant making the accusations were: the Duke of Gloucester and the earls of Warwick (Thomas Beauchamp), Derby (Henry Bolingbroke, John of Gaunt's son), Arundel (Richard Fitzalan), and Nottingham (Thomas Mowbray, Fitzalan's son-in-law). The next year King Richard, now nearly twenty-three, took up power himself and, although for some time all appeared to be going well, the dying years of the fourteenth century would see treachery, betrayal, Thomas Mowbray disgraced and banished, and King Richard deposed and murdered.

*John de Mowbray*, 29TH November 1310 - 4TH October 1361.
Third Lord Mowbray.

John, born at Hovingham in Yorkshire and baptised at All Saints

NO PLACE FOR A BOY AND HIS MOTHER.
*The Tower of London; John, 3rd Lord Mowbray and his mother, the Lady Alina, were incarcerated here by Edward II.*

Church there, was only eleven when he was sent to the Tower with Alina his mother, a month before his father was captured at Boroughbridge and executed. It appears that John could have already been promised in marriage to Maud de Holand, and some sources believe his little 'wife' was imprisoned too. However, the actual marriage ceremony seems not to have taken place, so it seems most unlikely that she was in the Tower with him, and John's elder sister, Christiana, was married by this time. (She was an ancestress of George Washington and the Bush Presidents, see Tables XIV and XXI). On the accession of Edward III in January 1327 they were given their freedom, and John's rightful lands were to be restored to him when he came of age, but in the meantime the wardship of the Isle of Axholme was granted to Joan (de Warenne) Countess of Surrey. In February John de Mowbray married, or was contracted to marry, Joan Plantagenet, fifth and youngest daughter of Henry, 3rd Earl of Lancaster, and great-granddaughter of King Henry III (Table III). Lancaster, the brother of the 2nd Earl, who had perished with John's father after Boroughbridge, was granted control over his marriage as a reward for services to Queen Isabella and was obviously going to marry off this rich young man to one of his own girls.

From an early age John was active in military and political events, the first summons for service against the Scots coming in the summer of 1327 when he was only sixteen and but a few months out of captivity in the Tower. He was ordered to escort personally a contingent of his men from Gower to Newcastle; too young, it would seem, to have control of his lands, but old enough to put his life in peril. Three months later, even though still under age, he was allowed control of his lands, perhaps as recompense for his imprisonment.

John served in Parliament between 1327 and 1360 and in 1340 was appointed Justice in those parts of Scotland occupied by the King of England, and Keeper of Berwick-on-Tweed, where he had with him, chroniclers tell us, 120 men-at-arms, 100 'hobelours' (hobelars: archers on horseback who could move around but who dismounted to fight, often used in raiding parties), 200 archers, 48 watchmen, one 'maistre angynour' (master engineer), and four 'valletz' (grooms) and was claiming he had not been paid monies due for their upkeep. In fact, four years later the King still owed him the very considerable sum of £1,826, about £700,000 at today's rates, towards his expenses. The description of the siege of Carlisle in John's father's day gives an idea of the duties the 'maistre angynour' had to perform in building siege towers, bridges and so forth for both attack and defence.

Between 1328 and 1359 John was frequently called to Councils as an advisor to the King, the large number of times that he was summoned showing him to have been a very important man whose opinions were respected. From 1332 onwards he was put on many Commissions of Array, that is, he decided who in his area was to be called-up for military service, and was also a judge on the 'Oyer and Terminer' (hear and determine) judicial circuit, presiding over cases involving serious breaches of the King's peace. These duties he fitted in around yet more service against the Scots and defending the south coast against the French. In 1341 he had to send men from his Yorkshire estates to the aid of Edward Balliol, John Balliol's son, and in 1343 was ordered to Court to be in the service of the Prince of Wales, the Black Prince, then aged thirteen.

Jean Froissart, one of the most famous of all the medieval chroniclers, places John de Mowbray at the Battle of Crécy in the summer of 1346, but this is an error, for although he sent 150 Welshmen from Gower, he was unable to go himself, since he and Lord Segrave were busy with the garrison at Berwick. The French were desolate after their defeat at Crécy and entreated their old ally, Scotland, to take some of the pressure off them. They reasoned that an invasion from north of the border could not be contained by the few fighting men left in England and, seeing that all of his realm was under threat, Edward III would be compelled to send a significant number of his troops home. David II of Scotland expected little opposition since thousands of English fighting men were involved at Crécy, and as many as 30,000 in the siege of Calais. However, Edward had anticipated just such a scenario, and in early March 1346 the Archbishop of York, the Bishop of Durham, the sheriff of Yorkshire and the northern magnates, including Mowbray, had been put in charge of defence plans, and the King issued a proclamation that able-bodied men between the ages of sixteen and sixty should be arrayed for the defence of the realm.

It is likely that the English forces thus mustered numbered about 6,000 - possibly 10,000 at the maximum. One Thomas Sampson, in a letter to a friend at the time, says there were 1,000 men-at-arms, more than 1,000 hobelars, over 10,000 archers, and a good 20,000 foot soldiers taken solely from the region 'between' the rivers Trent and Humber. This is typical of how the chroniclers and others grossly exaggerated the numbers involved in battles, possibly to make more exciting reading; in a relatively sparsely populated area this number would have been exceptional at the best of times, but when thousands were already deployed in France, it was impossible. Chronicles are invaluable, but not always reliable, and are by no means consistent. Rarely had the writers been at the scene of the events they described and had to rely upon hearsay, often long after the event, and did not interview participants in the way a modern war correspondent would do. Even men who had actually taken part in a battle would have a very limited idea of what was going on as a whole: a man fighting for his life and tussling with the constrictions of a heavy helmet with narrow slits for eyeholes was hardly going to be looking around him to try to get an overview of a battle.

Sometimes the work of chroniclers also took on a great deal of poetic licence, as was the case with Jean le Bel. A Hainaulter like his heroine Queen Philippa, he has her leading her absent husband's troops to a great victory over King David at Neville's Cross, a story later taken up by Jean Froissart, whose works included illustrations of the lovely lady resplendent on horseback at the head of the army outside the walls of Newcastle. Just two small problems here: the battle was outside the city of Durham, and the Queen was in Flanders at the time. The Chronicle of Meaux Abbey in Yorkshire tells us that King David led his army towards Hexham and spared nobody, not even women and children, and that English forces were under the leadership of William de la Zouche, Archbishop of York; Thomas Rokeby, sheriff of Yorkshire; the Baron of Bothal (Sir Robert Ogle, see Table VII); the Lords Percy, Mowbray, Neville, and Deincourt; and the Earl of Angus. The Chronicle of Geoffrey le Baker involves the Bishop of Carlisle, and sometimes the Bishop of Lincoln is also included in the accounts.

On the foggy morning of 17th October, Sir William Douglas and about 500 of his men were happily plundering the town of Merrington and were so engrossed in their work that they failed to realise that the

*DURHAM CATHEDRAL.*
*Durham monks prayed for an English victory at Neville's Cross.*
*Reproduced by kind permission of Durham County Council.*

English were upon them. Douglas lost half of his men but King David was not too troubled by this setback, instructing his servants to carry on preparing his breakfast, joking that he would soon be back for it after he had taken care of the English. However, his forces found themselves virtually trapped in a valley so that their vanguard and central divisions became mixed up and confused, which made them an ideal target. The Battle of Neville's Cross was very hard, with a good deal of hand-to-hand fighting, and it is suggested that the two sides had to lay down their arms and have a sort of 'half time'. The engagement seems to have lasted from about 1.30 p.m., the hour of Nones, to 5 p.m., the hour of Vespers. Both armies were arranged in three groups, most, but not all, of the chroniclers placing John de

Mowbray in the third line, the rearguard, with Thomas Rokeby. The English won the day.

King David received two arrow wounds, and after the Scots dispersed was captured by John de Coupland, a Northumbrian squire who is supposed to have seen his reflection in the water as he rested under a bridge. Apparently David planted his gauntleted fist firmly in Coupland's face and knocked out his front teeth, but the elated squire would not have been too upset, knowing that if a man could capture a king on another king's 'most wanted' list he would never be short of funds. Based on information from the Bank of England that £1 of 1350 would be worth £382.75 in 1997, Marie C. Dixon in *The Battle of Neville's Cross, 1346* writes that the annuity of £600 Coupland received for life would have an equivalent annual worth of about £229,650. He was murdered in December 1363.

According to Froissart, a fragment of an arrow remained lodged in David's head and gave him headaches at a new moon, but others believed the arrow miraculously worked itself out as he prayed at a holy shrine. It was 1357 before terms for his ransom were agreed at 100,000 marks (£66,666 – over £25,000,000 at today's rates) and he was released. Unable to raise the money, and having no children, (he was married to Joan, daughter of Edward II, in 1328 when he was four) he was later willing to agree that upon his death the throne should go to a candidate of Edward III, possibly his second son, Lionel Duke of Clarence, a proposition the Scots refused to back. When David died in 1371 he was succeeded by another Neville's Cross veteran, his nephew Robert Stewart, the son of his sister Marjorie Bruce and Walter Steward (see Chapter VII).

The Chronicler of Lanercost Abbey said of John de Mowbray, now nearly 36 and already famous and well-respected, that at the Battle of Neville's Cross he was,

> *"A man of grace and bounty, whose happy fame, worthy of extended praise, is widely known; he and his men so conducted themselves that glory shall be given them for long ages."*

This was fine praise indeed for a man who could so easily have been brutalised by his parents' ill-treatment at the hands of the late King, and by his own terrifying incarceration in the Tower when still an impressionable child. Sir William de Mowbray, his Scottish relative, was amongst those important prisoners taken for ransom by the Neville family after the battle. In December John was called to London to the Council as an advisor on Scottish affairs, and the next Easter was in Scotland with 50 men-at-arms and 50 mounted archers, whose total daily wages amounted to 77 shillings and 8 pence.

Three years after Neville's Cross John's wife, Joan Plantagenet, died early in July, possibly in the first wave of the plague, and was buried before the high altar at Byland Abbey; her very eligible widower is known to have been in Epworth the following September. John was still continually called-up for service against the Scots and French and when the truce with the latter expired in 1352 he was appointed chief of the commissioners charged with the defence of the Yorkshire coast. In 1354 the Earl of Warwick challenged him for the lordship of Gower, which generations before had been in the possession of his, Warwick's, family, and even though John's friend the Black Prince stepped in on his behalf, King Edward III ruled in favour of Warwick. After this Mowbray styled himself 'Lord of the Isle of Axholme and of the Honour of Bramber', and Gower was not restored to the family until the reign of Richard II. In January 1356 he was in Scotland with the King and was a witness to Edward Balliol surrendering his claim to the throne of Scotland in favour of Edward III. In December 1359 he was made a Justice of the Peace in the Holland district of Lincolnshire and the following February was also appointed a Justice in the counties of Lancashire, Nottinghamshire, Leicestershire, Derbyshire and Rutland.

A deed John de Mowbray granted on 1st May 1359 underlines what

*HAXEY CHURCH: 'THE CATHEDRAL OF THE ISLE'*
*The Mowbray Deed was kept here. The window on the right has a small Mowbray lion. There is no trace of the original stained glass portrait of John de Mowbray.*

was said of his good character at Neville's Cross. The marshy low-lying Isle of Axholme in the north of Lincolnshire was then an area where local people supplemented a meagre existence by fishing, fowling and collecting peat and, in order to end disputes between his steward and his tenants, John granted rights to the latter in perpetuity. This precious Mowbray Deed was jealously preserved in a stout ironbound chest under a stained glass window portrait of John in the church in the village of Haxey, the key being kept by 'some of the chiefest freeholders' of the area. In the time of King Charles I, the Commonwealth and Charles II, the rights of the Axholme commoners were overridden, the portrait of their hero destroyed, the deed removed and the land drained and re-allocated, leaving the people with only a fraction of what had traditionally been their greatest asset (see Appendix F).

John's last public duty was his summons to Parliament in May 1360, for the Bubonic Plague was no respecter of goodness and, having escaped the first outbreak of 1348-49, John de Mowbray too was struck down in the autumn of 1361 at the age of fifty. Dying in York on 4th October, he was buried at the Grey Friars Church in Bedford and was succeeded by his son, also called John. He had remarried after Joan's death, and his widow, Elizabeth de Vere, and her new husband abused her rights over Mowbray lands and properties (see Chapter VI).

*JOHN DE MOWBRAY*, JUNE 25TH 1340 - SEPTEMBER OR OCTOBER 1368. Fourth Lord Mowbray.

Born at Epworth, John was knighted at fifteen, and at sixteen was fighting in Brittany. He was summoned to Parliament regularly between summer 1362 and January 1366. This John brought great prestige to his family through his marriage, when he was about nine years old, to eleven-year-old Elizabeth Segrave, an heiress of John, the Lord Segrave who had been posted at Berwick with his father. There must have been mutual respect and understanding between the two families, for John's sister Blanche married Elizabeth's brother at about the same time, but he died young, his inheritance passing to his sister. Elizabeth was a great-granddaughter of Edward I on her mother's side, meaning that eventually the wealth of Edward's younger son, Thomas de Brotherton, would come to the Mowbrays. However, sometimes things do not work out as we anticipate they will, and unexpected events and complications meant that a large part of the Brotherton and Segrave wealth attached to Elizabeth's inheritance would be more difficult for them to secure than they could ever have thought, although Elizabeth's lands in Leicestershire, of which she had control after her father's death, added to the Mowbray holdings in the Melton Mowbray area, and she also brought them Caludon Castle and other lordships in Warwickshire.

Elizabeth Segrave's pedigree was impeccable indeed. Edward I was married to Eleanor of Castile for thirty-six years and was in his early fifties when she died, having borne him sixteen children but only one surviving son, later Edward II. He was inconsolable when she died, but devastated as he genuinely was, nine years later, at the age of sixty, King Edward married the Princess Margaret (Marguerite), sister of the King of France, as part of a truce between the two countries by which Gascony reverted to Edward; his son was to marry the French King's daughter Isabella, Margaret's niece. In 1300 Margaret, not yet twenty, gave birth to a son at Brotherton in Yorkshire, and this Thomas de Brotherton, half-brother of Edward II, was Elizabeth Segrave's grandfather, the Earl of Norfolk. As a young man he supported Edward II but realised he was never going to make a good ruler and was one of the first to offer support to Queen Isabella and Roger Mortimer. When he could see they were little better he transferred his allegiance to his young nephew Edward III.

Brotherton died aged thirty-eight leaving his daughters Margaret

Chart 5: *Two Great Mowbray Marriages*

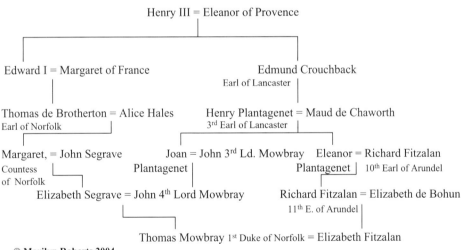

© **Marilyn Roberts 2004**

Joan Plantagenet, 1312-1349, was the fifth and youngest daughter of Henry, 3rd Earl of Lancaster (Table III). Her sister Eleanor married Richard Fitzalan, 10th Earl of Arundel, so not only were both Thomas Mowbray and Elizabeth Fitzalan descended from Henry III, their grandmothers were also sisters. Henry of Lancaster was the younger brother of the 2nd Earl, who had perished with John de Mowbray's father in 1322.
Margaret Plantagenet eventually came into the entire inheritance of her own father, Edward I's son Thomas de Brotherton. Her daughter Elizabeth Segrave outlived her brother and so looked forward to a considerable fortune in her own right. The deceased brother, John Segrave, had married Blanche de Mowbray, who went on to have four more husbands – see Chart 4.

and Alice as his coheirs; Margaret outlived her sister and inherited the earldom of Norfolk and the vast estates in East Anglia, as well as the hereditary title of Earl Marshal of England. She was styled 'Countess Marshal', and after all the centuries that have come and gone between her lifetime and the present day, the arrangements for such great state occasions as coronations, state funerals and the State Opening of Parliament are still made under the supervision of her descendants, the Dukes of Norfolk. It was true that the 3rd Lord Mowbray had also married a Plantagenet, but Joan was one of a large number of children of a father who himself had brothers and sisters, so her inheritance was considerably diluted, whereas Elizabeth Segrave was the only surviving child of an only surviving child of the son of a king. Margaret Plantagenet, Countess of Norfolk, would outlive her husband Lord Segrave, her daughter Elizabeth, her son-in-law John, 4th Lord Mowbray, her grandson John, and was only survived by his brother and heir Thomas Mowbray by a few weeks. Margaret's second husband, said to 'love honour more than silver' was Walter, Lord Mauny, a knight who had come to England with Philippa of Hainault and who went on to become one of the great soldiers of his day as well as being a very competent admiral. Deeply religious, he founded the London Charterhouse, near Smithfield, and died in 1372.

A document of the autumn of 1367 informs us that 'John de Mowbray of Axholme, chivaler' was about to go beyond the seas on the King's licence and had nominated lawyers to administer his affairs at home. Quite what his business abroad entailed is not clear, but in 1368, shortly after his wife Elizabeth's death, John was killed by Saracens in or near Constantinople, leaving behind a brood of very young children. The eldest, John, died young, but for the importance of the others – Thomas, Eleanor and Joan – see Table II. John, 4th Lord Mowbray's will was read at Lincoln on 17th May 1369.

*{By now the spelling of the name is predominantly Moubray or Mowbray, rather than de Mowbray.}*

JOHN DE MOWBRAY, DIED FEBRUARY 1383.
Earl of Nottingham.

Created Earl of Nottingham on the day of the coronation of Richard II in 1377, John died unmarried in 1383 at the age of no more than twenty-two. Buried in the Friars Carmelite, Fleet Street, London, he was succeeded by his brother, Thomas, who was arguably the most famous of all his family.

*Thomas Mowbray*, 22ND March 1366 - 22ND September 1399.
1st Duke of Norfolk, Earl of Nottingham, Earl of Norfolk, Earl Marshal; (succeeded his brother John).

Thomas, born at Epworth, and his brother and sisters had lost both parents by the time he was three years old and he was about the same age as his close kinsman Richard II. His mother particularly revered Thomas Becket, for whom she might have named her younger son. His first wife, Elizabeth Strange, whom he married in 1383 when he was seventeen, died shortly afterwards, still only in her tenth year. In 1384 Thomas married as his second wife the young widow Elizabeth Fitzalan, the 11th Earl of Arundel's daughter, an eighteen-year-old like himself and, like him, a great-great grandchild of Edward I; their grandmothers were the sisters Joan and Eleanor Plantagenet. (For Elizabeth Fitzalan see below, and for more on the Fitzalan family and the blood relationship with the Mowbrays see Table III and Chapter VII.)

In June 1385, King Richard invested Thomas as Earl Marshal of England for life, the office his great-grandfather Thomas de Brotherton had held, an honour made hereditary in the male line of his family just a few months later, and in 1386 his wife Elizabeth had a new Garter robe for the annual ceremony at Windsor, Thomas having been made a Knight of the Garter in 1383. In 1385 he fought against the Scots, becoming the Keeper of Berwick and Roxburgh in 1389, and in March 1387 served under Richard Fitzalan, Earl of Arundel, his father-in-law, against the French, Spanish and Flemish fleets off Margate. He was appointed Captain of Calais in February 1391, effective as from 1st June, which allowed him to wear as a medallion about his neck a golden leopard with a coronet of silver, and in November 1392 was made the King's Lieutenant in Calais, Picardy, Flanders and Artois. He became Chief Justice of North Wales in March 1394 and that year also accompanied the King to Ireland.

In February 1388 Thomas had supported Richard Fitzalan and the other Lords Appellant in their accusation of treason against the King's favourites, resulting in many exiles and executions that helped to unhinge King Richard's already disturbed mind still further. Particularly distressing, and, it could be said, vindictive, was the execution of Sir Simon Burley, who had been a close friend of the Black Prince and was devoted to his son Richard, whom as an exhausted little boy he had carried on his shoulders from Westminster

Abbey to his coronation feast in Westminster Hall, and to whom he must have seemed like a replacement father. In the space of ten years Burley had very heavily lined his own pockets it is true, but even some of those who wanted to be rid of him protested that he was hardly deserving of death. Thomas Mowbray, Henry Bolingbroke and even the mighty John of Gaunt, the latter's father, tried to intercede with the other Lords Appellant on Burley's behalf, and King Richard's beloved first wife, Anne of Bohemia, begged on her knees before the Earl of Arundel for three hours for his death sentence to be commuted to exile or imprisonment, but all their pleas fell on deaf ears and he was beheaded on Tower Hill.

It would seem that Richard decided his best move would be to make his peace with Mowbray and Henry Bolingbroke, and in the October he had a furious row with the Chancellor, William of Wykeham, who opposed his plan to grant Mowbray a large pension, but subsequently Richard gave Thomas a good deal of responsibility. Others were not so highly favoured. Thomas's father-in-law inadvertently arrived late for Queen Anne's funeral in 1394 and the distraught Richard, who could not erase the image of this staid and gentle woman's bravery and nobility as she had pleaded for the life of his mentor, attacked the Earl and wounded him. An insight into Richard's troubled mind can be had from the fact that he so detested the Sheen Palace where his wife had died that he had it demolished. In 1395 Thomas Mowbray negotiated terms for the widower Richard II's second marriage, to Princess Isabella, an eight-year-old child, but this French marriage was unpopular in many quarters and Mowbray was thereafter associated with having arranged it. A papal mandate and a licence to found a Carthusian House, or *Charterhouse*, at Low Melwood near Epworth in the Isle of Axholme were granted to Thomas in 1396 (see Appendix G).

In the January of 1397 Richard again confirmed that the office of Earl Marshal should be hereditary in the Mowbray House and Thomas was granted the right to bear a golden rod with a black ring at each end, at the top the royal arms, and the Marshal's arms at the lower end; up to this point, like his predecessors, Thomas had carried a wooden rod as his symbol of office. Another breakthrough in his favour was that Richard decided that Gower, out of the family since the time of Edward III and currently in the hands of the Beauchamp Earls of Warwick, should be restored to Mowbray. How sweet life must have seemed in the Earl of Nottingham's household during that English spring, for at 31 he had it all: money and position, the King's favour, a powerful father-in-law, a lovely wife and a brood of five healthy children.

*The Mowbray Lion.*
*Carving on remains of the Carthusian monastery founded by Thomas Mowbray near Epworth.*
*Photo M. Roberts, by kind permission of Mr. R. Thornton.*

In 1397 there were further plots hatching against Richard II, but this time Thomas Mowbray betrayed his former fellow Appellants, being invited to a meeting by Arundel and Gloucester (Thomas of Woodstock) and then revealing what he knew to the King, whom he then accompanied to arrest Gloucester at Pleshy in Essex in July. Gloucester, a royal duke and Richard's uncle, was sent to the Tower and from there to Calais; Arundel and Warwick were taken into custody at the same time. On 5th August Thomas was at a meeting with King Richard in Nottingham when it was decided to appeal the lords of treason at the Parliament due to meet at Westminster on 21st September. On that fateful Friday in early autumn, the latest Appellants, Thomas Mowbray included, attired in red silk robes banded with white silk and powdered with letters of gold, passed the death sentence on his father-in-law, Richard Fitzalan, the execution to be carried out three days later.

It seems inconceivable to us that Mowbray should be instrumental in the death of his wife's father, but, quite apart from the fact that he was doing very nicely under Richard's rule and wanted it to stay that

| | |
|---|---|
| Simon of Sudbury, Archbishop of Canterbury | 1381 |
| Sir Robert Hales | 1381 |
| Sir Simon de Burley, K.G. | 1388 |
| Richard Fitzalan, 3rd Earl of Arundel | 1397 |
| Rev. Richard Wyche, Vicar of Deptford | 1440 |
| John de Vere, 12th Earl of Oxford | 1462 |
| John Tiptoft, Earl of Worcester | 1470 |

TOWER HILL.
*One of the memorial plaques to victims of the axe. Notice that it was not long before Richard Fitzalan followed his own 'Victim' Sir Simon de Burley. (The makers have called Fitzalan 3rd earl – see Chapter VII)*

way, it could be argued that it was his duty to inform his sovereign if he knew that trouble was brewing, especially if it was treasonable. Thomas was present at the execution, and some enthusiastic sources, including the great chronicler Jean Froissart, state that he even bound Arundel's eyes and beheaded him himself but, although this was the popular gossip of the time, the execution was properly carried out under the direction of Lord Morley, the Earl Marshal's lieutenant. (For the life and death of Richard Fitzalan, 11th Earl of Arundel, see Chapter VII.)

The same day that Arundel was tried, Richard II issued a writ ordering Thomas Mowbray to bring the Duke of Gloucester before Parliament, but on 24th September, the day Arundel was killed, the Earl Marshal had to admit that he was unable to produce the royal duke because he was dead, last seen alive by one of the King's commissioners on 8th September. Thomas had returned to Calais, probably on 24th August, and the finger of suspicion was pointing firmly at him: at best he was guilty of a serious dereliction of duty in allowing an uncle of the King to be killed when in his custody, and at worst – and inevitably this was the road along which the gossip was running – he was himself guilty of the crime. Whether or not the King was already well aware of the death, or had even given the order for the murder to be carried out, will probably never be known. A confession supposedly made by Gloucester on 8th September to Sir William Rickhill, a justice of the common pleas, was read to Parliament, and he was posthumously found guilty of treason.

Five years later, in the reign of Henry IV and when Thomas Mowbray was long dead of the plague, John Hall, one of his former servants in Calais, made a statement to the effect that in September 1397 Thomas had called him from his bed in the middle of the night saying that the King wanted Gloucester killed and that he, Hall, had to be present with other servants and esquires to witness that the deed really had been done. When Hall refused, Mowbray apparently struck him very hard on the head and ordered him to obey or else he would die, so they all took an oath of secrecy and then Mowbray took them to a hostelry called *The Prince's Inn* where he left them to suffocate the Duke of Gloucester with a feather bed. Hall had been arrested quite some time after the event as an accomplice to the murder and was condemned and executed without having a proper trial. A note of caution is necessary here: those people relating the events and disseminating the gossip were chroniclers with a Lancastrian bias and it was in the interests of the Lancastrian Henry IV to make his late deposed cousin Richard and his associates look like irresponsible ogres. Another 'witness', one Serle, arrested in 1404, was similarly disposed of without the trial that could perhaps have set the record straight as to who had done what to the unfortunate Gloucester, and upon whose orders.

With the execution of his own father-in-law, and the part he himself was thought by many to have played in the murder of the King's uncle, September 1397 was a tempestuous month for Thomas Mowbray and culminated in his being created 1st Duke of Norfolk in Parliament on the 29th for services rendered. The other young appellant of ten years before, Bolingbroke, was made Duke of Hereford, Richard now accepting, or at least appearing to accept, that the two of them were 'innocent of malice' in the *Merciless Parliament* affair, having been only in their early twenties at the time. Could it have been that he recalled how both had vigorously tried to persuade Arundel and Warwick to spare Sir Simon Burley's life? Also honoured that day were Edward Earl of Rutland (Duke of Aumale), Thomas Holand Earl of Kent (Duke of Surrey), John Holand Earl of Huntingdon (Duke of Exeter) and Thomas Mowbray's grandmother, the aged Margaret, Countess of Norfolk and Countess Marshal, who was made Duchess of Norfolk for life, although she appears not to have been able to be present at the ceremony.

Other nobles, not impressed by the way some of the new dukes had earned their reward, felt that the dignity of the title had been debased and sneeringly referred to them as the *duketti* ['little dukes']. As a descendant of Thomas de Brotherton, Thomas Mowbray himself was allowed to impale the arms of Edward the Confessor, but when his descendant Henry Howard, Earl of Surrey revived the use of the arms in the reign of Henry VIII, he was executed for high treason. On the day before he received his dukedom, Thomas Mowbray was awarded the greater part of the late Arundel's estates in Sussex and Surrey as well as seventeen of Warwick's manors. What Fitzalan's daughter Elizabeth felt about the part her husband played in her father's sudden downfall and death one can only imagine.

All was not well, however, and for Thomas it all went very wrong very quickly, for King Richard had gathered around himself a new clique busily poisoning his mind against any person who had ever crossed him. Thomas had the dreadful feeling that, in his heart, Richard was still wanting revenge for the killing of his favourites, and so in December, as they were riding from Brentford to London, he warned Henry Bolingbroke to be on his guard in case the King could not be trusted. Bolingbroke told his father and Gaunt told him it was his duty to tell his cousin, which he did. By the same Parliament, now adjourned to Shrewsbury, that had created him Duke of Norfolk only weeks before, Thomas Mowbray was appealed of treason by Henry Bolingbroke, Duke of Hereford. Thomas's fears about the King proved to be well-founded, for now Richard, a complex and very disturbed man, saw his chance – an opportunity to punish both of them, even though his cousin Bolingbroke was now his staunch supporter. Very cleverly the evidence was manipulated so that the two *duketti* were accusing one another. Bolingbroke must have been dumbfounded, since in revealing Mowbray's rumblings of discontent his idea had been to ingratiate himself with his cousin the King by protecting him from harm. How their enemies, jealous of their illustrious new titles, must have relished every delicious nail-biting moment of their terror and confusion!

On 31st January 1398 the matter was referred to the King and a commission, and on 4th February Norfolk was ordered to answer the charges on pain of life and limb. Nineteen days later both men were summoned before the King at Oswestry, where Mowbray denied the charges. It was then decided that unless proof of his guilt could be found, the matter would be referred to the Court of Chivalry at Windsor on 28th April. The proof was not forthcoming, so the matter would have to be settled according to the Law of Chivalry, that is, the protagonists would have to fight it out. The two feuding noblemen were to settle their quarrel by trial by battle at Gosford Green, near Coventry, on 16th September 1398.

The greatest men and women in the land were present when the two knights came forth. Mowbray was wearing fine armour made in Germany and seated upon on a magnificent horse covered with crimson velvet embroidered with silver lions and mulberry trees. Hereford, however, outshone him, wearing the very best Italian armour from Milan and having no fewer than seven beautifully caparisoned horses to hand. The Gosford Green encounter appears in the opening scenes of Shakespeare's *King Richard II*. Norfolk having vigorously denied Bolingbroke's accusation of treason, murder and embezzlement, the King's herald then invites the two men to identify themselves to the spectators,

*My name is Thomas Mowbray, Duke of Norfolk;*
*Who hither come engaged by my oath, –*
*Which God defend a knight should violate! –*
*Both to defend my loyalty and truth*
*To God, my king and his succeeding issue,*
*Against the Duke of Hereford that appeals me;*
*And by the Grace of God and this mine arm,*
*To prove him in defending of myself,*
*A traitor to my God, my king and me:*
*And as I truly fight, defend me heaven!*

*Harry of Hereford, Lancaster and Derby*
*Am I; who ready here do stand in arms,*
*To prove, by God's grace and my body's valour,*
*In lists, on Thomas Mowbray, Duke of Norfolk,*
*That he is a traitor, foul and dangerous,*
*To God of Heaven, King Richard and to me:*
*And as I truly fight, defend me heaven!*
William Shakespeare: *King Richard II Act I, Scene III*

Perhaps Richard had been playing games all along to make them suffer more, for suddenly he stood up and the duel was called off. Maybe it dawned on him at the last moment that, should Bolingbroke win he would be dangerously embittered at his ill-treatment, but should Mowbray be the disaffected victor he could well go on to reveal to all and sundry what had happened to Gloucester in Calais – and upon whose orders the deed was done. The reason for his decision, Richard said, was that whatever the outcome, there would be dishonour of the blood royal, as both men were related to him. Both were sentenced to banishment, Bolingbroke to France for ten years, but the Duke of Norfolk was to be exiled for life, allowed to stay in Germany, Bohemia and Hungary, but nowhere else, although he could seek permission to visit the Holy Land. Thomas lost the Arundel and Warwick lands. Except for £1000 a year to be granted to him, the revenue from Thomas Mowbray's estates was taken into King Richard's hand to be used to pay off the debts his so-called maladministration of Calais had cost the Crown. A very rough idea of monetary values can be had from the John Coupland information in Chapter III, and Peter Hills in *The Priory of the Wood* tells us that in about 1400 a chicken could be bought for a farthing; there were 960 farthings in £1.

On Saturday 19th October 1398, Thomas Mowbray was to be allowed free passage out of the realm of England from any port between Scarborough and Orwell, with jewels, plate and other necessaries, as well as an entourage of forty people and a written request from King Richard to all other princes and nations to allow him safe conduct. He chose to depart for the Continent from a small Suffolk port near Lowestoft. Observers said that with good wind and surf he would be more than six leagues out to sea by sunset. The following February Richard requested the Senate in Venice, in whose records Thomas is given the alias 'Duke of Gilforth', to lend him a galley to take him on pilgrimage to the Holy Land, to which they agreed as long as he made it clear in his will that, should he not return, the Venetians had to be reimbursed for the expense incurred. A month later, on 24th March, his grandmother Margaret died, and Thomas found that he was to be allowed the title of Earl of Norfolk but would be denied the revenue from her vast Brotherton estates.

Whether or not Thomas Mowbray did embark on the pilgrimage is not known, for he died in Venice of the plague aged thirty-three on 22nd September 1399, only two years and one day since he had helped pass the death sentence on his own father-in-law, and only eight days before Henry Bolingbroke, Duke of Hereford, became King Henry IV. The creation of the Norfolk dukedom was annulled by Henry in 1399 and not forfeited in the reign of Richard II, as is sometimes stated. Indeed, one has to wonder whether Richard had entertained the idea of Thomas one day being allowed to return home. Documents in the Venetian archives show that in November 1403 Marcello Steno, the Doge, requested the new King's assistance in recovering the debt for the galley from Thomas's heirs on behalf of the noblemen 'Ser' Antonio Bembo, knight, and one Giovanni Zane.

Most sources say Thomas Mowbray was buried in Venice at the Abbey of St George, but others state that according to his son John's wishes his remains were brought home and buried in a tomb of alabaster in the chapter house in the monastery he had founded at Low Melwood, which is not borne out by later events. In 1532 Mowbray's descendant Thomas Howard, Duke of Norfolk, approached the Venetian Ambassador with a view to the return of the remains,

> "*The Duke of Norfolk requests the Signory to send to him from Venice by safe conveyance, the safest possible, at the least cost, the body or bones of Thomas [Mowbray] the first Duke of Norfolk, who was buried more than 150 years ago in a vault in St Mark's Church.*"

The ambassador's response was that he had not been able to ascertain where they were buried, and that he was in search of them. The search probably was not helped by the fact that Mowbray is believed to have been buried elsewhere. The nineteenth-century antiquarian Rawdon Brown claimed to have located his tombstone in Venice and attempted to explain the meaning of the carvings (see Appendix H).

Chart 6: *The Children of Thomas Mowbray and Elizabeth Fitzalan*

Thomas Mowbray Duke of Norfolk = Lady Elizabeth Fitzalan = Sir Robert Goushill

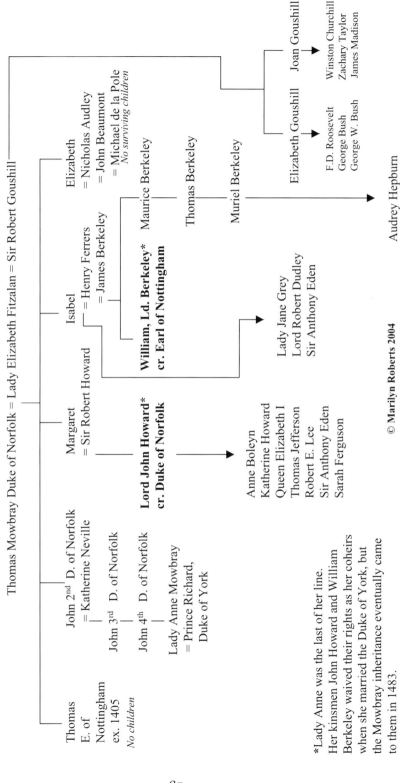

© **Marilyn Roberts 2004**

*Lady Anne was the last of her line. Her kinsmen John Howard and William Berkeley waived their rights as her coheirs when she married the Duke of York, but the Mowbray inheritance eventually came to them in 1483.

### *Elizabeth Fitzalan*, Duchess of Norfolk, c. 1366-July 1425.

A daughter of Richard Fitzalan, 11th Earl of Arundel, by his second wife Elizabeth de Bohun, Elizabeth married firstly Sir William Montagu, son and heir apparent of the Earl of Salisbury, and was still only about sixteen when he was accidentally killed by his own father in a joust in August 1382. Two years later, at her family home at Arundel Castle, in the presence of Richard II and his wife Anne of Bohemia, she married Thomas Mowbray, Earl of Nottingham, who thirteen years later was created Duke of Norfolk as a reward for betraying her father. With Mowbray she had the sons Thomas, executed in 1405, and John, who was restored as 2nd Duke of Norfolk in 1425, and the daughters Margaret, Isabel and Elizabeth.

After Thomas Mowbray's death in exile, Elizabeth, Dowager Duchess of Norfolk, recognised by the Crown as Countess of Norfolk, received as part of her dower the magnificent Framlingham Castle in Suffolk, which had come to the family as a result of the recent death of Mowbray's grandmother Margaret, and she also held lands throughout the eastern counties, including the Isle of Axholme in Lincolnshire. It would seem that with Framlingham Castle being fairly close to the sea and thus of great strategic importance, it was taken over by Henry IV in 1401, Elizabeth receiving lands of equivalent worth in Derbyshire, Leicestershire and Buckinghamshire, but it came back to the Mowbrays a short time later. She kept a firm grip on her Mowbray widow's entitlement to the end of her days, to the point that the settlement her late second husband Thomas had made on their son had to be adjusted to pay what she was due. It has been suggested that she is the Lady Mowbray of the Haxey Hood game

*Elizabeth Fitzalan and Sir Robert Goushill, Hoveringham.*
*Tomb effigies in St Michael and All Angels, Hoveringham, Nottinghamshire.*
*Photo. M. Roberts, by kind permission of the Churchwardens.*

Chart 7: Violent Deaths of Some of Elizabeth Fitzalan's Close Male Relatives.

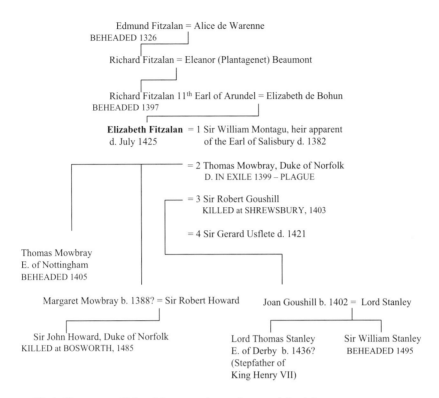

Edmund Fitzalan = Alice de Warenne
BEHEADED 1326

Richard Fitzalan = Eleanor (Plantagenet) Beaumont

Richard Fitzalan 11<sup>th</sup> Earl of Arundel = Elizabeth de Bohun
BEHEADED 1397

**Elizabeth Fitzalan** = 1 Sir William Montagu, heir apparent
d. July 1425          of the Earl of Salisbury d. 1382

= 2 Thomas Mowbray, Duke of Norfolk
D. IN EXILE 1399 – PLAGUE

= 3 Sir Robert Goushill
KILLED at SHREWSBURY, 1403

= 4 Sir Gerard Usflete d. 1421

Thomas Mowbray
E. of Nottingham
BEHEADED 1405

Margaret Mowbray b. 1388? = Sir Robert Howard       Joan Goushill b. 1402 = Lord Stanley

Sir John Howard, Duke of Norfolk       Lord Thomas Stanley       Sir William Stanley
KILLED at BOSWORTH, 1485       E. of Derby b. 1436?       BEHEADED 1495
                                       (Stepfather of
                                       King Henry VII)

Elizabeth's great-grandfather, father, son and a grandson were beheaded:
Edmund Fitzalan by Queen Isabella 1326 – as punishment for supporting her husband Edward II
Richard Fitzalan by Richard II 1397 – treason
Thomas Mowbray by Henry IV 1405 – treason                    **© Marilyn Roberts 2004**
Sir William Stanley by Henry VII 1495 – treason
Of her four husbands, all of whom she outlived, the first was accidentally killed by his father, the
second died in exile and the third in battle, as did another grandson, John Howard.

and that it was she who had the post with the Mowbray lion attached erected on Green Hill at Haxey in her late husband's memory.

In 1401, when in her mid-thirties, Elizabeth took as her third husband Sir Robert Goushill of Hoveringham, Nottinghamshire, who was probably about fifty at the time of the marriage and had been in her late husband's service. She had to surrender part of her dower lands for not having procured the correct royal licence for the marriage and then pay a huge fine in order to get them back, but she must have thought Sir Robert was worth it, and by him had two daughters, Elizabeth and Joan. Her happiness, however, was short-lived, for Sir Robert was killed in 1403 at the Battle of Shrewsbury.

Around 1414 Elizabeth Fitzalan was married for the fourth time, to Sir Gerard Usflete (or Afflete), whom she outlived, dying in July 1425. She is buried with Sir Robert Goushill in a lovely old tomb in the

Church of Saint Michael and All Angels in the village of Hoveringham, near Southwell. Unfortunately there is no trace of Sir Robert's family home remaining amongst the buttercups in the field beside the church, but it is a beautiful and tranquil spot and well worth a visit. The image seen in the South Choir Transept at York Minster above a stone shield bearing the Mowbray silver lion on a red background is very possibly of Elizabeth; the shield of her beheaded elder son Thomas, Earl of Nottingham, is nearby. One has to wonder how medieval women like Elizabeth coped with the uncertainties of life as far as the fate of their men folk was concerned. Her great-grandfather, Edmund Fitzalan, her father, her elder son, and her grandson, William Stanley, were all beheaded. She was a widow at sixteen, her second husband died in exile, her third in battle, and she outlived her fourth.

Elizabeth Fitzalan is one of the late medieval English nobles known to American genealogists as a 'gateway' ancestor because of the thousands of people descended from the children of her marriages to Thomas Mowbray and Sir Robert Goushill. Her daughters Elizabeth and Joan Goushill, between them forebears of Sir Winston Churchill, the Earls of Derby, several Presidents of the United States and Edward Maria Wingfield, first President of the Virginia Plantation, amongst others, were the half-sisters of Thomas Mowbray, Earl of Nottingham, who appears in Shakespeare's *The Second Part of King Henry IV*, and who was beheaded in York. Thomas's sister Margaret was an ancestor of Anne Boleyn and Elizabeth I; Lady Jane Grey and the actress Audrey Hepburn were descended from Isabel Mowbray, another of his sisters. (Elizabeth's sister, Joan Fitzalan, was also a forebear of Anne Boleyn and Queen Elizabeth. Another sister, Alice, was the mistress of the fabulously wealthy Cardinal Henry Beaufort, Chancellor of England and sometime Bishop of Lincoln and of Winchester, a son of John of Gaunt, Duke of Lancaster, and his mistress Katherine Swynford.)

# CHAPTER V

## 1400-1481: THE END OF THE DYNASTY

*...it is so fortuned, that whereas my Lord of Norfolk, yesterday being in good health, this night died about midnight ...*
Sir John Paston writing to his mother from Framlingham Castle with news of the sudden death of the last Mowbray Duke, 17th January 1476.

ENRY BOLINGBROKE was in exile when his father died in 1399. The terms of his banishment were meant to ensure that his inheritance would be safe and his properties unmolested until he had served out his ten years, so when the Crown confiscated everything that should have come to him and changed the banishment to life, panic broke out amongst the nobility. After all, John of Gaunt might have been grossly unpopular with the people, but he had been loyal and useful to his nephew King Richard and this was no way to treat his heir, who, although he had been one of the original Lords Appellant in 1388, had served his cousin loyally thereafter. If this could be happening to a grandson of Edward III, reasoned the great lords of the land, then what fate might there be in store for lesser mortals?

Bolingbroke returned and deposed Richard, but as King Henry IV he had a terrible reign beset by every conceivable problem, including his own poor health, rebellion at home and from the Welsh, skirmishes with the Scots, as well as the ongoing Hundred Years' War, for which he had much less relish than his son, Henry V. The younger Henry, after his 1415 victory at Agincourt, became a legend in his own lifetime, but it was to be a short life ended by dysentery, the scourge of the medieval armies. He in turn was succeeded by his ten-month-old son, Henry VI, whose mental illness and political ineptitude would lead to the conflict between the Lancaster and York branches of the Plantagenet family known today as the Wars of the Roses.

The family was divided over who should have succeeded the deposed Richard II in 1399, whose true heir was Edmund Mortimer, the great-grandson of his uncle, Lionel, Duke of Clarence. But Edmund was a child of eight, and the country had just had a bad experience of a ruler who had succeeded as a little boy, and anyway, Bolingbroke seemed to have the makings of ideal sovereign material. Mortimer himself, even as an adult, was satisfied to let matters lie – perhaps he just wanted to die of natural causes – but his sister Anne married her cousin Richard, Earl of Cambridge, grandson of Edward III's son the Duke of York, and the united Clarences and Yorks felt they were deserving of a very high, perhaps even the highest, profile, especially when Edmund Mortimer died young without an heir. Cambridge was executed in 1415 for rebellion against his cousin Henry V. His elder brother, who became Duke of York after their father's death, was killed at Agincourt, the dukedom eventually going to York's nephew, Cambridge's son, the Richard of York who years later challenged Henry VI for the crown (see Chart 2).

An added complication to the political life of the country, and one of the many contributory causes of the Wars of the Roses, was the eventful private life and resulting offspring of Edward III's middle son, John, Duke of Lancaster. John of Gaunt was married first to Blanche, daughter of Henry of Lancaster, who brought him great wealth and over thirty castles, but she perished of the bubonic plague, leaving young children, including Henry, born at Bolingbroke Castle in Lincolnshire. John then married Constance of Castile, in the hope of one day becoming King of that country, once his ousted bride had been restored as Queen, a dream destined never to come true. However, Gaunt's real love appears to have been Katherine Swynford, the widow of Sir Hugh Swynford, one of his knights. Katherine was governess to Gaunt's children but became his mistress after her husband's death in 1372 and bore him four children herself, and their offspring were given the family name of Beaufort, the name of one of John's estates on the Continent. The great Duke of Lancaster shocked the in-bred Court, and indeed the whole country, by marrying this woman of humble birth when Constance died in 1396, only three years before his own death. Their cousin Richard II recognised the Beauforts as being legitimate because their parents had eventually been able to marry, which opened-up endless possibilities for them, although legislation of their half-brother Henry IV (Bolingbroke) in 1407 excluded them from the succession.

Nevertheless, they prospered: the eldest, John, became Marquess of Somerset, and his brother Henry Beaufort, politician, Bishop of Lincoln, Bishop of Winchester, cardinal and man of unimaginable wealth, sat in judgement on Joan of Arc and also crowned the boy Henry VI of England as King of France at Notre Dame in December 1431. There was another brother, Thomas, and a sister, Joan, who was the second wife of Ralph Neville, Earl of Westmorland, and it was her daughter, Katherine Neville, who married John Mowbray, 2nd Duke of Norfolk (see Chart 8). The next two generations of Beauforts had the potential to hold enormous power in the reigns of Henry V and his feeble-minded son Henry VI, and one of them was particularly close to the latter's wife.

*Lady Margaret Beaufort, Mother of Henry Tudor.*
*Image on the gatehouse of a Cambridge College founded by her. Note the Tudor iconography –*
*the ubiquitous rose and portcullis, the latter being one of Lady Margaret's own badges.*

It is through the Beauforts that the virtually unknown Welshman Henry Tudor found himself head of the House of Lancaster and claimant to the throne of the Yorkist Richard III in 1485. Tudor's mother, the Lady Margaret Beaufort, daughter of the John, Duke of Somerset who died in 1444, survived after most of the rest of the Lancastrians had been wiped out by the Wars of the Roses, but Tudor's claim in right of his mother was flimsy indeed, as the legislation of Henry IV barring the Beauforts from the succession had never been repealed. They are mentioned here because the Dukes of Somerset were detested by both Richard of York and by the Mowbray Dukes of Norfolk who were suspicious of their activities, especially their manipulation of Henry VI, and it seems that John Mowbray, 3rd Duke of Norfolk was bitterly jealous of them when they were allowed to take precedence over him at Court.

1445 saw the marriage of Henry VI and Margaret of Anjou, a niece of the King of France, and there was no love lost between the new Queen and Richard, Duke of York, whom she tried to push out of the picture. Henry had inherited the mental illness of his maternal French grandfather, and York was appointed regent when he became unable to rule, much to the disgust of Queen Margaret, who thought she should have had that honour. York was biding his time, probably reasoning that, as there was no child for the King and Queen after seven years of marriage, his turn to rule would come eventually – as long as the Beauforts remained excluded from the succession. It was not to be; King Henry had another bout of mental illness, this time much more severe, where he understood nothing and knew no one. Once again York took on the rôle of regent, hoping that better times were not too far off, but his hopes were dashed when Queen Margaret gave birth to a son. Her bewildered husband believed she had had a visitation from the Angel Gabriel, but the fully *compos mentis* amongst those at Court, and the Yorkists in particular, thought that the angel in question was more likely to answer to the name of Edmund Beaufort, Duke of Somerset. Again Henry made some sort of recovery and immediately reinstated York's enemies, and by now the Queen had gathered a powerful group around her that became the core of the Lancastrian Party. Richard of York realised he was living in great danger and that the only way to survive was to gather a corresponding Yorkist faction, so by the mid-1450's, just as the Hundred Years' War was coming to its close, the battles of the Wars of the Roses between the Plantagenet Houses of Lancaster and York were beginning.

In September 1460, Richard of York entered London expecting to be welcomed as an alternative monarch to Henry VI, and was surprised to find this was not the wish of Parliament. Everyone wanted better government, but although Henry was an incompetent ruler, he was a kind and gentle man, and consequently was not unpopular. The Lords in particular shied away from York, possibly fearing the power his cronies such as the Mowbrays and Nevilles would assume should he become King. Therefore, a compromise was reached: Henry would live out his days as King and the succession would go to York rather than to the Prince of Wales. Henry would have accepted this arrangement but, perhaps understandably, his fiery wife refused to

*MICKLEGATE BAR, YORK*
*Detail of one of the medieval gates (or bars) to the city. The heads of Richard of York and his young son Edmund were exhibited here on spikes*

have her son's birthright taken away by a man she loathed.

On 30th December 1460, the Queen's army – King Henry was still wandering around in a daze – defeated the Yorkists at Wakefield. Richard of York fell in the battle and Edmund, Earl of Rutland, one of his young sons, was caught as he made his escape. He was murdered in cold blood by Lord Clifford in revenge for the boy's father having killed his own at the First Battle of St Albans in 1455. What a sad time it must have been for the people of York to have the heads of the father and son displayed on spikes above Micklegate Bar, one of the gates of that proud city, the Duke's adorned with a mocking paper crown. These deaths, and the Lancastrian slaughter of Yorkist prisoners after the Second Battle of St Albans, marked a significant turn for the worse in the conflict.

Richard Neville, Earl of Warwick, and other powerful nobles, including the 3rd Mowbray Duke of Norfolk, had had enough, and not long after the Battle of Wakefield York's eldest son, Edward, Earl of March was proclaimed King at the age of nineteen. Edward IV's relationship with Warwick started turning sour a few years later when the latter discovered he been on a fool's errand trying to find his young master a French bride without realising that the King was already married. As if that were not enough, his secret bride, Elizabeth Woodville, or Wydville, was a commoner, from a relentlessly upwardly mobile family, and, to add further insult to injury, she was the widow of a *Lancastrian* knight, John Grey, a great-grandson of Elizabeth Fitzalan and Thomas Mowbray (see Table V).

Ten years after Warwick put Edward IV on the throne of England he deposed him and reinstated Henry VI, hence his epithet *Kingmaker*, but it could not last, and Edward soon returned from exile on the Continent with mercenary soldiers, killing Warwick at Barnet in April 1471. The Lancastrian Prince of Wales, still only seventeen, was killed the following month at the Battle of Tewkesbury, or, more likely, was murdered afterwards as a prisoner of the Yorkists. His father was murdered in the Tower a few days later and Queen Margaret was eventually ransomed and sent back to France, where she died in poverty. Edward IV then reigned through a period of peace until the spring of 1483, when he died suddenly at the age of forty, leaving his younger brother, Richard, Duke of Gloucester, to be Protector during the minority of the child Edward V, aged twelve. In a matter of months the boy and his ten-year-old brother would disappear, presumably murdered in the Tower, and the Duke of Gloucester would be crowned King Richard III. The younger of the Princes, still only ten at the time of his disappearance, had been married some years earlier to the Lady Anne Mowbray, Countess of Norfolk, the only child of the last Mowbray Duke of Norfolk.

THOMAS MOWBRAY, 17TH SEPTEMBER 1385 - BEHEADED AT YORK 8TH JUNE 1405.
Earl of Nottingham, Earl of Norfolk, Earl Marshal.

Thomas was born in 1385 and was only fourteen when his father was banished, and at the time of Norfolk's death was a page to Queen Isabella, Richard II's little French bride. The Mowbray finances must have been in chaos at the time, and he and his brother were supported by a small income from the Gower estates, but in December 1399 he had to petition Henry IV for maintenance and was allowed 350 marks, about £250, for himself and £100 for his younger brother, John. It is hardly surprising that he took up arms against Henry, whom he must have held largely responsible for bringing disgrace and ruin on his late father and who had annulled the dukedom after the first duke's death in 1399. Thomas still held the office of Earl Marshal, but Henry had conferred the post of Marshal of England upon the Earl of Westmorland for life in 1399.

Perhaps by 1405 Thomas was dissatisfied that that he had not had the dukedom of Norfolk restored to him, and he also had an altercation at about this time with the Earl of Warwick, Richard Beauchamp, who claimed precedence over him at Court on the grounds that his earldom was of earlier creation, an opinion supported by King Henry. Thomas withdrew to his Yorkshire estates and became involved with Richard Scrope, Archbishop of York, and the Percy family, who were intent on the overthrow of King Henry, openly calling him a usurper. The powerful Percy family, the Earls of Northumberland, had initially helped with the overthrow of King Richard but turned against Henry IV and caused him years of trouble through a series of rebellions in the northern counties.

Mowbray and Scrope gathered a following of about 8,000 and hoped to rendezvous with Percy near Thirsk. However, they were intercepted by that other great northern magnate, Ralph Neville, Earl of Westmorland, at Shipton Moor five miles north of York, where, against Mowbray's better judgement, Scrope dismissed their men and hoped for constructive negotiations with Neville. In *Henry IV* (Part Two) Shakespeare puts the mature words of doubt into the young man's mouth as the others optimistically prepare to enter peace talks,

> *"There is a thing within my bosom tells me*
> *That no conditions of our peace can stand.*
> *... our valuation shall be such,*
> *That every slight and false-derived cause,*
> *Yea, every idle, nice and wanton reason*
> *Shall to the king taste of this action."*

The Thomas portrayed by the Bard was right to have misgivings. Instead of being involved in the fair and frank discussions Scrope expected, they were arrested and taken to Pontefract Castle, where Richard II had perished in recent history, and where King Henry himself arrived on or around 3rd June, and from there were removed to the Archbishop's own residence, Bishopthorpe Palace, outside York. They were condemned of treason on 8th June, and the same day, the feast day of St William of York, were beheaded before a large crowd in a field belonging to Clementhorpe Nunnery just outside the city; Nunnery Lane still runs alongside the city walls. Thomas, still only nineteen, was afraid, but Archbishop Scrope encouraged him to be of stout heart and then had to wait his own turn as Mowbray's young life was brutally extinguished before his very eyes. (The conspirators were tried by Lord Chief Justice Gascoigne, husband of Elizabeth Mowbray of the Kirklington branch of the family. The couple's tomb, depicting Gascoigne in his lawyer's robes rather than in the traditional attire of a fighting knight, can be found in the church at Harewood.)

In retrospect, Henry IV was horrified that he had sanctioned the execution of the prelate, especially as Gascoigne had refused to pronounce the death sentence upon such a prominent clergyman, so Scrope's remains were permitted to be buried in York Minster, but opinion is divided as to what happened to the remains of young Mowbray. In *The Heraldry of York Minster* by A.P. Purey Cust, Dean of the Minster, we are told that the head was set on the city walls and the body buried in the Minster, possibly in Scope's tomb, but *Complete Peerage* says he was buried at the Franciscan Friars (between Clifford's Tower and the river) and his head set on a spike above Bootham Bar, one of the city gates. Knight in his *History of the City of York* (1944) agrees with this alternative burial place but believes that the head was placed on a stake on Ouse Bridge. In *Eboracum*, published by one Francis Drake in 1738, we learn that,

> "The Earl's body was, by the King's permission, suffered to be buried in the cathedral at York. But his head fixed on a stake stood long on the walls of the city exposed to heat, wind and rain, which when the King at length granted it should be buried with the body, was found … neither fallen nor wasted nor scarcely discoloured but kept the same comeliness it had when living."

York's ancient Holy Trinity Church on Goodramgate has adjacent stained glass windows with the shields of Thomas Mowbray and Henry Percy, Shakespeare's 'Harry Hotspur', son of Northumberland. Both arms are lions rampant, Mowbray's being gules, a lion rampant argent, that is, a silver lion on its hind legs against a red background, whereas Hotspur's is or (gold) a lion rampant azure (blue). Hotspur had died at Shrewsbury in 1403 but his body was taken to York, beheaded and quartered, the quarters being nailed up in four different cities as a warning to others. After a spell of being impaled on a spike on Micklegate Bar, under which his own father had to pass at one stage, the head was buried at Holy Trinity and there is a grisly tradition that the parts of the body are still searching for it. Another casualty of the Battle of Shrewsbury was Sir Robert Goushill, whom Thomas Mowbray's mother had married after the death of the banished Duke of Norfolk.

Thomas Mowbray, who does not appear to have been attainted, that is forbidden from passing on or receiving an inheritance, had married Constance Holand, a granddaughter of John of Gaunt, but there were no children to succeed to his titles, which consequently passed to his brother.

*JOHN MOWBRAY*, 3RD AUGUST 1392(?) - OCTOBER 1432.
2nd Duke of Norfolk, Earl of Norfolk, Earl of Nottingham, Earl Marshal (brother of Thomas Mowbray Earl of Nottingham).

This John hardly had an ideal childhood and youth, being only five when his Fitzalan grandfather was beheaded, seven when his father died in exile and thirteen when his brother Thomas was beheaded at York. The extract from Inquisitions Post Mortem on his late brother below reveals that some of John's lands during his minority were in the wardship of Joan of Navarre, second wife of Henry IV, and that in order to secure control he could have been claiming to be older than he actually was. John Mowbray, Earl of Nottingham, produces witnesses to verify that he is of age. It may seem very odd to us that an earl with royal blood in his veins had to depend upon recollections of his late father's domestic servants to verify his date of birth, but these were times long before proper records of births were kept and this procedure as a way of confirming a date of birth was by no means uncommon. This entry provides one of the few fleeting glimpses into the home life of a great Mowbray Lord.

## Calais: Proof of age 1st December.

*John Bermycham*, alderman of Calais, and formerly mayor, aged 55 years and more, said that John Moubray, son and heir of Thomas was 21 in August having been born at Calais[1] 3rd August 1390[2] and baptised in St Mary's church there on 9th August. At that time he, Bermycham, was under-marshal and warned all the knights and other gentry to accompany John to the church for his baptism.

*William Hevering* remembered seeing Robert Goussel[3] carrying a sword erect to the house.

*John Laurens*, soldier, 48 and more, was sent to England by Elizabeth the mother to enquire about the status of the baptism and was given a new suit.

*Ralph Pamer*, 44 and more, was a servant of the earl, the father, and served in the pantry.

*William Noke*, burgess of Calais, 55 and more, ordered and prepared all the dinner in the house of the earl and carried it to the church.

*William Gate*, soldier, 50 and more, had a son Thomas born at that time and

John's nurse was godmother to Thomas.

*John Dene,* burgess, 60 and more, saw four honourable men, knights and squires, carrying a golden awning above John from the church after the baptism.

> ([1]In modern sources John's date of birth is often given as 1392. His father, Thomas Mowbray, then Earl of Nottingham, was appointed Captain of Calais in February 1391, so 1392 seems to be a more realistic date if his son was born there. The contradictory evidence about his date of birth is discussed by Mary Erler in "Hoccleve's Portrait?" *The Ricardian,* vol. 13, p. 228, note 27; 2003.
> [2]*Complete Peerage* gives his birth as 1392 but does not give sources for that information.
> [3]Preumably this is Sir Robert Goushill of Hoveringham who married baby John's widowed mother Elizabeth Fitzalan eleven (or nine) years later.)

In November 1407, at the age of fifteen, John was taken into the household of the King's mother-in-law, his great-aunt through the de Bohun/Fitzalan line of his family (see Table III), and three years later was taken into Henry IV's service at Court. John was allowed his late brother's earldoms, but still the dukedom of Norfolk was not restored to the family. At the age of nineteen (or 21) in 1412 he married, in the chapel at her Yorkshire home, Raby Castle, Katherine Neville, daughter of the Earl of Westmorland who held the office of Marshal of England for life after the first duke's exile, but who appears to have been willing to resign it to John on several occasions. Considering that John's new father-in-law had been responsible for the arrest and execution of his brother, this marriage seems a strange arrangement to us, but in the weird world of noble marriages of the Middle Ages the union would not have seemed out of the ordinary. Katherine's mother was Joan Beaufort, half-sister of Henry IV, and her sister Cicely was the mother of Edward IV and Richard III; see Chart 8.

The Hundred Years' War had been revived with some enthusiasm after Henry IV died, and John Mowbray fought for both Henry V and VI. As Earl Marshal he was the chief member of the judicial commission which investigated the conspiracy of Richard, Earl of Cambridge against Henry V in 1415, and he passed the death sentence a few days before the English left to fight the campaign which was to include the Battle of Agincourt. The accounts of his receiver-general, Robert Southwell, for Michaelmas 1414 - Michaelmas 1415 refer to members of the Mowbray household, some very appropriately named, such as John Foteman, William Sadelyer, Nicholas Armourer and not forgetting the trumpeter – Thomas Trumpet. In June 1415 the Earl spent £70 (over £35,000 at today's rates) on a suit of armour, and Nicholas Armourer carried out repairs on other items. His embroidered surcoat, essential so that his men could recognise him in the mêlée of the battlefield, set him back a further £40. He also treated himself to a new bed, mattress, bolster and seat for his latrine.

On 22nd September John Mowbray received the keys from the defeated citizens after the siege of Harfleur, but already dysentery was running riot in the army camps, and by the end of the month he and several of his company had to be invalided home, missing Agincourt. John lived, but Thomas Fitzalan, Earl of Arundel and his mother's brother, was not so fortunate. When Fitzalan died at Arundel Castle his estates and title went to a second cousin, but the inheritance that had come to the Fitzalans from the last Warenne Earl of Surrey in 1345 went to Thomas's three sisters. His will of October 10th 1415 made provision for a 'fair monument' to be erected over the body of his executed father and for the soldiers who had been with him at Harfleur to have all their arrears.

Although dysentery prevented John's own participation at Agincourt, he had earlier taken part in the siege of Harfleur with 50 men-at-arms and 150 horse-archers, and from 1417 onwards spent a great deal of time in France. He bore the sceptre at the coronation of Henry V's wife, Katherine de Valois, a younger sister of Isabella, Richard II's child bride, and was one of the Councillors of Regency to her baby son after her husband's early death in 1422. He performed the duties of Earl Marshal at the little boy's English coronation in 1429 and accompanied him to France the following year for a second ceremony. Mowbray had distinguished himself in action against the French in the 1420's and the 1422-3 accounts of Robert Southwell, as well as recording the receiver-general's visits to the estates and the collecting of revenues, also dealt with any expenses due from the exchequer, as in time of war. They show he drew nearly £3,400 in March 1423 on Mowbray's behalf for the French expedition, which included £20 back-pay for the retainer Sir Thomas Strangways, who many years later would marry Mowbray's widow, Katherine. Accounts reveal the Earl Marshal had in his household 64 yeomen, 11 pages, 6 minstrels and a herald, and that, although Epworth was still the preferred residence, there was frequent movement of the household, which would include transportation of large amounts of furniture and other moveable goods. In the autumn of 1422 the family is to be found at Bosham, Sussex, from where they went to London, arriving early November and leaving just before Christmas. They were in London again in April and then to Sandwich in Kent in May with part of the household sailing for France with the Earl Marshal and the remainder removing to Epworth with Katherine, from where they left in December and travelled south to welcome John home.

Then, as now, war proved a very expensive business, and especially difficult for a family still in the process of recovering from banishment and disgrace. Some sort of monetary comparisons can be made by the fact that Southwell's travel expenses for 6 months amounted to £12 and his wages £13. 6s. 8d. With the death of Elizabeth Fitzalan in July 1425 the slate of disgrace was wiped clean and the dukedom of Norfolk restored. It is from this point onward that the Mowbray interests became centred on East Anglia and magnificent Framlingham Castle in Suffolk became their main residence. According to the Chronicler of Brent, John Mowbray narrowly escaped drowning on 8th November 1428 when his barge capsized as it passed under London Bridge.

Most with him lost their lives but he jumped to safety onto one of the supports.

John Mowbray, 2nd Duke of Norfolk, died at Epworth on 19th October 1432 and was buried in the Carthusian monastery, or Charterhouse, founded by his father at Low Melwood a short distance away. Duchess Katherine, however, made three more marriages, the last in her late sixties, although some authorities even put her at eighty, to John Woodville, a lad of twenty, 'a diabolic match' according the chronicler William of Worcester. John Woodville was the brother-in-law of Edward IV and there must have been advantages in the union for both sides; he was a younger son in need of a fortune (Mowbray money!), whereas it would not do Katherine or her grown-up children (she had had a second family to Sir Thomas Strangways) any harm for her to be married to the Queen's brother. The Lancastrians beheaded John Woodville in 1469, five years after the marriage, but Katherine lived to be over eighty, and if the Lord Chamberlain's records showing that a gown was ordered for her on the occasion of the coronation of Richard III in 1483 are correct, she could have been nearer ninety when she died. A letter the Dowager wrote from Epworth to the Paston family in the 1440's indicates that she used the mansion there as her home at a time when the whole of Isle of Axholme was a part of her widow's settlement. (For details of Duchess Katherine's family see below and Chart 8; for the financial problems brought about for the Mowbray dynasty because of her longevity see Chapter VI.)

*JOHN MOWBRAY*, 12TH SEPTEMBER 1415 - 6TH NOVEMBER 1461.
3rd Duke of Norfolk, Earl of Norfolk, Earl of Nottingham, Earl Marshal.

Born in the autumn of 1415, John had a long military career fighting both Scots and French and served as an ambassador on various missions to both countries. He was Warden of the East March (Scottish borders) and captain of Berwick in 1437 and at the end of his year of service was appointed a guardian of the truce concluded with Scotland. In March 1443 he put down riots in Norwich and in 1452 he was sent by Henry VI to enquire into '…the great riots, extortions, horrible wrongs and hurts' happening in Norfolk and he resolved that after the King he himself would, '…have the principal rule and governance through this shire, of which we bear our name'. At this time he was addressed in his own territory as 'Your Highness' and 'Prince and Sovereign next our Sovereign Lord' (that is, the most important man after the King). In 1445 the King's Letters Patent confirmed the restoration of the dukedom, recognised by Parliament as long ago as 1425 when Henry VI was only three years old, and in the autumn of

*Richard Neville; 'Warwick the Kingmaker' Neville is seen here in the garb of a mourning figure, or 'weeper' on the tomb of Richard Beauchamp, his father-in-law. His daughter Anne Neville married Richard III.*

*Photo M. Roberts by kind Permission of St Mary's Church, Warwick*

1446 he went on pilgrimage to Rome, but had returned by the following July and was on a diplomatic mission to France. For a time his steward was Sir Robert Wingfield, son-in-law of his grandmother Elizabeth Fitzalan and her third husband, Robert Goushill, but the two kinsmen fell out and Wingfield became Mowbray's enemy; his sons and grandsons, however, supported the Duke, and his son after him. (For more on the Wingfields see Appendix L and Table XX.)

In the early days of the Wars of the Roses Mowbray was a supporter of Richard, Duke of York, his *'Uncle of York'*, married to his mother's sister. They were further related by the marriage of his own wife's brother, Lord Bourchier, to York's sister. Both John Mowbray and Richard of York hated and feared the leading Lancastrian, Edmund Beaufort, Duke of Somerset, whose 'nighness of blood and great zeal to do the King service' had given him precedence over John in the aristocratic pecking order. Mowbray and York met in Bury St Edmunds in October 1450 and illegally selected who should be the Parliamentary candidates for the area, but later Mowbray took advantage of an amnesty offered by Henry VI on Good Friday 1452 to those suspected of sympathising with the questionable activities of the disgruntled Duke of York. Queen Margaret and the Duke of Somerset insisted he distance himself from certain of York's known supporters, and by the early days of 1454 he found himself somewhat eclipsed by the further rising in the royal favour of Richard Neville, Earl of Warwick, his cousin on his mother's side.

Mowbray arrived a day late for the First Battle of St Albans in May 1455, the earliest of the battles of the Wars of the Roses, in which Edmund Beaufort was killed, and one has to wonder whether it was because his loyalties were still tending toward the Yorkists. The following year he was again promoting his own interests in the election of the Knights of the Shire to Parliament, when the disappointed hopeful John Paston was overlooked in favour of Mowbray's cousin, Sir John Howard. Howard's election caused something of a scandal: he might well have been Margaret Mowbray's son and a grandson of the 1st Duke of Norfolk, but he himself was a Suffolk man with no lands in Norfolk at the time. John Mowbray seems thereafter to have kept a fairly low profile, travelling on pilgrimage to holy places in Ireland, Scotland, Brittany, Picardy, Cologne, Rome and Jerusalem to try to obtain a miraculous cure for the King's mental illness, and we know that both he and his wife were in the service of Margaret of Anjou in 1458.

However, Mowbray was eventually drawn into the Lancaster/York conflict again, and although he swore allegiance to Henry VI and the Lancastrian succession in December 1459, less than a year later he emerged as one of the leading Yorkists, but even so, could have been amongst those lords who refused the crown to Richard of York. He managed to escape after the Battle of Wakefield in December 1460 after the Duke of York and one of his young sons were slain, and on 12th February 1461, the Duke of Norfolk set out from London taking with him the bewildered King Henry, now the Yorkists' prisoner. Near St Albans they met Warwick, who was waiting with an army, but five days later they were defeated by Queen Margaret's Lancastrians.

Either Mowbray had forgotten the King in the mayhem of battle, or Henry had given him the slip: whichever, he went missing. This poor soul was totally unsuited to the illustrious position fate had secured for him and would have been better off in a quiet backwater somewhere tending a little abbey garden. In an era when men's fashions were colourful and outrageous to the point of being ridiculous – Peter Idley in 1445 complained about some styles because, 'Cutted on the buttock, even above the rump, they inflame women with lecherous desires',– the chaste King, whose garments should have been the most magnificent of them all, preferred to wear the plain and dark understated clothing of a city merchant. The terrifying noises he heard on the battlefield and the horrific sights he saw there must have played havoc with his delicate mind, for he was found sitting under a tree laughing and singing in the hope that somehow it would all go away.

Reunited with her deranged husband, and determined that the Prince of Wales should in no wise grow up with his father's abhorrence for violence, the Queen had Yorkist prisoners brought before her son and is supposed to have asked him, 'Fair son, what manner of death should these knights whom ye see here die?' Knowing there was only one answer his mother wanted to hear, the Prince replied, 'Let them have their heads taken off'. The boy was seven years old. Whether or not this story is true, he was a child who would know nothing but war, violence, fear, and living like a fugitive throughout most of his short life. The only Lancastrian of note lost at the Second Battle of St Albans was Sir John Grey of Groby, a descendant of earlier Mowbrays, whose beautiful widow would soon secretly become the Queen of England. The Yorkists' revenge for atrocities the Lancastrians committed after Wakefield and St Albans would be released like a torrent in the aftermath of their next confrontation, which came at the end of March.

The Yorkists decided that drastic measures were called-for and the Duke of Norfolk was amongst those, with Richard Neville, who proclaimed York's eldest son, Edward, Earl of March, as King Edward IV, and at whose coronation he was Earl Marshal at the end of June 1461. Before that happy event, however, John Mowbray would be involved in the notorious Battle of Towton.

Margaret of Anjou was in North Yorkshire in the spring of 1461. Edward IV obviously had a pressing need to re-capture King Henry and met his military leaders for a council of war, possibly at Doncaster, and decided to proceed northward, even though there was no sign of the Duke of Norfolk, whose presence he very much needed, and who, Edward probably suspected, could just have changed his loyalties again. In fact, Norfolk was on his way, about a day's march behind the rest, and opinions differ as to why he was late. Some believe he was already a sick man and had to rest, possibly at Pontefract, en route – he died before the year was out – others that he was bringing up heavy artillery which was slow-going on the poor roads, while yet others speculate that he was late simply because he was finding it difficult to recruit enough men.

The Yorkists met the Lancastrians near the Yorkshire village of Towton, near Tadcaster, on Palm Sunday, 29th March 1461, each side having about 40,000 men, although, as usual, the chroniclers put the numbers higher, even up to 60,000. There were two Kings of England on the field that day and their attitudes could hardly have been more different. King Edward, as yet uncrowned, was still reeling from the loss of his father and brother the previous December and the disgraceful execution of his supporters after St Albans, and exhorted his men to take no prisoners. The deeply religious King Henry was begging his wife to postpone the battle on account of it being Palm Sunday.

*TOWTON MEMORIAL TO THE FALLEN; PALM SUNDAY 29TH MARCH 1461.*
*Site of the worst carnage of any battle fought on English soil; the arrival of John Mowbray,*
*3rd Duke of Norfolk and his men was said to have saved the day for the Yorkists.*

It was dreadful battle fought in a blizzard, the Lancastrians in particular suffering from having the snow driven into their faces by a strong southerly wind, which, in its turn, was advantageous to their enemies in that it helped the Yorkists' arrows travel further and hindered their own. Edward's experienced uncle, Lord Fauconberg, a Neville, took every advantage of the weather. He had all his archers shoot one flight only at the Lancastrians, who were taken completely by surprise as the deadly hail materialised from out of the falling snow, and, as he had anticipated, immediately retaliated without being able to see much through the blizzard, wasting their arrows that fell short. Fauconberg's men then advanced and finished off many Lancastrian archers with their own arrows pulled out of the ground. But still it went on. What the state of the ordinary men slipping on the bloodstained slush and falling over snow-covered bodies must have been like is unimaginable, but A.W. Boardman in *The Battle of Towton* paints a frightening picture of what it was like for knight in heavy armour, who could drown in mud or slush if he fell face down and was unable to get up,

*"The armoured knight in his sallet helmet, staring through eyeslots*
*and with blinkered vision and perspiring from the heat and pain*
*caused by, among other things, chafing neck armour, cannot have*
*lasted long in these conditions without rest. If he did not rest he was*
*fair game not only to exhaustion, but also to dehydration, both of*
*which could lead to death in the mêlée as reflexes became slower*
*and blows from the helmeted head's blind side rendered the victim*

*partially stunned, if not unconscious."* [Lord Clifford, who had murdered King Edward's younger brother Edmund after Wakefield three months earlier, was involved in a skirmish with the Yorkists at Dintingdale near Ferrybridge and, removing the armoured neckpiece, or gorget, that was probably chafing his skin, was killed by an arrow in his throat.]

By now, King Edward's intelligence coming in from his messengers and scouts had told him John Mowbray was close, but as the battle entered its fifth hour it looked as though he would be too late. Edward, only just nineteen, was a great soldier, preferring to fight on foot amongst his men, but even he must have had worries as his army was being pushed onto sloping terrain on which it would be difficult to keep their footing. Up to now the action was fairly even and the outcome could have gone either way, but the sudden arrival on the scene of the Mowbray lion standard and 5,000 men struck fear into the Lancastrians and joy into the hearts of their enemies. It is possible that the Duke of Norfolk found the Yorkists more by good luck than management, because the confusion and poor visibility through the falling snow would have made it difficult for him to pick out his side and find a safe place to station his men. It is believed that he entered them into the fray almost at once and the extra numbers eventually turned the tide in the Yorkists' favour; nevertheless, it was not a battle easily won and might have lasted up to ten hours in all. More were killed in the retreat than in the battle itself, not an unusual occurrence in medieval warfare, and the pursuing Yorkists were relentless. There were similarities with Bannockburn, in that the fugitives had to cross water where the bodies of the drowned acted as a human bridge for their fellow men. Where the Cock Beck met the River Wharfe three miles away its waters were said to be running red with blood. Between 20,000 and 30,000 died that day, the worst carnage of any battle on British soil.

A popular poem of the time, *The Rose of Rouen*, dedicated to Edward IV, who was born there, and celebrating the Towton victory, includes Mowbray. The 'Ragged Staff 'is the Earl of Warwick, while Mowbray is the 'White Lion'.

*For to save all England the Rose did his intent,*
*With Calais and with London with Essex and with Kent,*
*And all the south of England up to the water of Trent,*
*And when he saw the time was best the Rose from London went,*
*Blessed be the time that ever God spread that flower.*

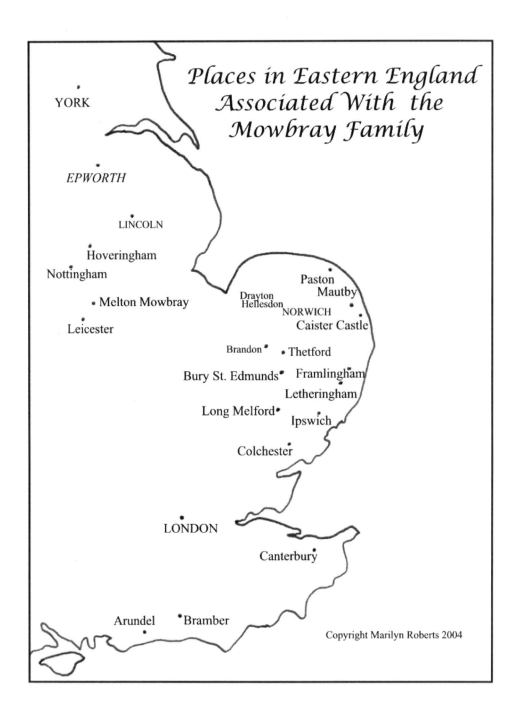

*Places in Eastern England Associated With the Mowbray Family*

YORK

EPWORTH

LINCOLN

Hoveringham

Nottingham

Paston
Mautby

Drayton
Heflesdon
NORWICH

• Melton Mowbray

Caister Castle

Leicester

Brandon • • Thetford

Bury St. Edmunds • Framlingham

Letheringham

Long Melford • 
Ipswich

Colchester

LONDON

Canterbury

Arundel • Bramber

Copyright Marilyn Roberts 2004

*The way into the North Country The Rose full fast he sought,*
*With him went The Ragged Staff that many men they brought,*
*So did The White Lion full worthily he wrought,*
*Almighty Jesu bless this soul, that their armies taught,*
*Blessed be the time that ever God spread that flower.*

*The northern party made them strong with spear and with shield,*
*On Palm Sunday afternoon they met us in the field,*
*Within an hour they were right fayne to flee, and eke to yield,*
*Twenty seven thousand The Rose killed in the field,*
*Blessed be the time that ever God spread that flower.*

In July 1461 the 3rd Duke of Norfolk was made steward and chief justice of the royal forests south of Trent and Constable of Scarborough. However, although his new young master was grateful for his efforts at Towton, he did not openly encourage his illegal occupancy of Caister Castle in Norfolk. The Wars of the Roses afforded those nobles so inclined ample opportunities to settle old scores or to acquire land and property to which they had no claim in the eyes of the law, and no case is better known than the struggle over Caister Castle between the Paston family and the last two Mowbray dukes.

Paston is a Norfolk village in the north of the county, not far from the coast. Clement Paston, who died in 1419, was a yeoman farmer with a hundred acres, an example of how a humble man surviving the bubonic plague could make a good living. The plague had decimated the country and precipitated such great changes in the social order that in three generations Clement's successors rose to be titled landowners with their own castle. He was prosperous enough to be able to educate his son William (1378 - 1444) as a lawyer, and William Paston 'a right cunning man in the law' was very successful and became a Justice of the Common Pleas. He bought more land, married Agnes, daughter of Sir Edmund Berry of Hertfordshire, and John Paston (1421 - 1466) was the eldest of their five sons.

John Paston married Margaret Mauteby, who inherited land and property of her own, and he too became a lawyer. His profession took him away to London a great deal, staying no doubt at his London home on Fleet Street where the Mowbray dowager Katherine Neville went to stay in 1444. Unfortunately, the 1450s and 1460s were lawless times and Margaret Paston, the most interesting member of the family, was often left at home to manage the estates with little support, a not unusual situation in those days when a woman was expected to cope in her husband's absence. But Margaret really was left 'holding the fort' against aristocratic predators when the men of her own family were away embroiled in the Lancaster and Yorkist struggles. The Pastons are famous for their correspondence with each other from 1422 - 1529 which sheds light on the minutiae of everyday middle-class life, such as where to get the best exotic spices in London, the difficulty of obtaining decent fabrics for a cloak in the local shops or for making clothes for the children – like many a modern woman of today Margaret Paston complains that she has 'done' all the shops in town and cannot find a thing she needs – and how to survive against powerful and violent neighbours like the Mowbrays and the de la Poles (see Appendix J).

Sir John Fastolf was a veteran of The Hundred Years' War who distinguished himself at Agincourt and became lieutenant and regent in Normandy for Henry V. He was Governor of Anjou and Maine from 1432-36 and retired in 1440. He grew very rich on ransom and the spoils of war, and wisely invested some of his money in the wool trade. With his accumulating wealth he increased his land holdings in Norfolk and built himself a castle at Caister for his retirement. Shakespeare turned him into Sir John Falstaff, a character nothing like his real self, and said that in his youth he was a page to the 1st Duke of Norfolk, but this is doubtful. In 1437 he sold Blickling Hall to the up-and-coming Bullen family of merchants, about to change their name to the more aristocratic sounding 'Boleyn'. Fastolf might have been related to the Pastons and certainly held them in high esteem, and when he died in 1459 left them Hellesdon, Drayton and Caister, three of his Norfolk estates, but unfortunately he had made two wills. By the terms of the first, made in the June before he died, he made clear his wish that a college for priests and poor men be founded at Caister and the residue of his estate be sold; by the second, made in November, not long before his death, he left his Norfolk and Suffolk lands to John Paston on condition that he went ahead with founding the college.

The 3rd Duke of Norfolk had coveted Caister Castle as far back as the early 1450s when he had tried to persuade Fastolf to sell it to him. He tried again just before the old knight died, but Mowbray was told that it was to go to John Paston (I). By the time the situation came to a head at the end of the 1460s both the 3rd Duke and John Paston (I) were dead, the family now headed by his son Sir John Paston (II), whose brother, just to complicate matters, was also called John Paston (III). Unfortunately the existence of the two wills, the chaos of living with civil war and the inability of the illustrious executors, who included the Bishop of Winchester, to agree what should be done, left the Pastons in a very difficult position, made worse by the fact that, given half a chance, Fastolf's relatives would have been delighted to sell Caister Castle to the Duke of Norfolk.

John Mowbray, 3rd Duke, died the November following Towton and was buried at Thetford Priory. His wife, Eleanor Bourchier, was a granddaughter of Thomas of Woodstock, the Duke of Gloucester many believed to have been killed in Calais with the connivance of Thomas Mowbray, John's own grandfather. Duchess Eleanor died in November 1474 and was also buried at Thetford.

*John Mowbray*, 18th October 1444 - 17th January 1476.
4th Duke of Norfolk, Earl of Norfolk, Earl of Nottingham, Earl Marshal, Earl of Surrey and Warenne.

Born on 18th October 1444, John was created Earl of Surrey and Warenne at only six years old when the earldom that had become extinct upon the death of his great-grandmother Elizabeth's brother, Thomas Fitzalan, was conferred upon him. By the age of eighteen he was engaged in fighting the Scots, at about the same time his neighbour Margaret Paston, to whom his greed and disrespect for the law would later bring such strife, wrote of him thus, 'The pepyll loveth and dredyth him more than any other lord except the King and my Lord of Warwick.'

The 4th duke had more contempt for the law than his late father ever had and was determined to have Caister, but he was not the only powerful nobleman engaged in questionable activities at this time and was matched in unpleasantness and greed by the de la Pole Duke of Suffolk; fortunately for the people of East Anglia, perhaps, the two ducal families were at loggerheads. Edward IV did not openly condone their activities, but well aware he needed their support, did not go out of his way to suppress their illegal doings either. Margaret Paston was far from enamoured of Suffolk, or his mother, and in a letter of 1464 tells us what the people thought of them, 'They love not in no wyse the Dwke of Sowthfolk nor his modyr. They sey that all the tretours and extorsyonerys of thys contre be meynteynyd by them.'

Margaret's husband was away when Suffolk took Hellesdon by force in 1465. Knowing that her property there would be attacked and vandalised, she had household valuables such as linen and pewter vessels stored in the church for safety, but the Duke's men looted what they could carry and smashed the rest, safe in the knowledge that many who would wish in their hearts to help Margaret Paston were too afraid of reprisals to do so. Margaret needed great courage and strength of character to stand her ground. Between November 1459 and his death in 1466, John Paston (I) was away from home a good deal: twice as a Knight of the Shire and three times imprisoned by Edward IV for being a Lancastrian. During this time, as well as the worry of the Hellesdon incident, Caister Castle was briefly occupied by Mowbray's father in 1461 and in 1465 by Anthony Woodville, the Queen's brother, who was also the brother of the Mowbray dowager Katherine Neville's new young husband.

The Pastons had once been on good terms with the Mowbrays, as the letter from Duchess Katherine written to them in the 1440s from the mansion at Epworth reveals (Appendix J), and might have entertained the faint hope that the Duke of Norfolk would come to their aid against Suffolk. Instead, they had to endure years of appalling behaviour from the Mowbray family over the rightful ownership of Caister Castle, a struggle that does nothing to endear the last of the Mowbray dukes to the modern researcher. Beneath the thin veneer of politeness, the Mowbrays saw the *nouveau riche* Pastons as upstarts, and when their relationship turned sour the latter were in trouble. As far back as April 1453, long before the Caister problem raised its ugly head, John Paston the father, a man of the law himself, made a complaint to the sheriff that one Charles Nowell, a Mowbray retainer, had attacked him in Norwich Cathedral, a surprise for Paston who thought himself to be a friend of the 3rd Duke, whose protection and goodwill he sorely needed,

> "[Nowell] *and five of his fellowship set upon me and one of my servants… he smiting at me whilst one of his fellows held mine arms at my back… Which was to me strange… I was my lord's man and his homager ere Charles knew his lordship… my lord was my good lord…"*

The Pastons were not the only ones suffering from Mowbray lawlessness, for in 1468 the 4th Duke forced Thomas Charles to convey to him his manors of Lodden, Kettlebury and Siseland that Charles's daughters only recovered ten years after Mowbray's death.

The 4th Duke of Norfolk was very much under the influence of William Brandon, a retainer who made his name and fortune in his service. Brandon married Elizabeth Fitzalan's granddaughter Elizabeth Wingfield, daughter of Elizabeth Goushill and Sir Robert Wingfield, and his family would eventually become Dukes of Suffolk. The most famous member of the Brandon family was the ill-fated Lady Jane Grey, also of Mowbray descent (see Table V). In June 1469 Elizabeth Wingfield's brother, Thomas, wrote to his friends the Pastons that Edward IV had warned Brandon that if John Mowbray broke the law over Caister Castle he would hold him, Brandon, responsible because he knew that Mowbray was under his thumb. Obviously things were getting out of hand and the King could not allow his laws to be flouted so openly. Edward IV was an impressive figure of a man about six-feet-four in height, so his outstanding physical presence and blunt words should have acted as a stern warning to someone of William Brandon's then relatively humble status. According to Thomas Wingfield the King said,

> *"Brandon, though thou can beguile the Duke of Norfolk, and bring him abow* [under] *the thumb as thou lyst* [like]*... thou shalt not do me so, for I understand thy false dealing well enough."*

Thomas continued to report that the King then said:

> *"...that if my Lord of Norffolk left not of his hold on that matter* [i.e. occupying Caister Castle] *that Brandon should repent it... and if my Lord did anything that were contrary to his laws, the King told him he knew well enough that it was by no body's means but by his."*

Shortly afterwards King Edward became a prisoner of Warwick the Kingmaker, and a local dispute over a castle was the last thing on his mind. Mowbray took Caister again, this time with great force, and life was lost. It was a desperate Margaret Paston who wrote to her son John (II) on 12ᵗʰ September, chiding him for not doing enough to help his younger brother and alleviate her plight,

> *"I greet you well, letting you know that your brother and his fellowship stand in great jeopardy at Caister, and lack victual; and Daubeney* [is] *dead... and divers others greatly hurt, and they lack gunpowder and arrows, and the place* [i.e. the castle] *is sore broken by the guns of the other party, so that unless they have hasty help, they are like to lose both their lives and the place..."*

(It is interesting to see that one of the Paston supporters was called Daubeney, a derivation of the ancient name d'Aubigny.)

As the premier nobleman in his area Mowbray could expect support. Like his father Sir Robert before him, it is possible that Thomas Wingfield was not a Mowbray admirer and was not his man from choice, but it would seem that commitment to his family and his fear of the Duke compelled him take up arms against his friends. Margaret Paston and her few supporters could not resist such an onslaught from some of the roughnecks pitched against them, including the formidable Gilbert Debenham, a one-time Mowbray steward, much feared in Ipswich and Colchester, and were forcibly evicted after a five-week siege. The Duke's rejoicing at having the castle in his clutches

*ELIZABETH TALBOT, DUCHESS OF NORFOLK AND MOTHER OF ANNE MOWBRAY*
*Wife of the last Mowbray Duke, Elizabeth was the daughter of Margaret Beauchamp who imprisoned Lady Isabel Mowbray.*
*Photo M. Roberts by Kind Permission of Rev'd Ian M.G. Friars, Long Melford Church, Suffolk*

at last was short-lived, however, for he was arrested twice as a Yorkist when Henry VI was briefly restored, in October 1470 and March 1471, and his ill-gotten gains had to be surrendered.

After the Battle of Tewkesbury in May 1471, John Mowbray sat in judgement at the hasty 'trial' of the poor Lancastrian souls dragged from the sanctuary of the abbey after the battle; one of his fellow judges was the King's brother, the eighteen-year-old Duke of Gloucester, later Richard III. Perhaps these two could have told what really happened to the young Prince of Wales – was he killed in the battle or taken prisoner and murdered? Mowbray's men William Brandon and the Wingfield brothers, Thomas and Henry, were knighted at Tewkesbury. The following month Mowbray was up to his old tricks and took Caister Castle yet again while the Pastons and their men slept, and the sheriff of Norfolk, his crony Sir John Wingfield, did absolutely nothing about it. (For further information on the Wingfield family see Table XX, *Presidents Bush and Franklin D. Roosevelt,* and Appendix L, *Palgrave Williams and Edward Maria Wingfield.*)

This was the era when the Dukes of Norfolk were trying to consolidate their interests in the eastern counties and obviously John Mowbray saw Caister Castle and its lands as a great prize worth pursuing. When he had first come into his inheritance the Mowbray finances were in a very bad way due to the legacy of the banishment of his great-grandfather, mismanagement of the estates and the burden of having to maintain aged dowagers in the manner appropriate to their station. However, with the death in 1474 of his mother, Duchess Eleanor, things improved, but not for long. The King suddenly gave him notice to provide and lead forty men-at-arms and 300 archers for an expedition to France, at his own expense of course, and in 1475 John was one of the captains for the invasion of France on behalf of the Duke of Burgundy. He managed to exchange his estates in Chepstow and Gower for lands in Norfolk and Suffolk, thus dispensing with the expense of administering far-distant holdings, which must have been something of a millstone to a man short of money. (For further information on the 4th Duke and his family's financial problems see Chapter VI.)

On January 16th – 17th 1476, that is, sometime in the middle of the night, John Mowbray died suddenly at Framlingham Castle at the age of thirty-one, and, he having a daughter but no son, the Mowbray dukedom of Norfolk and all the earldoms he held became extinct. After a lifespan of four hundred years, the great Mowbray dynasty was no more. According to a letter sent to Margaret Paston by her son Sir John, the death was totally unexpected, although as far back as May 1467 the Duke himself complained in a letter to his kinsman John Howard that God had visited him with great infirmity and disease.

The slightly severe image of John's wife, Elizabeth Talbot, daughter of the Earl of Shrewsbury, is to be found in the stained glass of Long Melford Church in Suffolk, together with the Mowbray lion shield and the more gentle likeness of ElizabethTilney, the grandmother of both Anne Boleyn and Kathryn Howard, wives of Henry VIII (Tables IV & V), and who, had she lived long enough, would have become the second Howard Duchess of Norfolk. Some say that the image of Elizabeth Talbot was John Tenniel's inspiration for the drawings of the Ugly Duchess in *Alice in Wonderland*, but that character is much more reminiscent of *A Grotesque Old Woman*, the wonderfully naughty comment on human vanity and self-delusion by Quentin Massys, now in London's National Gallery.

ANNE MOWBRAY, 10TH DECEMBER 1472 - NOVEMBER 1481.
Countess of Norfolk, Duchess of York and Norfolk.

Lady Anne, the long-awaited surviving baby, was born on 10th December 1472, baptised a week later at Framlingham by her godfather William of Waynflete, Bishop of Winchester, and was only just three years old when her father died. There being no male heir, the dukedom and all the earldoms held by John Mowbray became extinct and Anne took the title Countess of Norfolk. Her neighbours, the Pastons, were not alone in fearing that the little girl would become a pawn in a game of high finance and power, for Edward IV had two young sons, and was on the lookout for a good catch for the younger, Prince Richard, Duke of York. Sure enough, the children were soon

*JOHN TALBOT, EARL OF SHREWSBURY,
Anne Mowbray's grandfather.*

betrothed, and on 15th January 1478 were married in a splendid ceremony at St Stephen's Chapel in the Palace of Westminster, followed by feasting and jousting. She was five years old, and he only four. Prince Richard's father had already made him Duke of Norfolk in a new creation 'in contemplation of his marriage'.

In their *History of Framlingham* written in 1798, Hawes and Lodder, describing the events using old sources, painted a picture of handsome noblemen in a magnificent late-medieval setting escorting a lovely bride who could have come straight from the canvas of a romantic painting – were it not for her ridiculously young age,

*"This lady Anne Mowbray, the richest and most noble match of that time, being about four [sic] years old at her father's decease, was, two years after, married to Richard, duke of York, the King's second son, in the presence of the King, the Queen, the Prince and Princesses, the King's daughters. Accompanied with many dukes, earls, barons and ladies the young lady was led by the Earl of Lincoln on the right hand and on the left by the Earl Rivers, unto St Stephen's Chapel where, at the door, the Bishop of Norwich received her, and Dr Coke declared that*

*the high and mighty prince Richard duke of York, ought not to be
wedded to that high and excellent princess, for they were within the
Degrees of Marriage, the one at the fourth and the other at the
third, for which cause he forbad the spousal without there were a
special licence from the Pope, and a dispensation for the nighness of
blood. Then the Dean of the King's chapel showed an ample Bull
authorising them to proceed 'ad contractum et matrimonium'.
Whereupon the Bishop asked who would give the princess to the
Church and to him, which being done by the King, he proceeded to
the high altar to mass. And when the ceremonies were over, the Duke
of Gloucester led the bride on the right hand and the Duke of
Buckingham on the left, to St Edward's chamber, where a stately
feast was prepared for them."*

These are very interesting observations showing that Anne Mowbray
was attended by the greatest in the land on her wedding day. Whether
she really was 'the richest and most noble match of that time' is
debatable: noble certainly, but not as rich as we may think. As to
the 'third and fourth degrees of marriage', both were descended
from daughters of Ralph Neville, Earl of Westmorland, and Joan
Beaufort. The Prince mentioned is the future Edward V attending the
wedding with his sisters, all of whom were acknowledged to be very
handsome children, and Earl Rivers and the Duke of Gloucester are
respectively, Queen Elizabeth Woodville's brother Anthony and the
future Richard III, then aged twenty-five. It will probably never be
known whether Richard was responsible for the death of the little
bridegroom and his brother in the Tower only five years later, but
both Anthony Woodville and the Duke of Buckingham would perish
through him.

On 5th May 1479, the tiny Duke of York was appointed Lieutenant
of Ireland for two years, and the instrument of nomination reveals
that he had some very fine titles for one so young. He is styled:
*Recardus secundus filius Illustrissimi Principis Edw: quarti etc., Dux Ebor:
et Norff: Comes Warren: Surr: et Nottingham: Comes Marescallus, et
Marescallus Angliae, ac Dominus de Segrave, de Mowbray, et de Gower.*
(Richard, second son of the Illustrious Prince Edward IV; Duke of
York and Norfolk; Earl of Warenne, Surrey and Nottingham; Earl
Marshal and Marshal of England; Lord Segrave, Mowbray and
Gower.) His little wife would bear the female equivalent of all these.

Anne left her Suffolk home at Framlingham which was then settled
on Thomas Bourchier, the Archbishop of Canterbury, a relative
through her grandmother Duchess Eleanor, who held it in trust for
her and her heirs. She lived in the royal household in the comfort

and splendour befitting a great princess until her untimely death at Greenwich Palace in November 1481, days short of her ninth birthday. The whole Mowbray inheritance, probably illegally, went to her royal husband instead of to her co-heirs at law, Lord William Berkeley and Lord John Howard, and the financial outlook must have looked very promising to King Edward, who cannot have foreseen that the Dowager Duchess Katherine would outlive himself and his son, and they would never get their hands on the extensive Mowbray properties she still held. The Keeper of the Great Wardrobe, the government department responsible for, amongst other things, providing everything necessary for state occasions, paid out the enormous sum of £215. 16s. 10d. for the expenses of Anne's funeral and burial in Westminster Abbey, where she was interred in the St Erasmus Chapel.

Anne's coffin was moved to the convent of the Poor Clares, or Minoresses, in Stepney in the reign of Henry VII as a temporary arrangement when the St Erasmus Chapel was demolished to make room for his new Lady Chapel. It had always been assumed that she was reburied in Westminster Abbey once the works were finished, but the building went on for years, and it would seem that Anne was forgotten. In 1964, when buildings on the site of the old Stepney Convent were being demolished, a workman spotted a small lead coffin amongst the rubble. It was removed to a nearby police station, where a 'found property' label was attached to it, and from there was taken to the London Museum, then housed in Kensington Palace. A Latin inscription attached to the coffin revealed the occupant's name, the name of her father and the date of her death: it was Anne Mowbray, Duchess of York and Norfolk.

As newspaper cuttings of the time show, the find caused enormous interest. Limited forensic examinations were carried out on the remains and reports were promised, but there were those, including the then Duke of Norfolk (Bernard Marmaduke Fitzalan-Howard, 1908-1975, 16th Duke of Norfolk), who thought it was not right to be examining and reporting upon the remains of a princess, so some of the promised reports of findings failed to materialise. Due to an oversight, the necessary paperwork and licences to examine the body were not completely in order either, so the child's remains were reburied in Westminster Abbey in May 1965, not too far from the memorial sarcophagus designed by Sir Christopher Wren to hold the bones widely believed, but not proven, to be those of Anne's husband and his brother, the Princes in the Tower, found under a Tower staircase in the reign of Charles II.

Chart 8: *The Neville Family*

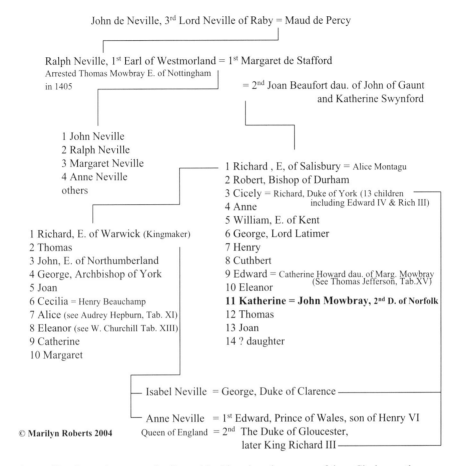

John de Neville, 3<sup>rd</sup> Lord Neville of Raby = Maud de Percy

Ralph Neville, 1<sup>st</sup> Earl of Westmorland = 1<sup>st</sup> Margaret de Stafford
Arrested Thomas Mowbray E. of Nottingham
in 1405

= 2<sup>nd</sup> Joan Beaufort dau. of John of Gaunt
and Katherine Swynford

1 John Neville
2 Ralph Neville
3 Margaret Neville
4 Anne Neville
others

1 Richard , E, of Salisbury = Alice Montagu
2 Robert, Bishop of Durham
3 Cicely = Richard, Duke of York (13 children
including Edward IV & Rich III)
4 Anne
5 William, E. of Kent
6 George, Lord Latimer
7 Henry
8 Cuthbert
9 Edward = Catherine Howard dau. of Marg. Mowbray
(See Thomas Jefferson, Tab.XV)
10 Eleanor
**11 Katherine = John Mowbray, 2<sup>nd</sup> D. of Norfolk**
12 Thomas
13 Joan
14 ? daughter

1 Richard, E. of Warwick (Kingmaker)
2 Thomas
3 John, E. of Northumberland
4 George, Archbishop of York
5 Joan
6 Cecilia = Henry Beauchamp
7 Alice (see Audrey Hepburn, Tab. XI)
8 Eleanor (see W. Churchill Tab. XIII)
9 Catherine
10 Margaret

Isabel Neville = George, Duke of Clarence

Anne Neville = 1<sup>st</sup> Edward, Prince of Wales, son of Henry VI
Queen of England = 2<sup>nd</sup> The Duke of Gloucester,
later King Richard III

© **Marilyn Roberts 2004**

The Nevilles show what a great family could achieve in a short space of time. Cicely was the mother of two kings, and her great-niece Anne Neville, by either of her marriages, was destined to become Queen of England.
In sharp contrast to the latter-day Mowbrays they were adept at producing large families, but the Kingmaker, who married the heiress of the great Richard Beauchamp, Earl of Warwick, had only two daughters, whose large inheritances made them very attractive to two of the Plantagenet brothers, the sons of their great-aunt Cicely.
Eleanor Neville, sister of Warwick the Kingmaker, married Lord Thomas Stanley.
Most of the Nevilles made very good marriages, with the exception of the clergymen, who instead managed to fill two of the greatest, and most lucrative, positions in the Church.

Bearing in mind that the Princes' grandmother, Cicely Neville, and Anne Mowbray's great-grandmother, Duchess Katherine, were sisters, modern scientific knowledge and sophisticated technology could, perhaps, shed some light on the identity of the remains supposed to be those of the Princes if further studies of the skeletons of the three children were to be sanctioned. Since the time of Queen Elizabeth I Westminster Abbey has had the status of a 'Royal Peculiar' and the sovereign's permission is required before remains interred therein may be exhumed. In 1933, George V allowed the Princes' remains to be examined, but the evidence for positive identification was inconclusive. There were found the incomplete skeletons of two children of four-foot-ten inches and four-foot-six-and-a-half inches in height, the bones indicating slim build and small hands. Dental evidence suggested the elder, who was suffering from a painful disease of the lower jaw, to be about thirteen years of age, the younger between nine and eleven, and also suggested the two were related. A stain on the facial bones of the elder was thought in some quarters to be a bloodstain indicating death by suffocation. It could not be determined whether the skeletons were male or female. Dental evidence on Anne Mowbray did not rule out the possibility of some familial affinity with these remains.

## THE BEAUCHAMP TOMB, ST MARY'S CHURCH, WARWICK

Richard Beauchamp, Earl of Warwick, was one of the greatest of the late medieval magnates and is mentioned here because of the connections his tomb figures have with the Mowbrays and the Nevilles featured in this chapter, and because his effigy has over it one of only three remaining medieval hearses, similar to the one mentioned in the Paston Letters with regard to the tomb of the last Mowbray duke (see Appendix J, Letter 768). The rich cloth covering the hearse would be lifted three times a day 'every day during the world', so that Masses

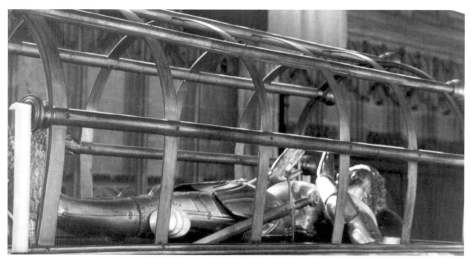

THE TOMB OF RICHARD BEAUCHAMP, EARL OF WARWICK
*One of the finest late medieval tombs in the country, it still retains the hearse over which a rich cloth would be draped when prayers were not being said for Beauchamp's soul.*
*Photo M. Roberts by kind permission of St Mary's Church, Warwick*

THE BEAUCHAMP TOMB
*The great man's son Henry and daughter-in-law, Cecilia Neville, lead the mourners depicted on*
*the sides of the tomb.*
*Photo M. Roberts by kind permission of St. Mary's Church, Warwick*

could be said for his soul. Beauchamp was an internationally famous soldier under Henry V and was appointed Lieutenant in France in 1437. He was appointed 'maistre', or tutor, to the baby Henry VI in the 1420's and had authority to chastise him. When he died a new chantry chapel was built at St Mary's Church in Warwick, one of the finest ever constructed in the 'decorated' style of Gothic, where priests would pray for his soul.

The tomb with its mourning figures, or 'weepers', and their exquisitely attired wives, is one of the great treasures of English medieval art and we have to wonder if it bears any resemblance to lost Mowbray tombs, but the Mowbrays, although eventually achieving a dukedom, somehow seem never to have quite 'made it' in the way the Beauchamps and the Nevilles did. Beauchamp married two wealthy women: Elizabeth, daughter of the 3rd Lord Berkeley and Lisle, with whom he had only daughters, and Isabel Despenser, through whom he became heir to the Despenser fortune, and who bore him further daughters and one son, Henry, Duke of Warwick.

The males on the tomb are wearing the long cloaks and large hoods typical of mourning figures; their wives, depicted on the opposite side, are a different matter altogether, putting on for our delight a late medieval fashion parade of the first order. Their husbands might well be looking downcast, as five of the seven of them would die in battle.

### THE LADIES OF THE BEAUCHAMP TOMB:

#### CECILIA NEVILLE (DIED 1450)
WIFE OF BEAUCHAMP'S ONLY SURVIVING SON, HENRY DUKE OF WARWICK.

A daughter of Richard Neville, Earl of Salisbury, sister of Warwick the Kingmaker and niece of Duchess Katherine and John Mowbray, 2nd Duke of Norfolk.

Her husband died in 1445 leaving no children; his sister Anne Beauchamp (see below) was his heiress.

*CECILIA NEVILLE*

*ALICE MONTAGU*

## ALICE MONTAGU (DIED 1462)
WIFE OF RICHARD, EARL OF SALISBURY.

Sister-in-law of Duchess Katherine, mother of Warwick the Kingmaker and of Alice Neville who was an ancestor of the actress Audrey Hepburn.

Her husband, a grandson of John of Gaunt, was killed at the Battle of Wakefield in 1460.

*ELEANOR BEAUCHAMP*

## ELEANOR BEAUCHAMP (DIED 1467)
WIFE OF EDMUND BEAUFORT, DUKE OF SOMERSET.

A daughter of Beauchamp and Elizabeth, daughter of Lord Berkeley and Lisle. Yorkist gossip accused Eleanor's husband of being the father of Margaret of Anjou's only son, the Prince of Wales. (Edmund Beaufort seems to have been something of a ladies' man. When he was younger Henry V's young widow, Katherine de Valois, was thought to have taken a shine to him, so legislation was introduced making it necessary for her to seek the permission of Parliament before she remarried.) Edmund Beaufort was killed at the First Battle of St Albans, the first of the Wars of the Roses, in 1455.

*ANNE NEVILLE*

## ANNE NEVILLE (DIED 1480)
WIFE OF HUMPHREY STAFFORD, DUKE OF BUCKINGHAM.

A daughter of Ralph Neville, Earl of Westmorland; a sister of Duchess Katherine and also of Cicely Neville, Duchess of York, making her, like her sister Katherine, the aunt of Edward IV, Richard III and their brother, the Duke of Clarence who drowned in a barrel of wine.

Her husband was killed at the Battle of Northampton in 1460.

### MARGARET BEAUCHAMP (DIED 1467)
WIFE OF JOHN TALBOT, EARL OF SHREWSBURY.

The eldest daughter of Richard Beauchamp and Elizabeth, daughter of Thomas, Lord Berkeley and Lisle; her uncle James Berkeley, 'the Just', married the Lady Isabel Mowbray. The two Berkeley branches became locked in a quarrel over money and property, including Berkeley Castle, and Isabel died Margaret Beauchamp's prisoner in Gloucester Castle (see Chapter VII). It seems rather odd that Margaret's daughter, Elizabeth Talbot, should marry Isabel's great-nephew, John, 4th Duke of Norfolk, who appears to have tried to keep out of the Berkeley family's feud. Margaret Beauchamp was the grandmother of the Lady Anne Mowbray, but had died before the child was born.

MARGARET BEAUCHAMP

Her husband, a famous soldier of his day, was killed at the Battle of Castillon, when defeat for England led to the loss of Gascony in 1453.

### ANNE BEAUCHAMP (DIED 1492)
WIFE OF RICHARD NEVILLE, 'THE KINGMAKER'.

A daughter of Beauchamp and his second wife Isabel Despenser. Her daughter Isabel was married to the Duke of Clarence who famously drowned in the butt of Malmsey wine. When the Kingmaker changed sides and threw in his lot with Henry VI he married his other daughter, another Anne Neville, to the young Prince of Wales. After the Prince was killed at Tewkesbury Anne married Clarence's brother, Richard, Duke of Gloucester, and in 1483 became Queen of England, making Anne Beauchamp mother-in-law to a Prince of Wales and a King of England.

ANNE BEAUCHAMP

Warwick the Kingmaker was killed at the Battle of Barnet in 1471.

### ELIZABETH BEAUCHAMP (DIED 1480, NOT SHOWN)
WIFE OF GEORGE NEVILLE, LORD LATIMER.

A daughter of Beauchamp and his first wife.

Her husband, Duchess Katherine's brother, died in 1469.

## Postscript to Anne Mowbray

In the seven years since the original publication of *The Mowbray Legacy* the author has researched the Mowbrays' London residence at Broken Wharf near the Millennium Bridge, the old Fitzalan-Mowbray residence in Lambeth known as Norfolk House, which was the home of Kathryn Howard before her marriage to Henry VIII, and has also looked at the bigger picture surrounding the marriage of Anne Mowbray and Prince Richard and the 1964 discovery of her remains. One of the biggest surprises was to find how Elizabeth Talbot, one of the finest ladies of the land, was reduced to poverty by Edward IV and Henry VII to the extent she had no means of leaving bequests to her relatives and friends. In her will of 6th November 1506, ten days before her death, she made what provision she could for the poor of Whitechapel and Hackney and poor gentlemen and servants that were,

*"...fallen in povertie and decaye, and especially thoos that have bee[n] in service with my lord and me."*

She apologised to those close to her and her few remaining relatives for the lack of means to make bequests to them because,

*"... my poor substance ys little ynough to pay and content my dettes... and to recompense theym that moost truely have served me."*

The Dowager had been living at the Convent of the Poor Clares north of the Tower, and was buried in the nuns' choir of the convent church, and this is why her daughter's coffin was taken there for, what was expected to be, temporary interment while the alterations were happening at Westminster Abbey. Elizabeth Tilney, Anne Boleyn and Kathryn Howard's grandmother, who appears with Elizabeth Talbot in the stained glass at Long Melford Church in Suffolk, was also buried in the convent. No trace of these two ladies was found during excavations following the discovery of Anne's remains.

Anne Mowbray's story (and what little information there is on Broken Wharf) is to be published under the title *The High and Excellent Princess: Lady Anne Mowbray, the bride of a Prince in the Tower.*

# CHAPTER VI

## THE MOWBRAY INHERITANCE

*Let us all pray that God send my Lady of Norfolk a son.*
Sir John Paston, January 1476, writing in the hope that the
Duchess could be carrying her late husband's son and heir.

ITH THE DEATH of the last male of the Mowbray line it is easy to think of his daughter Anne as a vulnerable little girl with a huge fortune in danger of being snapped up by the most cunning operator. But, even in the time of her grandfather, the fortune was nowhere near as great as we may think and would have been better suited to the lifestyle of an affluent baron than a mighty duke with royal blood in his veins, massive financial commitments and an opulent lifestyle to maintain.

The famous Bess of Hardwick, a contemporary of Elizabeth I, is the archetypal example of a woman who made her fortune through being a widow, each time collecting her third of her late husband's estates for the rest of her life, but this practice, with all the attendant pitfalls for the son and heir, was the law in medieval England and the longevity of a succession of widows almost bled the Mowbray family to death financially. A twice or thrice-widowed noblewoman could be rich indeed, and some, with their own financial security, must have allowed themselves the luxury of marrying for love rather than duty, at the risk of having to pay a huge fine of £1000 for failing to procure the necessary licence from the Crown.

A comfortable financial situation sometimes allowed a widow to choose a social inferior for a husband, as appears to have been the case with Elizabeth Fitzalan, who chose Sir Robert Goushill, one of her late husband's retainers. Henry V's widow, a daughter of the King of France, went so far as to marry, or at least co-habit with, her late husband's squire, Sir Owen Tudor, albeit in secret, and this illicit liaison produced the foundations for the most colourful ruling dynasty Britain has ever had. Their great-great-granddaughter Queen Elizabeth I (1558-1603), herself descended from the Mowbrays through Anne Boleyn, had obviously given the wealthy widow situation some thought, for shortly after the death of her favourite, Robert Dudley, Earl of Leicester, yet another Mowbray descendant, she called in his debts before his widow, also of the Mowbray blood,

## Chart 9: *The Mowbray Inheritance*

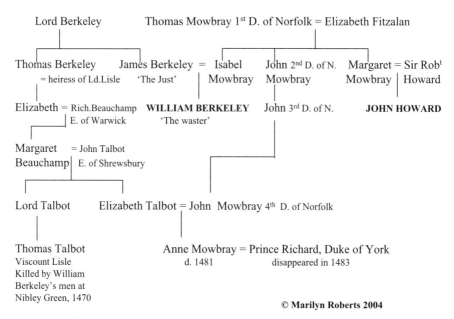

Lord Berkeley     Thomas Mowbray 1st D. of Norfolk = Elizabeth Fitzalan

Thomas Berkeley    James Berkeley = Isabel    John 2nd D. of N.    Margaret = Sir Robt
= heiress of Ld.Lisle   'The Just'   Mowbray   Mowbray     Mowbray | Howard

Elizabeth = Rich.Beauchamp   **WILLIAM BERKELEY**   John 3rd D. of N.    **JOHN HOWARD**
E. of Warwick    'The waster'

Margaret    = John Talbot
Beauchamp | E. of Shrewsbury

Lord Talbot     Elizabeth Talbot = John Mowbray 4th D. of Norfolk

Thomas Talbot      Anne Mowbray = Prince Richard, Duke of York
Viscount Lisle        d. 1481      disappeared in 1483
Killed by William
Berkeley's men at
Nibley Green, 1470

© **Marilyn Roberts 2004**

After the Duke of York's incarceration in the Tower in the summer of 1483 Lord John Howard became Duke of Norfolk and Earl Marshal, while William Berkeley was made Earl of Nottingham. Howard was killed two years later at Bosworth, and William Berkeley, nicknamed *the Waster,* sold or gave away his lands to buy popularity, including the Isle of Axholme that was sold to the Stanleys.
Viscount Lisle was only 20 when he was killed at Nibley Green and his wife miscarried after his death; these events were seen by some as God's punishment upon his grandmother Margaret Beauchamp (Talbot) for imprisoning the Lady Isabel Mowbray (Berkeley) in Gloucester Castle, where she died in 1452. The dispute between the Berkeleys and Lisles was not resolved until the seventeenth century.

and her new husband could enjoy the fruits of the wealth that she, Elizabeth, had lavished upon Robert over a period of thirty years (see Tables IV & VI).

Dowagers and avaricious stepfathers must have been a real thorn in the side for the head of a great family, a bad enough situation when the dowager was the mother of the heir, but intolerable when she was a stepmother who had had no children within the family and so was no blood relation at all. John, 4th Lord Mowbray had to sue his stepmother, Elizabeth de Vere, and her new husband for widespread neglect and damage to Mowbray properties and the cutting down of 12,000 trees; his action was successful but she outlived him and the practices continued into the time of his son. As mentioned earlier, John's own father had difficulty retrieving some of his late mother Alina's estates from his stepfather, Sir Richard Peshale.

Financial disappointments for the Mowbray family began during the long life of Margaret, Countess (briefly Duchess) of Norfolk, mother-in-law of John, 4th Lord Mowbray who had married her daughter, Elizabeth Segrave. As Margaret was an heiress of Edward I's son Thomas de Brotherton, the marriage would have been welcomed by the Mowbray family as a passport to vast wealth, but Margaret lived to be over eighty, keeping a tight hold of the Brotherton estates and of her entitlement for life to the Segrave widow's third, outliving her daughter and son-in-law and one of her grandsons. She died in 1399 shortly before another grandson Thomas, 1st duke, who was already in exile and was consequently deprived of the Brotherton inheritance. The exile of Thomas Mowbray itself caused considerable financial upheaval as his assets were frozen until his so-called embezzlement of funds when governor of Calais had been sorted out, and we have already seen that his sons had to petition Henry IV for financial support in their youth.

Serious financial problems for the family can also be linked to Katherine Neville, wife of the 2nd Duke, an incredible woman who manipulated resources to the advantage of some of the children of a later marriage, all the more galling for the Mowbrays because her own dowry had never been paid in full, even though her father, Ralph Neville, Earl of Westmorland, was astonishingly wealthy. *The Sunday Times* 'Rich List' estimated his worth to be the equivalent of nearly £7 billion in the year 2000. Soon after the Duke died, Katherine married Sir Thomas Strangways one of his knights, and after his death had two more husbands, John Beaumont and the young John Woodville, both killed in the Wars of the Roses. In a will made at

Epworth on the day of his death, Duchess Katherine's Mowbray husband left her all his estates in the Isle of Axholme and in Yorkshire, together with land in Norfolk and at least seven other counties, for the rest of her life. Since she outlived not only her son, but also her grandson and great-granddaughter Anne, Katherine was a severe strain on the Mowbray family fortune, and even the Carthusian monastery at Low Melwood was kept waiting years for money promised in its early days.

Long before the 1470s there had been an effort by the Mowbrays to concentrate the family lands in the very prosperous counties of East Anglia, the area that was now their main sphere of influence, and when the Gower lands and Chepstow Castle were sold in 1469 to William Herbert, guardian of the child Henry Tudor, the revenue was earmarked as part of the settlement of the 4th Duke's mother, Duchess

*ELIZABETH TALBOT*

Eleanor, and would not come to him until she died. John, the 4<sup>th</sup> Duke, had married Elizabeth Talbot, daughter of the Earl of Shrewsbury, as early as 1448, when he was Earl of Nottingham and still a very young child, Over the years Elizabeth became a shrewd operator manipulating and taking control of lands, including some held by her grandmother-in-law Duchess Katherine, so that in the event of her husband's death she would have a great deal of control over what was to happen to the estates. By 1467 the couple still had no children and at twenty-five John was already describing himself as suffering from great infirmity and disease, and if he died childless the heir at law to half

MARGARET BEAUCHAMP

of his lands would be William, Lord Berkeley. However, Duchess Elizabeth, herself of Berkeley stock, had a long-standing and bitter feud with William's branch of her family that went back fifty years and involved a dispute over land and Berkeley Castle. The other co-heir in the event of Norfolk having no child was Lord John Howard; Berkeley and Howard were the sons of the 4<sup>th</sup> Duke's great-aunts, Isabel and Margaret Mowbray, daughters of Thomas, 1<sup>st</sup> Duke, and Elizabeth Fitzalan.

Thomas, Lord Berkeley's granddaughter, Margaret Beauchamp, married the Earl of Shrewsbury and it is her daughter, Elizabeth Talbot, who married the 4<sup>th</sup> Duke of Norfolk. Isabel Mowbray had married as her second husband Lord Thomas's brother, James Berkeley, and died at Gloucester Castle in 1452, a prisoner of Margaret, Countess of Shrewsbury. At the time of her husband's death, Elizabeth Talbot still detested the other Berkeleys, who had killed her nephew, Viscount Lisle, in 1470 at Nibley Green, but she had the satisfaction of knowing, or thought she had, that they would not get their hands on the Mowbray inheritance, once she had given birth to a live baby, the Lady Anne, in December 1472. Three years later the Mowbray finances were in such a dire state that the newly-widowed Duchess Elizabeth had to forego some of her own widow's entitlement in order to make up a decent dowry for her little daughter's royal marriage, but in time, once Duchess Katherine passed-way, and if the dowager Elizabeth were not so long-lived as her predecessors, the Norfolk fortune had every chance of recovery, and Edward IV must have been congratulating himself upon his choice of daughter-in-law.

On 15th January 1478, five-year-old Lady Anne and her four-year-old fiancé were married. The Mowbray estates were settled on the young couple jointly, with the addition, put through Parliament the day after their wedding, that if Anne predeceased her husband and there was no issue, Prince Richard would inherit the whole. (The other business of Parliament that day was the reading out of the charges against the Duke of Clarence, King Edward's brother, later found conveniently drowned in a barrel of wine.) William, Lord Berkeley gave up his right to his share of the Mowbray inheritance in exchange for his astronomical debts of £34,000 being settled by the Crown, while John Howard appears to have made no objection to the arrangements, although there were those amongst the nobility who took exception to his shabby treatment and the flouting of the ancient laws of inheritance.

With Anne's death in November 1481, the whole inheritance, with the exception of that part legally held by the dowagers Katherine Neville and Elizabeth Talbot, went to the boy. In the early spring of 1483 further arrangements were made through Parliament for him to retain it, and, in the event of his death for it to go to his father, the King. Little did anyone realise that by the autumn not only would King Edward IV be dead at forty, his youthful good looks having run to seed long ago through excesses of every kind, or that his two sons would have been declared illegitimate on the grounds that he had already made another contract of marriage before he married Elizabeth Woodville. Nor could it have been foreseen that the children would disappear and their uncle of Gloucester would usurp the throne as King Richard III.

Elizabeth Talbot, Dowager Duchess of Norfolk, must have been mortified to see Richard III settle the Mowbray inheritance on the Howards and the hated Berkeleys. If the young Princes were murdered there is no real evidence that either Berkeley or Howard was complicit in the deed. On the other hand, accepting the inheritance of Edward V's brother was a risky thing to do if there was any chance that the boys were still alive, as in the strange world of medieval politics there was always the possibility the illegitimacy allegation could be withdrawn and the elder brother restored to power: then where would they all stand? And, of course, we cannot deny that it was John Howard who persuaded Elizabeth Woodville to give up her younger son, whom she had with her in sanctuary at Westminster Abbey.

The ambitious and powerful Woodvilles had not informed Richard, Duke of Gloucester, then at Middleham Castle in Yorkshire, of the King his brother's death on 9th April 1483 and hoped to have the son crowned and themselves in power before the designated Protector could do anything about it. Richard, for his part, moved quickly when he realised what was going on, and when news reached Elizabeth Woodville on the last day of April that the Duke of Gloucester had kidnapped her son, supposedly for his own good, on his way from Ludlow to London with his uncle, Anthony Woodville, she was distraught, and not only because of fears for his safety, but also because she realised that the power and privilege her family had enjoyed for twenty years was suddenly over. She also knew that Richard held her partly responsible for his brother the Duke of Clarence's demise in the butt of malmsey wine and that she and her self-seeking family were very unpopular generally. In desperation she thought about trying to get an army together but had to resort to the only avenue left, namely the seeking of sanctuary in Westminster Abbey. Elizabeth was no stranger to this situation, having sought refuge there before during the Wars of the Roses; indeed, her elder son, now suddenly King Edward V, had been born there in 1470. It is a measure of the nature of her late enemy, King Henry VI, that during her previous spell in the Abbey he took pity on her children and sent clothes and gifts for them.

On 1st May she arrived at the Abbey Sanctuary building, a very strong and ancient cross-shaped structure, demolished in the mid-eighteenth century, in which were housed all types of refugees from guilty criminals evading the law to the totally innocent seeking a place of safety from their pursuers. Elizabeth and her second son and his five beautiful sisters, ranging from two-year-old Bridget to the stunning seventeen-year-old Elizabeth, their half-brother Thomas Grey, Marquess of Dorset, and Lionel Woodville, bishop of Salisbury and the Queen Dowager's brother, were registered by the Abbot of Westminster as 'sanctuary persons'. Elizabeth also had with her as many of her goods and chattels as she had been able to get together in the space of a few hours, and it was rumoured that a sizeable portion of the royal treasury was transported to the Abbey as well.

All this presented the Duke of Gloucester with a real problem: one could hardly drag the King's little brother from sanctuary in such a public place, but to secure his own position as Protector – or had he already decided an even more exalted position could be his – he needed to have both boys under his control. The Archbishop of York visited Elizabeth, and even though the Abbot of Westminster had made over his lodgings to her, he found her in a desolate state and assured her that if they tried to crown anyone else but Edward, '...we shall on the morrow crown his brother, whom you have here with you'. Archbishop Rotherham of York seems to have been rather naïve, and indeed, Richard already had the place staked out and knew who came and went.

Something had to be done quickly, so enter Lord John Howard and his son Thomas. The Howards hired and paid for eight boats to take Richard of Gloucester, various supporters, including themselves, and a large number of soldiers down the Thames to Westminster where the grim-looking two-storey Sanctuary building was then surrounded. Thomas Bourchier and Lord Howard entered the Abbot's lodgings and put before Elizabeth the case for releasing her younger son into the custody of his uncle. Bourchier, the Archbishop of Canterbury, seems to have implied that the boy could come back to his mother after his brother's coronation, but when he asked her why she feared her children would come to harm, Howard is said to have interrupted before she could reply. This was the Thomas Bourchier who had taken charge of Framlingham Castle for his great-niece Anne Mowbray upon her marriage to the Duke of York; now Anne's little widower, once described as 'joyous and witty', must have been a very frightened little boy indeed.

The two men put forward the argument that that the bothers wanted to be together and that it would look very bad in the eyes of the world for the family of a king to be hiding in sanctuary on his coronation day. Then they came up with the trump card: it was believed, they said, that Elizabeth was holding her son at the Abbey against his will. Howard promised that the child would be reunited with his brother and that they would be safe and well cared for. Elizabeth, surrounded by hundreds of armed men and accused of holding the King's brother against his wishes, knew from the experience of Tewkesbury that the right of sanctuary in a church stood for little in the eyes of the Yorkists and there could well be bloodshed if she held out. She let her little boy go with Bourchier and Howard to be reunited with his brother, who was lodging in the Tower, and never saw either of her sons again.

On 28th June 1483 William Berkeley became Earl of Nottingham, but he was never a strong Richard III supporter. John Howard, on the other hand, saw a monumental advance in his fortunes, becoming Duke of Norfolk and Earl Marshal. A month later, at the Palace of Woodstock in Oxfordshire, he was made Lord Admiral of England, Surveyor of Array in thirteen counties, Steward of the Duchy of Lancaster, Member of the Council, was given forty-six manors in East Anglia and rents from many others, and property and lands of Elizabeth Woodville's executed brother Anthony, Lord Rivers, who was guilty of no crime and executed at Pontefract with no trial. Howard had already had a distinguished career before his advancement by Richard III and, although a Yorkist, had been created Lord Howard by Henry VI in October 1470. His mother, the Lady Margaret

Mowbray, seems to have married beneath her, socially at any rate, when she became the wife of Sir Robert Howard, son of the sheriff of Essex, but the new powers given their son, now one of the wealthiest subjects in the whole land, would excel any the Mowbrays ever held, and it seems that Richard had great hopes of John Howard, whose son and heir was created Earl of Surrey. John ('Jockey', or 'Jacky') Howard, fell in the early stages of the Battle of Bosworth in 1485, a blow to the Yorkists from which they never recovered. There is a portrait of him in the Royal Collection on which are written words taken from an ominous note supposedly found on Bosworth Field, *'Jockey of Norfolk be not too bold, for Dickon* (Richard III) *thy master is bought and sold.'*

After Bosworth, the new Tudor monarch made Howard's cousin, William Berkeley, Marquess of Berkeley, but he was a foolish and irresponsible man who had no respect for money or for his heritage and squandered his funds in trying to ingratiate himself with high society, and it was he who sold the Isle of Axholme and the Mowbray Yorkshire estates to Henry Tudor's stepfather, Thomas Stanley, 1st Earl of Derby. In a manner of speaking it was keeping it in the family, since Stanley was a grandson of Elizabeth Fitzalan and Sir Robert Goushill (see Table XIII and Appendix K).

# Chapter VII

## The Mowbray/d'Aubigny/Fitzalan/Howard Connection

*I have touched the highest point of all my greatness!*
*And from that full meridian of my glory,*
*I haste now to my setting: I shall fall*
*Like a bright exhalation in the evening, and no man see me more.*
William Shakespeare *King Henry VIII, Act III*

HE LINK BETWEEN the Mowbray and d'Aubigny families and the decree of Henry I resulting in the great name of Mowbray surviving in the form of Roger d'Aubigny have already been explored in Chapter II. As we have also seen already, Roger's cousin William married the widow of Henry I and was the first of the d'Aubigny (d'Albini) earls of Arundel and it is important that we appreciate the fact that it is through marriage into this d'Aubigny branch that the Fitzalan family rose to such prominence in England, although they never quite matched the illustrious career of their Fitzalan cousins who settled in Scotland.

The Fitzalans, Lords of Oswestry and Clun in Shropshire, were of a very ancient family originally from Brittany. It was not unusual in those times for younger sons of English nobility to seek their fortune in Scotland, as was the case with Philip de Mowbray in 1200, but the Walter Fitzalan who died in 1177 could hardly have foreseen that the High Stewards of Scotland, of which he was the first, would eventually adopt the name Steward (later Stewart, then Stuart), marry into the Bruce family and become Kings of Scotland themselves. Through Mary Stuart, Queen of Scots, they are the forebears of Queen Elizabeth II.

By the time the d'Aubigny male line of the Earls of Arundel died out, a John Fitzalan had already married Isabel, the sister of Hugh d'Aubigny, the last earl. Isabel and John predeceased Hugh, but when he died without heir it was their son, also John, who was awarded the Castle and Honour of Arundel in right of his deceased mother. It appears that neither this John nor his son, yet another John, used the Arundel title; they did not use the castle as much as they would have liked either, for Hugh d'Aubigny's widow resided there for forty years and refused to move.

The March 2000 *Sunday Times* 'Richest of the Rich' supplement suggested that the Richard Fitzalan who was 10<sup>th</sup> Earl of Arundel from

Chart 10: *Mowbray/D'Aubigny/Fitzalan/Howard Connections – Much Simplified*

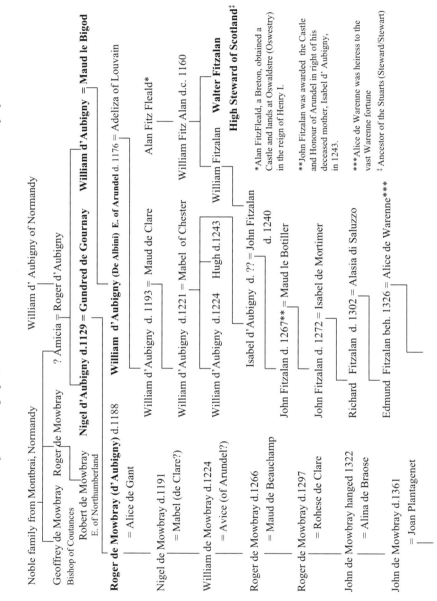

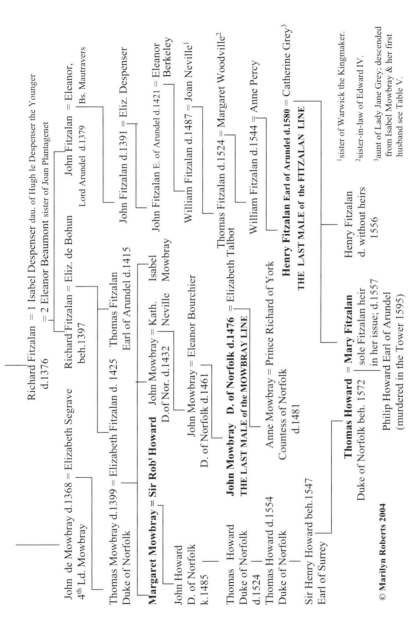

Richard Fitzalan = 1 Isabel Despenser dau. of Hugh le Despenser the Younger
d.1376                = 2 Eleanor Beaumont sister of Joan Plantagenet

John Fitzalan = Eleanor,
Lord Arundel d.1379        Bs. Mautravers

Richard Fitzalan = Eliz. de Bohun
beh.1397

John Fitzalan d.1391 = Eliz. Despenser

Thomas Fitzalan
Earl of Arundel d.1415

John Fitzalan E. of Arundel d.1421 = Eleanor
Berkeley

William Fitzalan d.1487 = Joan Neville[1]

Thomas Fitzalan d.1524 = Margaret Woodville[2]

William Fitzalan d.1544 = Anne Percy

Henry Fitzalan **Earl of Arundel d.1580** = Catherine Grey[3]
**THE LAST MALE of the FITZALAN LINE**

Henry Fitzalan
d. without heirs
1556

John de Mowbray d.1368 = Elizabeth Segrave
4th Ld. Mowbray

Thomas Mowbray d.1399 = Elizabeth Fitzalan d. 1425

**Margaret Mowbray = Sir Rob[t] Howard**

John Mowbray
D.of Nor. d.1432

John Mowbray = Kath.
D. of Norfolk d.1461     Neville

Isabel
Mowbray

John Mowbray = Eleanor Bourchier

**John Mowbray   D. of Norfolk d.1476** = Elizabeth Talbot
**THE LAST MALE of the MOWBRAY LINE**

Anne Mowbray = Prince Richard of York
Countess of Norfolk
d.1481

**Mary Fitzalan**
sole Fitzalan heir
in her issue; d.1557

John Howard
D. of Norfolk
k.1485

Thomas  Howard
Duke of Norfolk
d.1524

Thomas Howard d.1554
Duke of Norfolk

Sir Henry Howard beh.1547
Earl of Surrey

**Thomas Howard = Mary Fitzalan**
Duke of Norfolk beh. 1572

Philip Howard Earl of Arundel
(murdered in the Tower 1595)

© **Marilyn Roberts 2004**

[1] sister of Warwick the Kingmaker.
[2] sister-in-law of Edward IV.
[3] aunt of Lady Jane Grey; descended
from Isabel Mowbray & her first
husband see Table V.

Thomas Howard was beheaded in 1572 for plotting to marry Mary Queen of Scots and depose or assassinate Elizabeth I. His son Philip was held prisoner in the Tower
for 11 years because of his Catholic faith; he was poisoned there in 1595, at the age of 38. The dukedom of Norfolk was not restored to the Howards until 1660.

## Chart 11: The Fitzalan Ancestors of Mary Queen of Scots

A branch of the Fitzalan family became Hereditary Stewards of Scotland and took the name of Steward, which evolved into Stewart and finally, Stuart.

William Fitz Alan

William Fitzalan

William Fitzalan

John Fitzalan

John Fitzalan

John Fitzalan

Richard Fitzalan

Edmund Fitzalan

Richard Fitzalan

Richard Fitzalan

Elizabeth Fitzalan
= Thomas Mowbray

Walter Fitzalan 1st High Steward of Scotland

Alan Fitzwalter 2nd High Steward of Scotland

Walter Fitzalan 3rd High Steward of Scotland

Alexander Steward 4th High Steward of Scotland

James Steward 5th High Steward b. 1243

**WALTER STEWART = MARJORIE BRUCE**
**dau. of Robert I (the Bruce)**

ROBERT II b.1316
(Very badly injured by a fall from a horse)

ROBERT III b. 1337
(Collapsed and died upon learning that his young son had been captured by pirates, sold to the English and imprisoned by Henry IV)

JAMES I b. 1394
(In captivity 1405 – 1424; assassinated in 1437)

JAMES II b. 1430
(Killed by an exploding cannon in 1460)

JAMES III b. 1451
(Assassinated in 1488)

JAMES IV b. 1473   = Margaret Tudor, = Archibald Douglas
(Killed by forces of his brother-in-law   dau. of Henry VII
Henry VIII at Flodden Field, 1513)

JAMES V b. 1512                    Margaret = Matthew Stuart
(Came to the throne at only 17 months old.   Douglas   E. of Lennox
Died of grief in 1542 after the Battle of
Solway Moss)

MARY STUART, QUEEN of SCOTS = Henry Stuart
b. 1542                        Lord Darnley
(Came to the throne at only a week old;
beheaded by Elizabeth I in 1587)

JAMES I of England and VI of Scotland
(Came to the throne of Scotland at one year old)

Adapted from
*The Bare Bones of British Royal Family Trees*
**© Marilyn Roberts 2004**

**PRESENT ROYAL FAMILY OF GREAT BRITAIN**

1331-1376, was the second richest Briton of all time with a fortune worth the equivalent of £48 billion today. Edward II had beheaded his father Edmund, and Richard had to petition Edward III, whom he served faithfully, for the restoration of his estates and titles, and in 1353 he also succeeded to the earldom of Warenne and Surrey through right of his mother. Rewards resulting from his loyalty to Edward, together with booty and ransom money from the ongoing Hundred Years' War, added to his vast wealth, and the King actually had to borrow from him to finance the wars.

In 1321 Richard married Isabel Despenser, daughter of the dreaded Hugh the Younger, he then being only seven and she eight years of age. Later he cohabited for some time with Isabel's first cousin, Eleanor Beaumont, née Plantagenet, (see Table III) and then had his marriage annulled after twenty-three years and three children in order to marry her, his union with Isabel conveniently dissolved on the grounds that at the age of seven he had been too young to have properly given his consent. Unusually for the males in his family, this Richard Fitzalan died peacefully in his bed at Arundel Castle in his seventieth year, to be succeeded by his and Eleanor's son, also Richard, and it is this son who became father-in-law to Thomas Mowbray.

Richard Fitzalan, 11th Earl of Arundel, was as wealthy as his father but did not significantly increase his family's astounding fortune and so had no position on the *Sunday Times* list in 2000. He was bearer of the crown at the coronation of Richard II and had a distinguished military and naval record, being one of the best sea captains of his day. His famous escapades included the taking of a hundred French, Spanish and Flemish ships with their cargoes of wine, making him very popular because he took little or no profit from it and good wine was cheap for a whole year. In 1388 he was one of the five Lords Appellant who coerced King Richard into parting with his favourites, including Sir Simon Burley. In July 1397 Fitzalan's latest fears about the unstable Richard were betrayed by his own son-in-law and erstwhile supporter, Thomas Mowbray, and he was beheaded for treason on 24th September, at the age of fifty-one. An eyewitness said that on the way to the scaffold in Cheapside he was, 'no more shrinking or changing colour than if he were going to a banquet', and that he had exhorted the executioner to make sure the axe was sharp; he was buried at the Church of the Augustine Friars in Bread Street. He had married Elizabeth de Bohun, daughter of the Earl of Northampton, by whom he had a son, Thomas, and the daughters Elizabeth, Alice and Joan Fitzalan.

All Richard Fitzalan's honours were forfeit, and in 1398 John Holand, Duke of Exeter, had a grant of the Castle and Honour of Arundel and the wardship of Richard's son and heir, whom he was said to have

CHART 12: DIFFERING NOTATION FOR THE EARLS OF ARUNDEL, 1067-1397

This information was kindly provided by Mrs. Sara Rodger,
Assistant Librarian to the Duke of Norfolk.

| DATE ACCEDED TO TITLE | A | B | C* | D | E | F |
|---|---|---|---|---|---|---|
| Roger de Montgomery 1067 | 1 | 1 | | | | |
| Hugh de Montgomery 1094 | 2 | 2 | | | | |
| Robert de Bellême 1098 | 3 | 3 | | | | |
| William d'Albini (d'Aubigny) 1138 | 4 | 4 | 1 | 1 | 1 | |
| William d'Albini 1189 | 5 | 5 | 2 | 2 | 2 | |
| William d'Albini 1193 | 6 | 6 | 3 | 3 | 3 | |
| William d'Albini 1221 | 7 | 7 | 4 | 4 | 4 | |
| Hugh d'Albini 1224 | 8 | 8 | 5 | 5 | 5 | |
| John Fitzalan 1243 | 9 | 9 | 6 | | | |
| John Fitzalan 1267 | 10 | 10 | 7 | | | |
| Richard Fitzalan 1272 | 11 | 11 | 8 | 6 | 6 | 1 |
| Edmund Fitzalan 1302 | 12 | 12 | 9 | 7 | 7 | 2 |
| Edmund Earl of Kent 1327 | 13 | | | 8 | | |
| Richard Fitzalan 1331 | 14 | 13 | 10 | 9 | 8 | 3 |
| Richard Fitzalan 1376 (ex. 1397) | 15th | 14th | 11th | 10th | 9th | 4th |

A Includes all who held, or may be said to have held the title Earl of Arundel between 1067 and 1397.
B Excludes the Earl of Kent, who briefly held the Castle and Honour of Arundel (1327-1330) and may be considered to have become Earl of Arundel.
C Commences with the d'Aubigny earls and excludes Kent. *This is the notation used in *Complete Peerage* and in this book.
D Excludes Kent and the two Fitzalans who did not use the title.
E Includes Kent but not the two early Fitzalans.
F The system used at Arundel Castle today.

treated very badly. Thomas managed to escape the country and returned with Henry Bolingbroke, who put the seventeen-year-old in charge of the Tower and delivered Richard II into his hands for safe keeping. The earldom was restored in 1400 but Thomas Fitzalan died of dysentery contracted while serving in France in 1415. His earldom went to a cousin, and part of his fortune to his sisters.

There can be some confusion as to whether the Richard Fitzalan beheaded in 1397 was 15th, 14th, 11th, 10th, 9th, or 4th Earl of Arundel, any of which would be correct, depending from where we begin counting. There were three Montgomery earls, then five from the d'Albini (d'Aubigny) family and then came two Fitzalans, both named John, who did not take the title, but whom some sources regard as being earls. Today at Arundel they regard the Richard Fitzalan who finally got possession of the Castle and Honour of Arundel in 1290 as being the 1st Earl of his family and count from him, making the Richard beheaded in 1397 the 4th Earl. *Complete Peerage* begins counting from the d'Aubigny earls, and includes all the Fitzalans, which makes *our* Richard Fitzalan the 11th earl of Arundel, the system used by the present writer. *C.P.* further complicates matters by giving the option of including Edmund, Earl of Kent, who very briefly held the Castle and Honour of Arundel after the beheading of *our* Richard's grandfather, Edmund; this would enable us to call Richard 15th Earl if we included them all.

The present Dukes of Norfolk, whose family name is Fitzalan-Howard, also hold the Arundel title and a question sometimes asked is whether this is a result of Thomas Mowbray's marriage to Elizabeth Fitzalan, but directly it is not. Their daughter, Margaret Mowbray, married Sir Robert Howard of Stoke Neyland, Suffolk, and it is their son, John Howard, who became the first Howard Duke of Norfolk in the reign of Richard III, and the dukedom has remained in the Howard family ever since, except for a period of attainder in the sixteenth/seventeenth century. The earldom of Arundel came into the family when Thomas Howard, the fourth Howard Duke of Norfolk, who was later beheaded by Elizabeth I for treason, married Lady Mary Fitzalan, daughter and sole heir of Henry, Earl of Arundel. The first duke to use the name Fitzalan-Howard was Henry Grenville Fitzalan-Howard, 14th Duke of Norfolk who died in 1860. Thomas Howard, 4th Duke of Norfolk, also married Margaret Audley, heir of Lord Audley of Walden, who was a descendant of the Mowbrays through the Greys. So, by the third quarter of the sixteenth century the Howards, of relatively humble origin, had inherited all or part of Mowbray, Fitzalan and Audley fortunes and titles.

In his entertaining and hugely informative little book *They Came with the Conqueror* Leslie G. Pine tells us that the Howards,

> *"...cannot be got back earlier than John Howard, a plain and honest yeoman of Wiggen Hall, St Peter, in Norfolk, who in 1267 had by Lucy his wife a son, Sir William Howard, Justice of the Common Pleas in 1297, who started the royal and ducal Howards on the road to Arundel Castle, Westminster Abbey – and the Tower!"*

Regarding the story that Howard was a medieval English contraction of Hereward (as in Hereward the Wake) Pine was light-heartedly sceptical,

> *"I believe that the legend in the Howard case owed much of its currency to the Baroness Herries, a peeress in her own right, who married the fifteenth Duke of Norfolk (1847-1915) as his second wife and was the mother of our present Earl Marshal. I understand that she stood guard over the Hereward legend, as the dragon in Beowulf shielded the fairy gold, and none durst touch it while she lived."*

The History of the Howards, powerful though it is, is not the purpose of this book, the Mowbray/Howard family having largely moved away from Lincolnshire by the time they began their rise to wealth and

Chart 13: *The Origins of the Howard family*

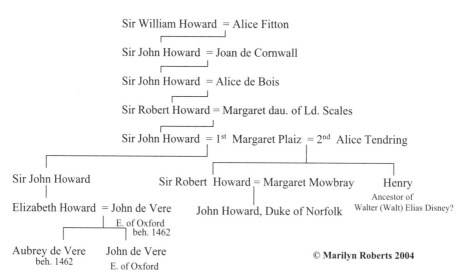

Elizabeth Howard's husband John de Vere, Earl of Oxford, and his elder son Aubrey were attainted after Towton and beheaded by the Yorkists at Tower Hill in 1462. Although a Yorkist himself, John Howard helped his cousin Elizabeth regain and administer her estates but her son John also became a Lancastrian, one contemporary account making him personally responsible for Howard's death at Bosworth in 1485.

power in the late fifteenth century, and so the present writer has been somewhat economical on research and confesses to relying upon *Great Governing Families of England* by Sanford and Townsend and *Complete Peerage* for the following.

The Sir John Howard who died in 1437 had, by his first wife, a son, also Sir John, who died in his father's lifetime. In 1429 this younger John's daughter Elizabeth married John de Vere, Earl of Oxford and 'carried away most of the Howard estates' leaving her grandfather's two other sons, Sir Robert and Henry, born to his second wife, Alice Tendring, with a greatly reduced inheritance. The brother Henry, is, I am informed, an ancestor of Walter Elias (Walt) Disney (d'Isney), but as yet I have not worked on this line myself.

Sir Robert Howard, born in the mid-1380's, courted and married Lady Margaret Mowbray, of about the same age and of impeccable pedigree, but probably with very little fortune at a time when her family was at a low ebb following the death of her father in exile and the execution of her brother at York. We may wonder where the young Mowbray sisters Margaret, Isabel and Elizabeth stood financially with their mother Elizabeth Fitzalan at this time – the historian K. B. McFarlane describes them as 'scarcely coveted brides' – she having remarried, had two more daughters and been widowed again and married for the fourth time by 1414. It would appear that the match offered Robert Howard nothing financially and would not have been seen as a way of advancing his family. Neither was he a good catch for Margaret as far as wealth and position were concerned. They lived with and were supported by the widowed Alice Tendring, and it would seem that the £200 Margaret's brother John promised her never materialised. According to Sanford,

> *"Nothing could therefore have less of a mercenary match on both sides than that on which – as it turned out – the greatness of the Howard family was built."*

He also refers to a 'probable' portrait of Sir Robert painted on glass, which,

> *"represents a pleasing open countenance, with fair, straight flowing hair, much resembling that of his mother, who was a great beauty of those times."*

Margaret was still alive in 1437 but her husband was dead by 1436. Their son, John, the first Howard Duke, was born between 1420-25 and was killed at Bosworth in 1485. His son, Thomas, Earl of Surrey, was taken prisoner and held in the Tower but became a Henry VII supporter and the Norfolk dukedom was restored to him in the early years of the reign of Henry VIII. The photograph on the right shows his first wife, Elizabeth Tilney, portrayed in stained glass at Long Melford Church in Suffolk. Their daughter, Elizabeth Howard, was Anne Boleyn's mother, and their son Edmund the father of Kathryn Howard. Both girls married Henry VIII and were beheaded by him and interred beneath the floor of the church within the walls of the Tower of London (see Table IV).

ELIZABETH TILNEY

# CHAPTER VIII

## THE MOWBRAY AND SEGRAVE CASE OF 1877

*The Lords of the Committee… subordinated their intelligence to that of the not very scrupulous Mr. Fleming, and one of them, though he had attended every meeting of the Committee except the first, does not appear to have had, even on the last day of the hearing, any idea of what the case was about.*
*Complete Peerage Vol. IX, Appendix G*

This chapter relies heavily upon *Complete Peerage* Vol. IX, Appendix G, but see also preface to *C.P.* Vol. I for the 1283 Assembly at Salisbury, and J. Horace Round's *Peerage & Pedigree: Studies in Peerage Law and Family History*, especially the sections entitled 'The Muddle of the Law', and 'The Abeyance of the Barony of Mowbray' which deal with this case and others. See also the various Appendices to *C.P.* quoted at the end of this chapter.

N 1877 LORD STOURTON'S petition for the determination in his favour of the barony of Mowbray came before the House of Lords Committee for Privileges. Winifred Howard, who died in 1753, was the niece of Edward Howard, Duke of Norfolk, who died without heir in 1777, the dukedom then passing to another branch of the Howard family. Winifred had married William Stourton in 1749, and Alfred Joseph Stourton, the Lord Stourton making the appeal in 1877, was descended from them. The author of Appendix G to *Complete Peerage* Volume IX could barely conceal his contempt for the way the case was handled, calling it one of the most unsatisfactory cases the Lords had ever decided, despite the Committee containing some of the most eminent lawyers of the day. The case was not without its complications from the start,

*"… there was no opposing petitioner, for the legitimacy of the Lord Berkeley who was coheir with Lord Stourton in the ancient barony had not then been established. There being no one to represent the Berkeley interest, there was the greater need for the Attorney-General's vigilance, but he allowed the one-sided evidence proffered by Mr. Fleming, Lord Stourton's Counsel, to pass without challenge,*

*although much of it was manifestly questionable. The Lords of the Committee... subordinated their intelligence to that of the not very scrupulous Mr. Fleming, and one of them, though he had attended every meeting of the Committee except the first, does not appear to have had, even on the last day of the hearing, any idea of what the case was about."*

The writer goes on to complain that the Committee's time was spent almost entirely on futilities, and that their Lordships were mainly engaged in drawing wrong conclusions from evidence that was always insufficient and often misrepresented and that,

*"Owing to their unfamiliarity with the social customs and forms of the fifteenth century, they were easily persuaded to believe that what were mere commonplaces of the period had a profound significance...[and] never once got into touch with realities."*

So, what were those realities? The baronies of Mowbray and Segrave were first joined in the John de Mowbray who succeeded his parents John, 4th Lord Mowbray and Elizabeth Segrave, both of whom died in 1368. *Complete Peerage* states that this John, however, at his creation as Earl of Nottingham in 1377 was styled simply John de Mowbray, Earl of Nottingham, without mention of the barony titles and when, upon his early death, the earldom passed to his brother Thomas, he too was simply styled Earl of Nottingham. This, however, does not mean that the Mowbrays were never addressed as Lords Mowbray and Segrave and does not appear to square with other evidence. An original document of 1392 unearthed at Lincoln Archives during the present writer's research shows that Thomas Mowbray, writing to the Abbot of Selby, called himself *Earl Marshal and of Nottingham, Lord of Mowbray and of Segrave*, and the Instrument of Nomination appointing Anne Mowbray's little husband as Lieutenant of Ireland in 1479 calls him Lord Segrave, Mowbray and Gower, as do Hawes and Lodder writing in 1798, nearly eighty years before Lord Stourton made his petition,

*"Then the Duke of York did receive of the King* [at the time of his marriage] *the additional titles of Duke of Norfolk, Earl of Warren, Surrey and Nottingham, and Earl Marshal of England; and in right of his lady he was lord of Segrave, Mowbray and of Gower."*

The lawyer Fleming told the Lords that after the death of Anne Mowbray the baronies of Mowbray and Segrave fell into abeyance between Lord John Howard and William, Lord Berkeley, sons of

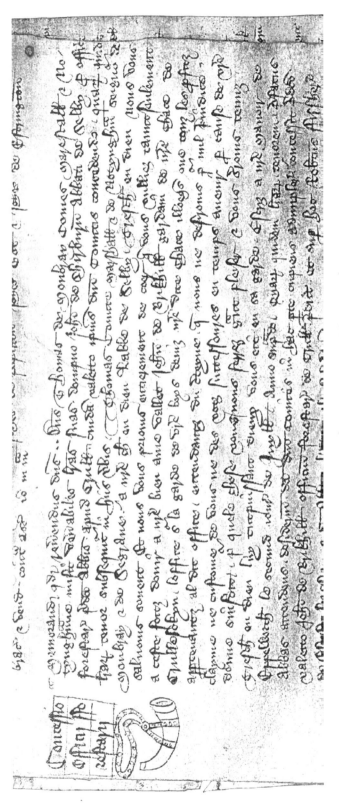

*DOCUMENT OF THOMAS MOWBRAY, EARL OF NOTTINGHAM, FROM THE COURT ROLL OF THE MANOR OF CROWLE, 1392*

"Memorandum that the Reverend Lord Lord Thomas de Mowbray, Earl Marshal and Nottingham, sent his venerable letters to Dominus John de Shireburn, Abbot of Selby, concerning granting the office of forester of the said abbot at Crowle to a certain valet of him the lord Earl, the tenor of which letter follows in these words…"

(Notice that the beginning of the fifth line Thomas Mowbray is called "Lord of Mowbray and of Segrave…".)

145

Anne's great-great aunts, Margaret and Isabel Mowbray. However, the complex concept of abeyance, which can leave a title in limbo for generations, and is concerned with certain criteria in the female line being met before a title can be called out of abeyance, did not develop for another two centuries and would have been a mystery to both Howard and Berkeley. Between 1368 and the time of the Stourton Case no one had been summoned to Parliament as Lord Mowbray and Segrave, although there had been a new creation of the Mowbray title alone for Henry Francis Howard in 1640. It was for this new barony that Alfred Joseph, Lord Stourton, mistakenly made his original petition in 1876; a mistake soon rectified.

Fleming's case, virtually unchallenged in the Lords, rested on two main pieces of evidence that would more than likely have been destroyed by a third piece, had it been disclosed. The first was a Letter Missive signed by Richard III and dated 24th September 1484, which was a treaty for a marriage between one of his nieces and the heir of the King of Scotland; in it two of the Ambassadors he introduces are 'John, Duke of Norfolk, Earl Marshal, and Admiral of England, Lord Mowbray, Segrave and Howard', and 'William Berkeley, Earl of Nottingham'. The use of Mowbray and Segrave was probably an error on the King's part and other such examples occur that could have been cited in this case; indeed, King Richard had made another such error only one month earlier, when Edmund Grey was wrongly addressed as Hastings and Waysford [Wexford], Wexford being a title that did not really exist. Another point overlooked is that even if John Howard did hold the baronies of Mowbray and Segrave under Richard's rule, they were lost under attainder upon the accession of Henry VII, and when Howard's son, the Earl of Surrey, was restored there was no mention of the Mowbray or Segrave baronies. [Attainder was the forfeiture of the peerage and all property and a *'corruption of blood'*, that is, title and property could not be passed to or inherited from the attainted person unless or until the attainder was lifted.]

Mr. Fleming's second piece of evidence was a Garter Stall Plate of 1611 in St George's Chapel, Windsor, upon which Thomas, Earl of Arundel and Surrey, is described as 'Seigneur Howard, Fitzallen, Mautravers, Mowbray, Segrave, Bruse [Braose] et Clun'. Except for Howard and Mautravers all these titles were assumed. The assumption of titles, a mere vanity, was not at all uncommon and countless examples existed, but in 1877 their Lordships were kept in ignorance of this, although, surely, many must have known of such irregularities and might even have held assumed titles themselves. There were so many assumed titles in Tudor and Stuart England that it was difficult for a monarch to know which were genuine and which fake, and between 1559 and 1601 even the exceptionally mentally alert

Elizabeth I unwittingly allowed a dozen Garter Stall Plates at Windsor to be incorrectly inscribed with imagined titles.

When the Lord Chancellor asked Fleming what difference it would make to the case if it could be shown that the Berkeleys had also used the Mowbray and Segrave titles he replied, 'Of course, if there were contradictory evidence, the one would destroy the other.'

Had anyone asked whether such evidence existed, and had Fleming then replied truthfully, the whole case would have collapsed, but the Committee allowed itself to be sidetracked. The *Complete Peerage* writer says that Fleming, having previously been Counsel for Sir Maurice F. Fitzharding Berkeley in his claim to the barony of Berkeley, knew full well that the Berkeleys had used the Mowbray and Segrave titles over a period of two hundred years but chose not to disclose the fact. When John Howard died at Bosworth, his cousin William, created Marquess of Berkeley by Henry VII, assumed the titles, and, although the Berkeley title became extinct at his death, his nephew and heir styled himself Lord Berkeley, Mowbray and Segrave, an assumption of titles that continued until 1698. There is also a document of 9th July 1528 in which 'the Most Noble Prince Thomas [Howard], Duke of Norfolk' becomes a trustee for his cousin Thomas Berkeley 'Lord Berkeley, Mowbray and Segrave'.

Alfred Joseph Stourton won his appeal and became the 23rd Lord Mowbray, the title said to date from 1283, the first time Roger de Mowbray was summoned to a Parliament of Edward I. The Resolution of the Committee for Privileges with respect to origin of the Mowbray Barony was,

> *"It is proved by the Writ of summons addressed to Roger de Mowbray in the 11th year of Edward I (1283) and the other evidence adduced on behalf of the Petitioner that the barony of Mowbray was in the reign of Edward I vested in Roger de Mowbray."*

This case, and it is not alone, appears to show that the criteria in question are something of a moveable feast, because prior to this case the 1283 Assembly at Salisbury had not been regarded as a Parliament and the earliest baronies were said to have dated from the summonses to the Model Parliament of 1295, Roger de Mowbray being summoned on 24th June of that year. The Segrave barony also dates from 1295, while Stourton was created in 1448. (There is further confusion in that the status of Premier Baron passes to the holder of the Mowbray title when the barony of Roos, supposedly dating from 1264, is held by a woman. This is the reason the present Lord Mowbray's grandfather represented his rank of the peerage at the coronation in 1953.) The present Lord Mowbray, Segrave and Stourton is Edward William Stephen Stourton,

24th Baron Stourton, 28th Baron Segrave, 27th Baron Mowbray (born 1953) who succeeded his father Charles Edward Stourton in 2006.

The Stourton family's subsequent efforts to secure the ancient earldom of Norfolk, once belonging to Thomas de Brotherton, were unanimously rejected by the Lords in 1906 on the grounds that Edward I had actually been in error in conferring the earldom on his son because it had been illegally surrendered by Roger Bigod. Bigod had no heirs and surrendered the earldom and Marshalship in 1302. The 1906 decision that the earldom was held in error is somewhat surprising, since the Crown was willing for the title to be passed down through Brotherton's daughter Margaret, who also held the office of Countess Marshal. After her grandson Thomas Mowbray's banishment in 1398, and both their deaths the following year, his widow Elizabeth was styled Countess of Norfolk when the dukedom was annulled by Henry IV, who of all people might have been expected to cause the title to be forfeited if there were any hint of illegality. Neither, it would seem, was the question of legal or assumed title raised when Thomas Mowbray, Elizabeth's son, sued for precedence over the Earl of Warwick: surely one would have expected Warwick to make much of it, were it true, and then there was the Lady Anne, styled Countess of Norfolk before becoming Duchess of York. In 1906 the then Duke of Norfolk also strongly opposed the Stourton petition, which might have had some influence on their Lordships' decision. The Dukes of Norfolk now hold the earldom.

Various *Complete Peerage* appendices of relevance:

| | |
|---|---|
| Vol. III A/ | *The Surrender of Peerages in England* |
| Vol. IV H/ | *Earldoms and Baronies in History and in Law, and the Doctrine of Abeyance* (100+ pages) |
| Vol. V F/ | *Peerage Titles Assumed by Peers* |
| Vol. VI E/ | *The Claim to the Earldom of Norfolk* |
| Vol. VII C/ | *The Barony of Berkeley* |
| Vol. IX G/ | *Some observations on the Mowbray and Segrave Case of 1877* |
| Vol. XII Part I A/ | *Baronies by Writ* |

# CHAPTER IX

## THE MOWBRAY LEGACY

*And yet time hath his revolution; there must be a period and an end of all temporal things…*
*An end of names and dignities…*
*For where is Bohun? where is Mowbray? where is Mortimer?*
*Nay, which is more and most of all, where is Plantagenet?*
*They are entombed in the arms and sepulchres of mortality.*
Sir Ranulphe Crewe, Judge at the Oxford Peerage Case of 1626

HERE IS MOWBRAY INDEED? 'Mowbray' is a name that is very familiar in our own times, possibly through its association with Melton Mowbray in Leicestershire and the production of the famous pork pies, but like de Bohun and Mortimer it is a name that was heard of little in the pages of history once the male line became extinct. And yet, their legacy remains alive and well in the most illustrious household in the kingdom. The Tudors and Stuarts came and went and the House of Hanover became the House of Saxe-Coburg-Gotha, which itself was transformed into the House of Windsor in 1917. Even so, our present Queen is of the ancient Mowbray blood through her mother, and in Prince William we shall have a king who is of Mowbray stock through both his parents. At the time of writing, the Western World is in conflict with the Middle East, where Roger de Mowbray was on crusade in 1147, making a name for himself by beating a Saracen champion in single combat; it appears that his 25-times-great-grandson, George Walker Bush, 43rd President of the United States, is having a much tougher time in Iraq. I see that tonight following the television news, on which President Bush will no doubt be struggling again to put across his thoughts to a somewhat baffled world, there will be a classic Hollywood film starring Roger's descendant Audrey Hepburn, so we can safely say that the Mowbray blood has lived on in the rich and famous.

The Howard dukes of Norfolk at some stage chose to preserve the Fitzalan name for posterity but nowadays give us little clue as to their Mowbray roots, unlike David Peter Mowbray Algernon Howard (1939 - ) the current Earl of Effingham and his son and heir Edward Mowbray Nicholas Howard (1971- ). Are the Howards to blame for us forgetting the family? Not really, the damage was already done by Edward IV. If

Anne Mowbray had married a younger son of another noble house then, perhaps, we might have expected a change of name, but her marriage with a prince of the House of York, itself of recent creation, made this unthinkable. The world of the 1480's was moving on, away from the medieval past, and Lord John Howard would have been more than a little aggrieved at being told to surrender his own family name as he stood on the brink of founding a great new dynasty. Under the Tudors, supported by new nobility, the old families like the Bohuns, Mortimers and Mowbrays slipped from memory, their ancient blood flowing unheeded in the veins of the Dudleys, Greys, and Howards; the 'new men' even forgot to rebury Lady Anne in Westminster Abbey. The world after Bosworth was a different world about to face great changes, challenges and revelations, and the noble dynasties of today, such as the Cavendishes, Russells and Cecils, were already waiting in the wings.

Some of the ancient families who have held onto their titles and castles until the present day, Percy, for example, have been extinct in the male line more than once and the name has been able to survive, but for Mowbray it was not to be, and the family name of the present Lord Mowbray is Stourton. But is their great name really lost? Of course not: there are Mowbrays and Moubrays and the rest throughout the length and breadth of the land. They are to be found in significant numbers in Scotland, Ireland, the United States, Canada, Australia, and New Zealand, and there are still Mowbrays living in York not too far from where their ancestors were executed all those centuries ago.

The Mowbrays were involved in everything that happened in England for four hundred years, from Hastings to the Wars of the Roses, and played their part in its development as a nation. Their lives, and those of their contemporaries, reveal glimpses of a world very different from our own, another aspect of their legacy. They show us too that the splendid and colourful lives of the great medieval magnates often hung in the balance and their fortunes could change in blinking of an eye, and back again equally quickly: John, 3$^{rd}$ Lord Mowbray, was no sooner out of the Tower than he was betrothed to a close relative of the very king who had put him away and killed his father. Anxiety for position, and an individual being rewarded with high office and power for having 'nighness of blood' to the king caused many a bitter and bloody feud. In modern parlance we would probably say that circumstances conspired to force these great men of medieval England continually to 'watch their backs'.

The Mowbray story demolishes some of our pre-conceived ideas about medieval knightly life as well. Knighthood was about death.

They lived to kill: going onto the field of battle for the first time was the culmination of what they had been trained for from their early youth. We see through them that the high ideals of chivalry were all very well when it suited, but there are many known cases of refugees being torn from the sanctuary of a church and carried off to their certain deaths, and the more we see of it, the more chivalry seems to have been a figment of the imagination. John and his Mother Alina survived their incarceration in the Tower, but some noble mothers and sons were not so fortunate and died there. Surely one would expect the laws of chivalry, as the modern world has interpreted them, to be rather more gentle with, and protective of, women and children. The knight in shining armour rescuing the beautiful damsel in distress – did he really exist? Probably not. But if he did, we may be forgiven for suspecting that he was a very rare commodity, and was more than likely to have been promised in marriage to another damsel when he was still a babe in arms.

Considering their power, connections and wide sphere of influence over such a long period, the Mowbrays and their possessions can be tantalisingly elusive, and small or portable artefacts with a connection to them are very thin on the ground. They must have owned and commissioned a large number of expensive and exquisite items, many of which probably found their way into other collections after 1476 and 1483, but to the layman they are not immediately obvious or accessible. The legacy in bricks and mortar is rather disappointing too. The Vinegarth at Epworth has given up a few secrets, but so little remains it is not possible even to draw a reconstruction. Of the Mowbray castles, acquired through marriage, most have suffered either neglect or the ravages of the Civil War, and the best-known, Framlingham, is more readily associated with Mary Tudor at the time of the Lady Jane Grey conspiracy, and with the Howards, whose grand tombs can be seen in the church there. Arundel, the main residence of the Howard dukes of Norfolk, came to them through the Fitzalans, not the Mowbrays. However, the Mowbray story is a substantial part of the rich history of these places and as such must form a part of their legacy to us.

There is no extant miracle of religious architecture such as the remarkable Beauchamp Chapel in Warwick either. The Dissolution of the Monasteries in the reign of Henry VIII was not kind to Mowbray foundations, although the beautiful ruins of Byland Abbey seen against a January setting sun are a sight never to be forgotten. There would have been some wonderful tombs and effigies in the various religious houses the Mowbrays aided, including the alabaster tomb at the Low Melwood monastery, but their superstructures are now destroyed. Even so, who would have thought that the Lady Anne was lying eleven feet down in a vault in Stepney, so who knows how many of her family are lying at peace beneath the grass at Fountains, Byland or Thetford, yet to be discovered? The Mowbrays were always very well-connected but never quite reached the dizzy heights of their Howard descendants, or of the Nevilles, another northern dynasty, and it was left to the little Lady Anne to be their lone representative in Westminster Abbey, and that only because she married the king's son. York Minster, however, is a treasure house of Mowbray memorabilia and here we find their trusty lion rubbing shoulders with the most powerful of heraldic beasts, both in stone and glass: a fine and pleasing legacy.

The changes that have come about in all aspects of life since the times of the Mowbrays have been phenomenal. That a mysterious tail-bearing star appeared in the night sky in 1066, caused panic and was seen as an ill-omen, is well known from a scene on the Bayeux Tapestry. It was not until 1705 that the astronomer Edmond Halley was able to reveal that 'star' for what it really was, but before he reached that conclusion man had first to realise that explorers were not going to fall off the ends of the earth, and the aged Galileo Galilei would have to do battle with the Church in his efforts to demonstrate the relationship between the sun and the planets. That Church itself, in England at any rate, faced revolutionary changes in the days of Henry VIII, the man indirectly responsible for the loss of so many of the Mowbray tombs. When Henry's own future in-laws (the first of many), Ferdinand of Aragon and Isabella of Castile, sent Columbus on his great voyage of discovery in 1492, Anne Mowbray had already been dead for eleven years.

Leonardo da Vinci was twenty-nine when Lady Anne died. His near contemporary, Michelangelo Buonarroti, another genius of the Italian Renaissance, was born in 1476, the year her father died. Over the centuries art has 'progressed' from Leonardo's *Mona Lisa* and Michelangelo's Sistine Chapel ceiling, through Rembrandt, Constable, Monet, Picasso and Warhol to the pickled sheep and unmade beds that are so prized by some connoisseurs in our own times. Thomas Mowbray, 1ˢᵗ Duke of Norfolk, was a contemporary of Geoffrey Chaucer, whom he would know through the royal Court, and the lives of both Thomas and his son Thomas were scrutinised by Shakespeare and can be seen sometimes being played out on the stage of the Royal Shakespeare Theatre in Stratford. The hand-written books and illuminated manuscripts familiar to the Mowbrays gave way to the printing press and, more recently, to desktop publishing. Roger de Mowbray's journey to the Holy Land in 1147 would have been a most remarkable and challenging adventure; the great voyagers and explorers travelling since his family died out have found the Americas and Canada, Australia and New Zealand, and man has walked on the moon. The time is long gone since uttering 'abracadabra' would ward off plague and 'ananizapta' help protect sufferers from epilepsy, yet for a very long time after the last of the Mowbrays these spells were still in use. What would they have made of the transplant surgery and antibiotics we take for granted – and what use would the wonderful

*THE MOWBRAY LION AT HAXEY*

and enduring Duchess Katherine have made of cosmetic surgery?

Why make these comparisons? It is done because, despite all the incredible changes and discoveries in the world at large since their final demise in 1481 with the death of Anne, the Mowbrays are still remembered. The Mowbray lion in the porch at St Andrew's Church in Epworth was already hundreds of years old when local man John Wesley, the bringer of another kind of revolution to the Church, was refused entry and so stood on his father's tomb in the churchyard overlooking the Vinegarth to deliver his sermon. That Lion still lingers there in the porch, in need of a little care and attention nowadays it is true, and its brothers are still watching us from stained glass windows and carved shields in the great Minster at York. Another brother, on his stone post in Haxey village, joins them in giving us continuity with the past, enabling us to keep contact with the memory of their masters and mistresses after all these years. From the Crusades through The Hundred Years War, the Spanish Armada, Trafalgar, Waterloo and two World Wars, these lions have kept watch, and now one of their own family is embattled in the East again. From a dragon slayer defending Jerusalem to a U.S. President doing battle in Iraq, the Mowbray lions have seen it all, and so the ancient Castle Hill in Owston Ferry.

The British Library on Euston Road is a stone's throw from King's Cross Railway Station and I am drawn to it whenever I visit London. It is somewhat off the beaten track for tourists and for that reason its exhibition galleries are seldom packed with people like the National Gallery or the Tower are, and it is possible to be just about the only person in the Library's wonderful John Ritblat Gallery with its exhibition of national treasures. On more than one occasion I have marvelled at being the only person in the whole world at that particular moment to be looking at the genuine Lindisfarne Gospels or reading Lady Jane Grey's prayer book or one of Henry VIII's smudgy, messy letters to Cardinal Wolsey. In my travels near and far I have been fortunate that so many kind people have taken an interest in what I was doing and have actually put into my hands items as varied as a tiny lead pilgrim badge representing a cheap souvenir dropped and lost in the fourteenth century, a chalice used by John and Charles Wesley when they took communion, and

*MOWBRAY LION FLOOR TILE FROM EPWORTH.*

the 'new' seventeenth-century key to the Treasury of Westminster Abbey.

To see items such as these is a privilege; to be allowed to touch them is an unexpected honour. They form a bridge across the years to people who were in many respects just the same as ourselves, with hopes and aspirations, joys and sorrows, and they give one a feeling of making contact with the past in a way that cannot quite be explained. It was like that for me when I had my first sight of the Mowbray tile on display at the Epworth Old Rectory. I wanted to know about the fine ladies whose daintily-shod feet had tripped along the lion pavement, whose rich fur mantles and silk gowns had trailed along the floors in that vanished mansion on land they now call *the Vinegarth*. I wondered about the great lords returning home from the hunt, but I have to admit, it had not occurred to me they would be returning from the Scottish and French wars or from their regular stints as valued advisors to the monarch. For me that simple tile helped make sense of Epworth's Mowbray Street with the The Mowbray Arms public house, the lion in Haxey and the Haxey Hood game.

I believe that this ancient and powerful family deserves a higher profile than it currently has, but the present dukes of Norfolk taking the name Fitzalan-Mowbray-Howard does not seem a very likely proposition in the near future. No matter. As long as the people of the Isle of Axholme keep remembering John and his Deed with pride and admiration, and as long as the Lord, the Fool, the Boggins and hundreds of local people keep turning out to rescue a mysterious lady's hood on Twelfth Night, the great name of Mowbray will outlive us all.

# GENEALOGICAL TABLES

*Showing the Mowbray Family's links to royal and noble houses, Presidents of the United States and Hollywood film stars.*

TABLE I

## *The Mowbray Family and Some of Their Descendants as far as Queen Elizabeth I*

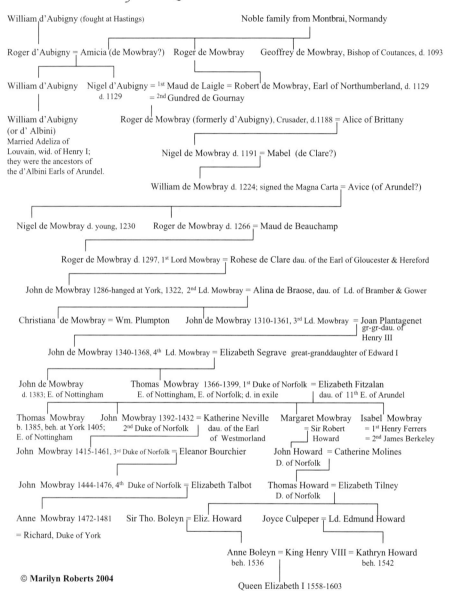

© **Marilyn Roberts 2004**

TABLE II

## *The Mowbray Family - Connections Revealed so Far*

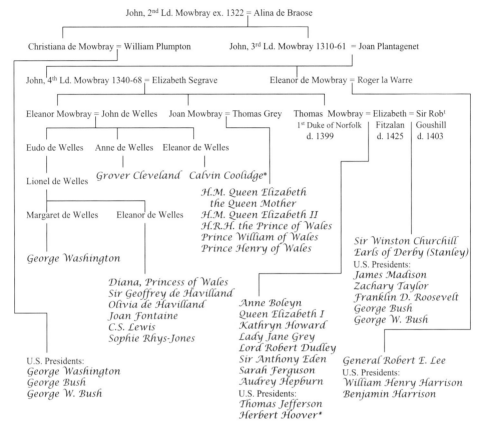

John, 2nd Ld. Mowbray ex. 1322 = Alina de Braose

Christiana de Mowbray = William Plumpton      John, 3rd Ld. Mowbray 1310-61 = Joan Plantagenet

John, 4th Ld. Mowbray 1340-68 = Elizabeth Segrave      Eleanor de Mowbray = Roger la Warre

Eleanor Mowbray = John de Welles    Joan Mowbray = Thomas Grey    Thomas Mowbray = Elizabeth = Sir Robt
                                                        1st Duke of Norfolk   Fitzalan   Goushill
                                                            d. 1399     d. 1425   d. 1403

Eudo de Welles    Anne de Welles    Eleanor de Welles

Lionel de Welles    *Grover Cleveland*   *Calvin Coolidge\**

*H.M. Queen Elizabeth*
*the Queen Mother*
*H.M. Queen Elizabeth II*
*H.R.H. the Prince of Wales*
*Prince William of Wales*
*Prince Henry of Wales*

Margaret de Welles    Eleanor de Welles

*George Washington*

*Sir Winston Churchill*
*Earls of Derby (Stanley)*
U.S. Presidents:
*James Madison*
*Zachary Taylor*
*Franklin D. Roosevelt*
*George Bush*
*George W. Bush*

*Diana, Princess of Wales*
*Sir Geoffrey de Havilland*
*Olivia de Havilland*
*Joan Fontaine*
*C.S. Lewis*
*Sophie Rhys-Jones*

*Anne Boleyn*
*Queen Elizabeth I*
*Kathryn Howard*
*Lady Jane Grey*
*Lord Robert Dudley*
*Sir Anthony Eden*
*Sarah Ferguson*
*Audrey Hepburn*
U.S. Presidents:
*Thomas Jefferson*
*Herbert Hoover\**

U.S. Presidents:
*George Washington*
*George Bush*
*George W. Bush*

*General Robert E. Lee*
U.S. Presidents:
*William Henry Harrison*
*Benjamin Harrison*

\* Tables for Presidents Calvin Coolidge and Herbert Clark Hoover require more work and are not included.

ABBREVIATIONS USED ON THE TABLES:

| | |
|---|---|
| arr. arrived | ex. executed |
| b. born | E. earl |
| beh. beheaded | emig. emigrated (to America) |
| c. circa, at about this time | k. killed |
| cr. created or creation | wid. widow |
| D. duke | = married |
| d. died | (=) not married |
| dau. daughter | ⬇ many generations ahead |

© Marilyn Roberts 2004

# TABLE III

## Some Intermarriages Affecting Mowbray Loyalties and Relationships

There will, of course, be further intermarriages not shown here.

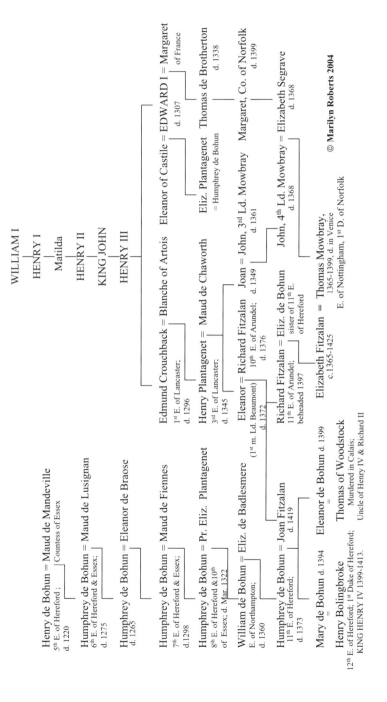

© Marilyn Roberts 2004

TABLE IV

*The Mowbray Ancestry of Anne Boleyn and Her Daughter Queen Elizabeth I*

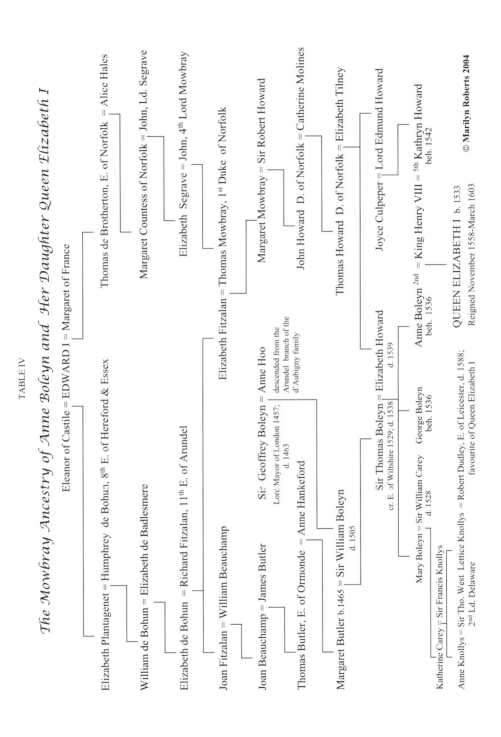

TABLE V

## The Mowbray Family, the House of Tudor and Lady Jane Grey

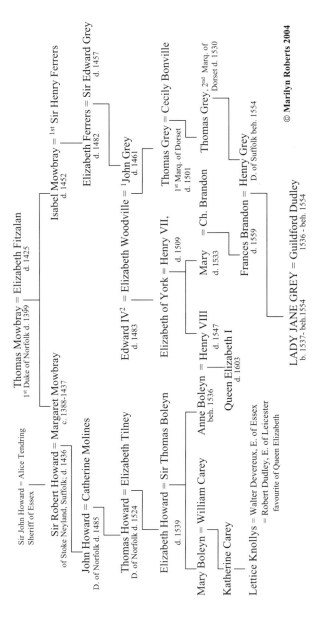

© **Marilyn Roberts 2004**

In order to secure the continuation of Protestantism in England, the dying teenager Edward VI made a will in favour of Lady Jane Grey, who had married Guildford Dudley, son of the King's chief minister, John Dudley. Edward's will was a worthless document and the rightful queen, the Catholic Mary, had John Dudley executed. 'Queen' Jane, the Dudley brothers Guildford, Ambrose and Robert, together with Henry Grey, were imprisoned in the Tower, but Jane, her father and her husband were executed the following year after Sir Thomas Wyatt's rebellion in favour of Princess Elizabeth. Wyatt, too, was descended from the Mowbrays.

TABLE VI

# Mowbray Blood in the Veins of Some of Queen Elizabeth's Leading Courtiers
## (Tudor/Boleyn/Devereux/Dudley/Grey/Knollys)

The Mowbrays would have been related to most of the great families of the time

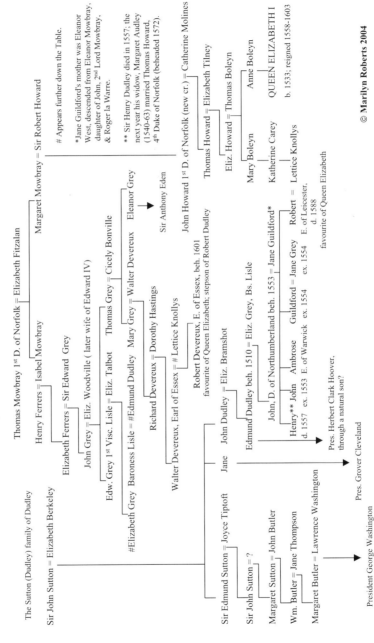

\# Appears further down the Table.

\*Jane Guildford's mother was Eleanor West, descended from Eleanor Mowbray, daughter of John, 2nd Lord Mowbray, & Roger la Warre.

\*\* Sir Henry Dudley died in 1557: the next year his widow, Margaret Audley (1540-63) married Thomas Howard, 4th Duke of Norfolk (beheaded 1572).

© **Marilyn Roberts 2004**

163

TABLE VII

# Descent of the Present Royal family from the Ogle and Mowbray Families through H.M. Queen Elizabeth, the Queen mother*

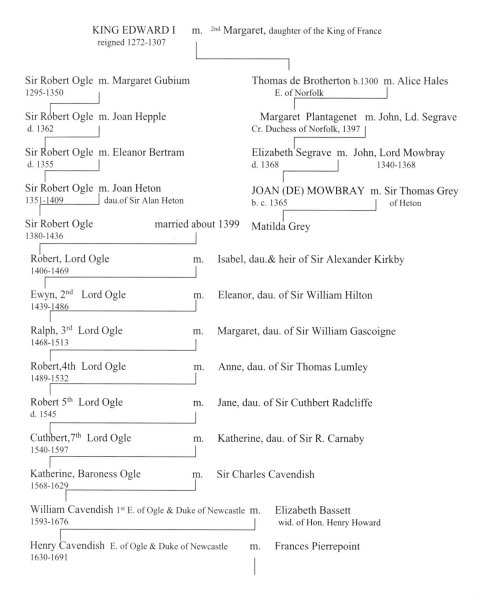

KING EDWARD I   m.   2nd Margaret, daughter of the King of France
reigned 1272-1307

Sir Robert Ogle  m. Margaret Gubium
1295-1350

Thomas de Brotherton b.1300  m. Alice Hales
E. of Norfolk

Sir Robert Ogle  m. Joan Hepple
d. 1362

Margaret  Plantagenet  m. John, Ld. Segrave
Cr. Duchess of Norfolk, 1397

Sir Robert Ogle  m. Eleanor Bertram
d. 1355

Elizabeth Segrave  m.  John, Lord Mowbray
d. 1368                        1340-1368

Sir Robert Ogle  m. Joan Heton
1351-1409            dau.of Sir Alan Heton

JOAN (DE) MOWBRAY  m. Sir Thomas Grey
b. c. 1365                              of Heton

Sir Robert Ogle                married about 1399   Matilda Grey
1380-1436

Robert, Lord Ogle                    m.    Isabel, dau.& heir of Sir Alexander Kirkby
1406-1469

Ewyn, 2nd  Lord Ogle              m.    Eleanor, dau. of Sir William Hilton
1439-1486

Ralph, 3rd  Lord Ogle             m.    Margaret, dau. of Sir William Gascoigne
1468-1513

Robert,4th Lord Ogle              m.    Anne, dau. of Sir Thomas Lumley
1489-1532

Robert 5th  Lord Ogle             m.    Jane, dau. of Sir Cuthbert Radcliffe
d. 1545

Cuthbert,7th  Lord Ogle          m.    Katherine, dau. of Sir R. Carnaby
1540-1597

Katherine, Baroness Ogle        m.    Sir Charles Cavendish
1568-1629

William Cavendish 1st E. of Ogle & Duke of Newcastle m.    Elizabeth Bassett
1593-1676                                                            wid. of Hon. Henry Howard

Henry Cavendish  E. of Ogle & Duke of Newcastle      m.    Frances Pierrepoint
1630-1691

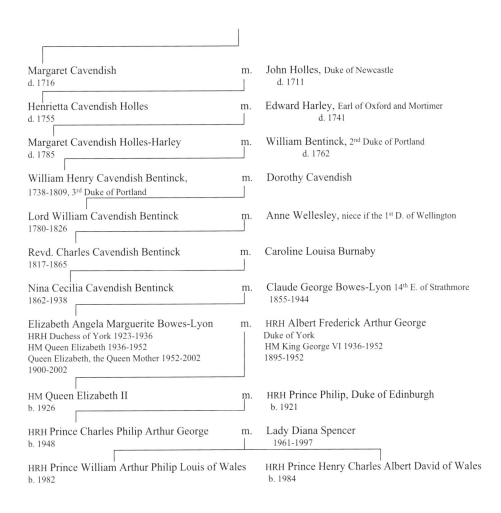

Margaret Cavendish       m.    John Holles, Duke of Newcastle
d. 1716                                        d. 1711

Henrietta Cavendish Holles    m.    Edward Harley, Earl of Oxford and Mortimer
d. 1755                                         d. 1741

Margaret Cavendish Holles-Harley    m.    William Bentinck, 2nd Duke of Portland
d. 1785                                         d. 1762

William Henry Cavendish Bentinck,    m.    Dorothy Cavendish
1738-1809, 3rd Duke of Portland

Lord William Cavendish Bentinck    m.    Anne Wellesley, niece if the 1st D. of Wellington
1780-1826

Revd. Charles Cavendish Bentinck    m.    Caroline Louisa Burnaby
1817-1865

Nina Cecilia Cavendish Bentinck    m.    Claude George Bowes-Lyon 14th E. of Strathmore
1862-1938                                      1855-1944

Elizabeth Angela Marguerite Bowes-Lyon    m.    HRH Albert Frederick Arthur George
HRH Duchess of York 1923-1936                           Duke of York
HM Queen Elizabeth 1936-1952                            HM King George VI 1936-1952
Queen Elizabeth, the Queen Mother 1952-2002      1895-1952
1900-2002

HM Queen Elizabeth II    m.    HRH Prince Philip, Duke of Edinburgh
b. 1926                                        b. 1921

HRH Prince Charles Philip Arthur George    m.    Lady Diana Spencer
b. 1948                                        1961-1997

HRH Prince William Arthur Philip Louis of Wales      HRH Prince Henry Charles Albert David of Wales
b. 1982                                        b. 1984

*This pedigree is the work of Mr. Stanley Johnson of Epworth, with whose kind permission it is reproduced here. Mr Johnson is descended from the Ogle family of Ogle Castle, Ogle, Northumberland.

**© Stanley Johnson 2004**

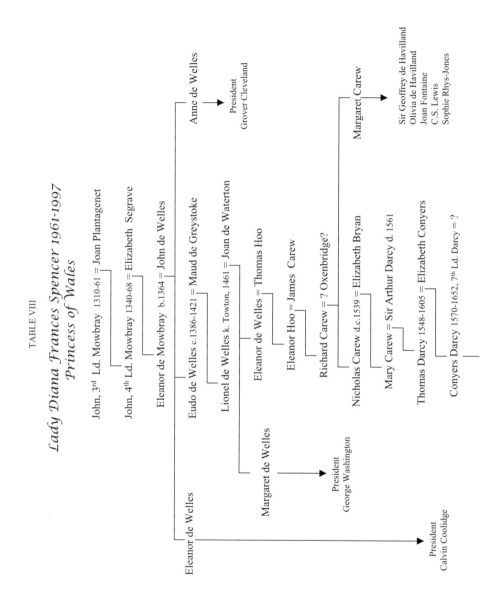

TABLE VIII

*Lady Diana Frances Spencer 1961-1997*
*Princess of Wales*

John, 3rd Ld. Mowbray 1310-61 = Joan Plantagenet

John, 4th Ld. Mowbray 1340-68 = Elizabeth Segrave

Eleanor de Mowbray b.1364 = John de Welles

Eudo de Welles c.1386-1421 = Maud de Greystoke

Lionel de Welles k. Towton, 1461 = Joan de Waterton

Eleanor de Welles = Thomas Hoo

Eleanor Hoo = James Carew

Richard Carew = ? Oxenbridge?

Nicholas Carew d.c.1539 = Elizabeth Bryan

Mary Carew = Sir Arthur Darcy d. 1561

Thomas Darcy 1548-1605 = Elizabeth Conyers

Conyers Darcy 1570-1652, 7th Ld. Darcy = ?

Anne de Welles

President
Grover Cleveland

Margaret Carew

Sir Geoffrey de Havilland
Olivia de Havilland
Joan Fontaine
C.S. Lewis
Sophie Rhys-Jones

Margaret de Welles

President
George Washington

Eleanor de Welles

President
Calvin Coolidge

166

Conyers Darcy, b. 1596; created 1st Earl of Holderness = ?

Conyers Darcy 1622-92, 2nd E. of Holderness = Frances Howard

John Darcy 1658-88 = ?

Robert Darcy b. 1681, 3rd E. of Holderness = ?

Caroline Louise Darcy d. 1778 = William Henry Kerr

Louisa Kerr d. 1830 = George Henry Lennox, Lord Lennox

Charles, 4th Duke of Richmond & Lennox b. 1764 = Lady Charlotte Gordon

Charles Lennox, 5th D. of Richmond & Lennox 1791-1860 = Lady Caroline Paget

Cecilia Catherine Gordon Lennox 1838-1910 = George Bingham, 4th Earl of Lucan

Rosalind Cecilia Caroline Bingham b. 1869 = James Hamilton, 3rd Duke of Abercorn

Cynthia Elinor Beatrix Hamilton 1897-1972 = Albert Edward John Spencer, 7th Earl Spencer

Edward John, 8th Earl Spencer 1924-1992 = Frances Roche (dau. of Lord Fermoy)

LADY DIANA FRANCES SPENCER 1961-1997 = Charles Philip Arthur George, Prince of Wales

TABLE IX

## Sarah Margaret Ferguson, Duchess of York

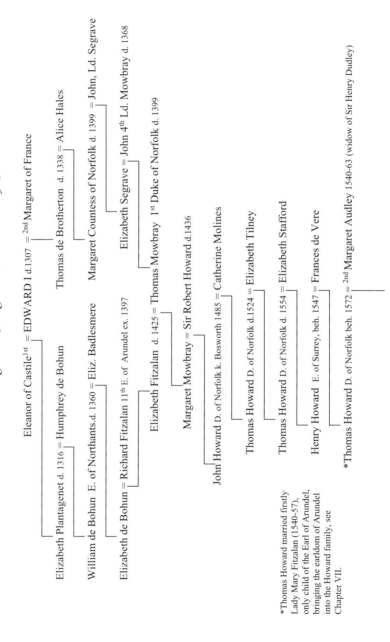

Eleanor of Castile 1st = EDWARD I d.1307 = 2nd Margaret of France

Thomas de Brotherton  d. 1338 = Alice Hales

Margaret Countess of Norfolk d. 1399 = John, Ld. Segrave

Elizabeth Plantagenet d. 1316 = Humphrey de Bohun

William de Bohun  E. of Northants. d. 1360 = Eliz. Badlesmere

Elizabeth Segrave = John 4th Ld. Mowbray d. 1368

Elizabeth de Bohun = Richard Fitzalan 11th E. of Arundel ex. 1397

Elizabeth Fitzalan  d. 1425 = Thomas Mowbray  1st Duke of Norfolk d. 1399

Margaret Mowbray = Sir Robert Howard d.1436

John Howard D. of Norfolk k. Bosworth 1485 = Catherine Molines

Thomas Howard D. of Norfolk d.1524 = Elizabeth Tilney

Thomas Howard D. of Norfolk d. 1554 = Elizabeth Stafford

Henry Howard  E. of Surrey, beh. 1547 = Frances de Vere

*Thomas Howard D. of Norfolk beh. 1572 = 2nd Margaret Audley 1540-63 (widow of Sir Henry Dudley)

*Thomas Howard married firstly
Lady Mary Fitzalan (1540-57),
only child of the Earl of Arundel,
bringing the earldom of Arundel
into the Howard family, see
Chapter VII.

Thomas Howard 1st E. of Suffolk d.1626 = Catherine Knyvet

Theophilus Howard E. of Suffolk d. 1640 = Elizabeth Hume

Frances Howard d. 1677 = Sir Edward Villiers

Alice Villiers d. 1685 = William Bentinck E. of Portland

Henry Bentinck 1st D. of Portland d.1756 = Elizabeth Noel

William Bentinck D. of Portland d. 1762 = Margaret Cavendish Holles-Harley

Elizabeth Bentinck d. 1825 = Thomas Thynne 1st Marquess of Bath

Charlotte Anne Thynne d. 1895 = Walter Montague-Douglas-Scott 5th D. of Buccleuch

Wm. Montague-Douglas-Scott d.1914 = Louisa Jane Hamilton

Herbert Montague-Douglas-Scott d. 1944 = Marie Josephine Edwards

Marian Montague-Douglas-Scott d. 1996 = Col. Andrew Henry Ferguson

Maj. Ronald Ivor Ferguson d. 2003 = Susan Mary Wright

SARAH MARGARET FERGUSON = Prince Andrew, Duke of York (divorced)
b. 1959

TABLE X

# Sir Geoffrey de Havilland, Olivia de Havilland, Joan Fontaine, C.S. Lewis, Sophie Rhys-Jones*

John, 3rd Ld. Mowbray, 1310-61 = Joan Plantagenet

John 4th Ld. Mowbray, 1340-68 = Elizabeth Segrave

Eleanor (Alianore) Mowbray 1364-1417 = John de Welles

Eudo de Welles = Maud de Greystoke

Lionel de Welles, 1406-61 = Joan de Waterton

Eleanor de Welles = Thomas de Hoo, 1st Baron Hoo, d. 1455

Eleanor Hoo = James Carew of Beddington, d. 1492

Sir Richard Carew, 1469-1520 = ? Oxenbridge?

Margaret Carew, b. 1510 = John St. John of Cornwall

Nicholas St. John, 1526-89 = Elizabeth Blount

Elizabeth St. John = Sir Richard St. George, d. 1635

Sir George St. George, b. 1583 = Catherine Gifford

Mary St. George, d. 1701 = Sir Richard Coote, 1st Baron Coote, 1620-83

Letitia Coote, 1658-1729 = Robert Molesworth, 1st Viscount Molesworth, 1656-1725

Anne de Welles → President Grover Cleveland

Margaret de Welles → President George Washington

Nicholas Carew → Diana, Princess of Wales

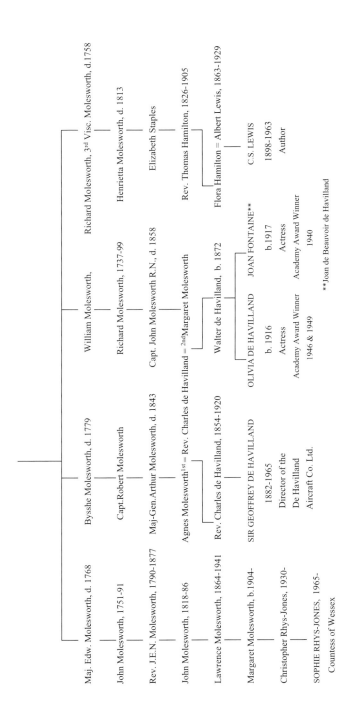

The de Havillands of Guernsey derived their name from Haverland near Valognes in Normandy, where it is known they were the lords in 1050; they settled in Guernsey in 1176.

*I am indebted to Tony Scupham-Bilton for the Molesworth family details.*

© **Marilyn Roberts 2004**

TABLE XI

*Audrey Hepburn (Edda Kathleen Van Heemstra Hepburn-Ruston) 1929-1993*

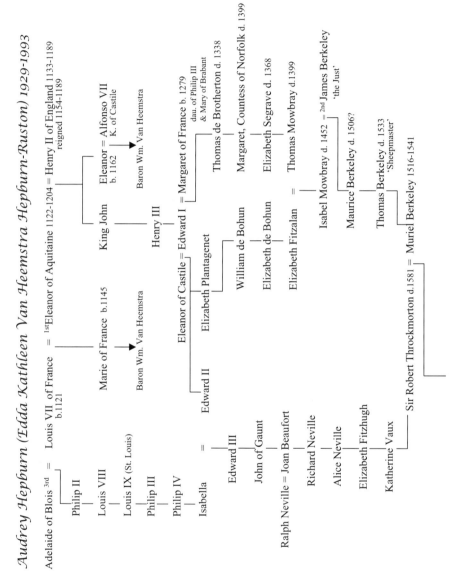

The royal and noble lineage of Audrey Hepburn is well-known and includes the Plantagenets and El Cid (Rodrigo Diaz de Vivar) as well as the dukes of Burgundy, the Battenburg and Pallandt families and Mary Queen of Scots.

This table, included to give some idea of that illustrious ancestry, has been pieced together from a wide number of sources and requires further work regarding some of the dates.

"What is needed to become a real star is an extra element that God can give you or not. You are already born with it. You can't learn it. God kissed the face of Audrey Hepburn and there she was."
Billy Wilder

Anne Throckmorton 1541-1603 (of Coughton Court, Warwickshire) = Ralph Sheldon

Philippe (Philippa) Sheldon b. 1578? = John Sulyard 1572-1626 of Suffolk

Ralph Sulyard b. 1612? = Elizabeth Willford of Wandsworth

Thomas (or John) Sulyard b. 1637 = Johanna de Lietdael

Agnes Sulyard 1696-1744 = Pieter Anthony Godin of Utrecht

Pieter Anthony Godin 1726-1776 = Isabella Lucretia Winjtiers

Antoinette Charlotte Godin b. 1756 = Aernaud Jan Van Westreenen

Cornelia Anna Van Westreenen 1775-1839 = Willem Hendrick De Beaufort

Arnoud Jan De Beaufort 1799-1866 = Anna Aleida Stoop

Wilhemina Cornelia De Beaufort 1843-1927 = Baron William Hendrik Johann Van Heemstra
(of an ancient Dutch noble family)

Baron Arnoud Jan Van Heemstra 1871-1957 = Elbrig Willemine Van Asbeck

Baroness Ella Van Heemstra  d. 1984 = Joseph Victor Hepburn-Ruston (Anglo-Irish Banker)
1889-1980

AUDREY HEPBURN (EDDA KATHLEEN VAN HEEMSTRA HEPBURN-RUSTON) 1929-1993
Academy Award Winner 1953
= 1st Mel Ferrer (actor)
= 2nd Andrea Dotti (psychiatrist)

Sean Ferrer b. 1960        Lucca Dotti b. 1970

© Marilyn Roberts 2004

TABLE XII

## *The Rt. Hon. Sir Anthony Eden, 1897-1977, Prime Minister of Great Britain 1955-57; Earl of Avon*

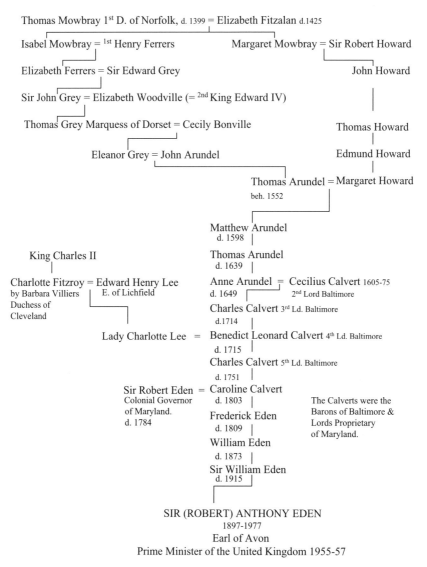

Thomas Mowbray 1ˢᵗ D. of Norfolk, d. 1399 = Elizabeth Fitzalan d.1425

Isabel Mowbray = ¹ˢᵗ Henry Ferrers

Margaret Mowbray = Sir Robert Howard

Elizabeth Ferrers = Sir Edward Grey

John Howard

Sir John Grey = Elizabeth Woodville (= ²ⁿᵈ King Edward IV)

Thomas Grey Marquess of Dorset = Cecily Bonville

Thomas Howard

Eleanor Grey = John Arundel

Edmund Howard

Thomas Arundel = Margaret Howard
beh. 1552

Matthew Arundel
d. 1598

King Charles II

Thomas Arundel
d. 1639

Charlotte Fitzroy = Edward Henry Lee
by Barbara Villiers   E. of Lichfield
Duchess of
Cleveland

Anne Arundel = Cecilius Calvert 1605-75
d. 1649   2ⁿᵈ Lord Baltimore

Charles Calvert 3ʳᵈ Ld. Baltimore
d.1714

Lady Charlotte Lee =

Benedict Leonard Calvert 4ᵗʰ Ld. Baltimore
d. 1715

Charles Calvert 5ᵗʰ Ld. Baltimore
d. 1751

Sir Robert Eden = Caroline Calvert
Colonial Governor   d. 1803
of Maryland.
d. 1784

Frederick Eden
d. 1809

The Calverts were the
Barons of Baltimore &
Lords Proprietary
of Maryland.

William Eden
d. 1873

Sir William Eden
d. 1915

SIR (ROBERT) ANTHONY EDEN
1897-1977
Earl of Avon
Prime Minister of the United Kingdom 1955-57

© **Marilyn Roberts 2004**

174

TABLE XIII    *Sir Winston Churchill - descent from Elizabeth Fitzalan and her third husband*

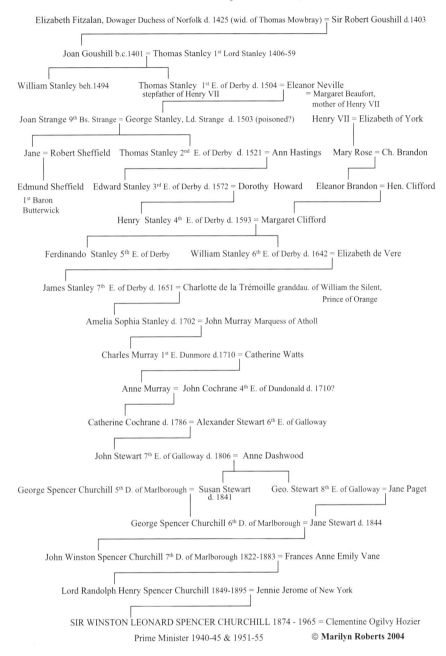

Elizabeth Fitzalan, Dowager Duchess of Norfolk d. 1425 (wid. of Thomas Mowbray) = Sir Robert Goushill d.1403

Joan Goushill b.c.1401 = Thomas Stanley 1ˢᵗ Lord Stanley 1406-59

William Stanley beh.1494    Thomas Stanley  1ˢᵗ E. of Derby d. 1504 = Eleanor Neville
                                    stepfather of Henry VII             = Margaret Beaufort,
                                                                          mother of Henry VII

Joan Strange 9ᵗʰ Bs. Strange = George Stanley, Ld. Strange  d. 1503 (poisoned?)    Henry VII = Elizabeth of York

Jane = Robert Sheffield    Thomas Stanley 2ⁿᵈ  E. of Derby  d. 1521 = Ann Hastings    Mary Rose = Ch. Brandon

Edmund Sheffield    Edward Stanley 3ʳᵈ E. of Derby d. 1572 = Dorothy  Howard    Eleanor Brandon = Hen. Clifford
1ˢᵗ Baron
Butterwick              Henry  Stanley 4ᵗʰ  E. of Derby d. 1593 = Margaret Clifford

Ferdinando  Stanley 5ᵗʰ E. of Derby    William Stanley 6ᵗʰ E. of Derby d. 1642 = Elizabeth de Vere

James Stanley 7ᵗʰ E. of Derby d. 1651 = Charlotte de la Trémoille granddau. of William the Silent,
                                                                           Prince of Orange

Amelia Sophia Stanley d. 1702 = John Murray Marquess of Atholl

Charles Murray 1ˢᵗ E. Dunmore d.1710 = Catherine Watts

Anne Murray =  John Cochrane 4ᵗʰ E. of Dundonald d. 1710?

Catherine Cochrane d. 1786 = Alexander Stewart 6ᵗʰ E. of Galloway

John Stewart 7ᵗʰ E. of Galloway d. 1806 =  Anne Dashwood

George Spencer Churchill 5ᵗʰ D. of Marlborough =  Susan Stewart    Geo. Stewart 8ᵗʰ E. of Galloway = Jane Paget
                                                      d. 1841

George Spencer Churchill 6ᵗʰ D. of Marlborough = Jane Stewart d. 1844

John Winston Spencer Churchill 7ᵗʰ D. of Marlborough 1822-1883 = Frances Anne Emily Vane

Lord Randolph Henry Spencer Churchill 1849-1895 = Jennie Jerome of New York

SIR WINSTON LEONARD SPENCER CHURCHILL 1874 - 1965 = Clementine Ogilvy Hozier
Prime Minister 1940-45 & 1951-55         © **Marilyn Roberts 2004**

TABLE XIV

## George Washington 1732-1799
### 1st President of the United States

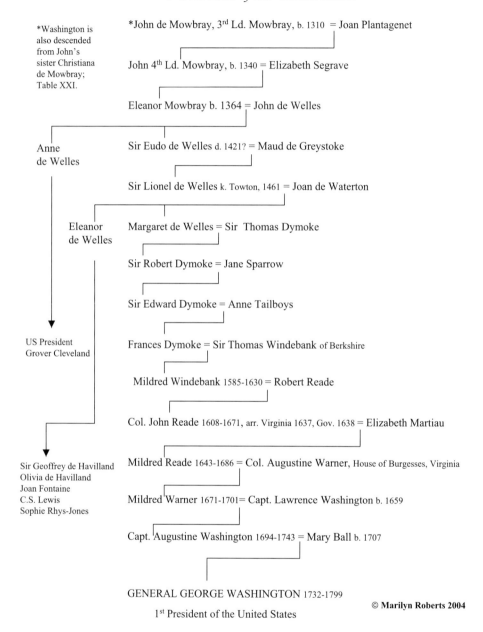

*Washington is also descended from John's sister Christiana de Mowbray; Table XXI.

*John de Mowbray, 3rd Ld. Mowbray, b. 1310 = Joan Plantagenet

John 4th Ld. Mowbray, b. 1340 = Elizabeth Segrave

Eleanor Mowbray b. 1364 = John de Welles

Anne de Welles

Sir Eudo de Welles d. 1421? = Maud de Greystoke

Sir Lionel de Welles k. Towton, 1461 = Joan de Waterton

Eleanor de Welles

Margaret de Welles = Sir Thomas Dymoke

Sir Robert Dymoke = Jane Sparrow

Sir Edward Dymoke = Anne Tailboys

US President Grover Cleveland

Frances Dymoke = Sir Thomas Windebank of Berkshire

Mildred Windebank 1585-1630 = Robert Reade

Col. John Reade 1608-1671, arr. Virginia 1637, Gov. 1638 = Elizabeth Martiau

Sir Geoffrey de Havilland
Olivia de Havilland
Joan Fontaine
C.S. Lewis
Sophie Rhys-Jones

Mildred Reade 1643-1686 = Col. Augustine Warner, House of Burgesses, Virginia

Mildred Warner 1671-1701 = Capt. Lawrence Washington b. 1659

Capt. Augustine Washington 1694-1743 = Mary Ball b. 1707

GENERAL GEORGE WASHINGTON 1732-1799

1st President of the United States

© **Marilyn Roberts 2004**

TABLE XV

## Thomas Jefferson, 1743-1826
### 3<sup>rd</sup> President of the United States

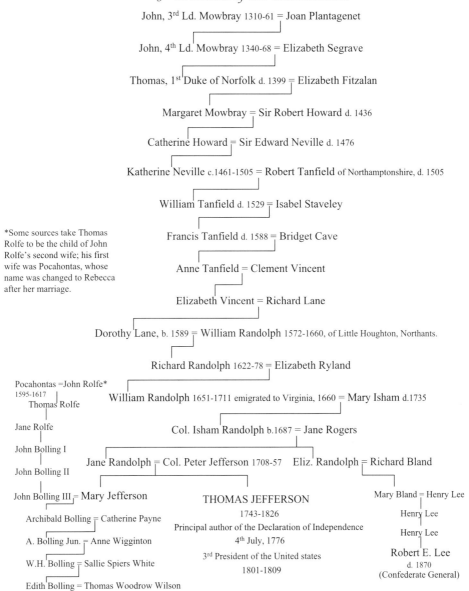

John, 3<sup>rd</sup> Ld. Mowbray 1310-61 = Joan Plantagenet

John, 4<sup>th</sup> Ld. Mowbray 1340-68 = Elizabeth Segrave

Thomas, 1<sup>st</sup> Duke of Norfolk d. 1399 = Elizabeth Fitzalan

Margaret Mowbray = Sir Robert Howard d. 1436

Catherine Howard = Sir Edward Neville d. 1476

Katherine Neville c.1461-1505 = Robert Tanfield of Northamptonshire, d. 1505

William Tanfield d. 1529 = Isabel Staveley

Francis Tanfield d. 1588 = Bridget Cave

Anne Tanfield = Clement Vincent

Elizabeth Vincent = Richard Lane

Dorothy Lane, b. 1589 = William Randolph 1572-1660, of Little Houghton, Northants.

Richard Randolph 1622-78 = Elizabeth Ryland

William Randolph 1651-1711 emigrated to Virginia, 1660 = Mary Isham d.1735

Col. Isham Randolph b.1687 = Jane Rogers

Jane Randolph = Col. Peter Jefferson 1708-57      Eliz. Randolph = Richard Bland

*Some sources take Thomas Rolfe to be the child of John Rolfe's second wife; his first wife was Pocahontas, whose name was changed to Rebecca after her marriage.

Pocahontas = John Rolfe*
1595-1617
Thomas Rolfe

Jane Rolfe

John Bolling I

John Bolling II

John Bolling III = Mary Jefferson

Archibald Bolling = Catherine Payne

A. Bolling Jun. = Anne Wigginton

W.H. Bolling = Sallie Spiers White

Edith Bolling = Thomas Woodrow Wilson
28<sup>th</sup> President of the United States

THOMAS JEFFERSON
1743-1826
Principal author of the Declaration of Independence
4<sup>th</sup> July, 1776
3<sup>rd</sup> President of the United states
1801-1809

Mary Bland = Henry Lee

Henry Lee

Henry Lee

Robert E. Lee
d. 1870
(Confederate General)

© **Marilyn Roberts 2004**

TABLE XVI  *The Harrison Presidents & Confederate General*
*Robert E. Lee*

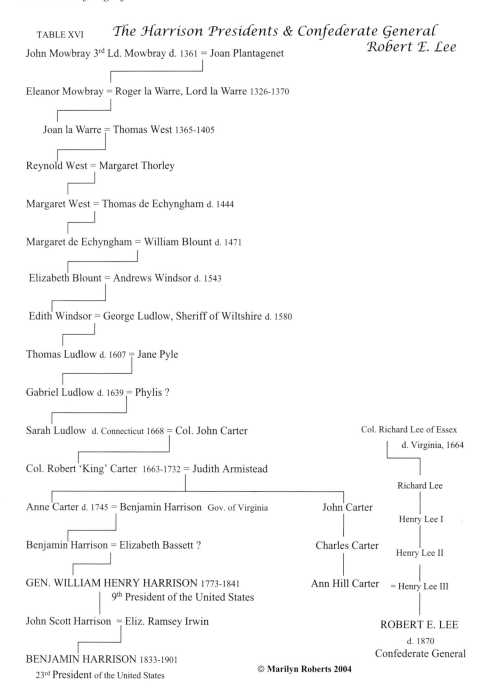

John Mowbray 3rd Ld. Mowbray d. 1361 = Joan Plantagenet

Eleanor Mowbray = Roger la Warre, Lord la Warre 1326-1370

Joan la Warre = Thomas West 1365-1405

Reynold West = Margaret Thorley

Margaret West = Thomas de Echyngham d. 1444

Margaret de Echyngham = William Blount d. 1471

Elizabeth Blount = Andrews Windsor d. 1543

Edith Windsor = George Ludlow, Sheriff of Wiltshire d. 1580

Thomas Ludlow d. 1607 = Jane Pyle

Gabriel Ludlow d. 1639 = Phylis ?

Sarah Ludlow  d. Connecticut 1668 = Col. John Carter

Col. Robert 'King' Carter  1663-1732 = Judith Armistead

Anne Carter d. 1745 = Benjamin Harrison  Gov. of Virginia

Benjamin Harrison = Elizabeth Bassett ?

GEN. WILLIAM HENRY HARRISON 1773-1841
9th President of the United States

John Scott Harrison = Eliz. Ramsey Irwin

BENJAMIN HARRISON 1833-1901
23rd President of the United States

John Carter

Charles Carter

Ann Hill Carter  = Henry Lee III

Col. Richard Lee of Essex
d. Virginia, 1664

Richard Lee

Henry Lee I

Henry Lee II

ROBERT E. LEE
d. 1870
Confederate General

© **Marilyn Roberts 2004**

178

TABLE XVII

## *Grover Cleveland, 22ⁿᵈ and 24ᵗʰ U.S. President*

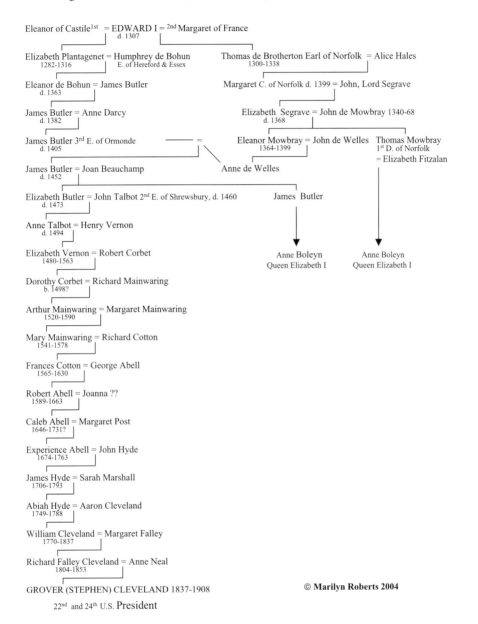

Eleanor of Castile[1st] = EDWARD I = [2nd] Margaret of France
d. 1307

Elizabeth Plantagenet = Humphrey de Bohun          Thomas de Brotherton Earl of Norfolk = Alice Hales
1282-1316          E. of Hereford & Essex          1300-1338

Eleanor de Bohun = James Butler          Margaret C. of Norfolk d. 1399 = John, Lord Segrave
d. 1363

James Butler = Anne Darcy          Elizabeth Segrave = John de Mowbray 1340-68
d. 1382          d. 1368

James Butler 3ʳᵈ E. of Ormonde    ———    =    Eleanor Mowbray = John de Welles    Thomas Mowbray
d. 1405          1364-1399          1ˢᵗ D. of Norfolk
          = Elizabeth Fitzalan

James Butler = Joan Beauchamp          Anne de Welles
d. 1452

Elizabeth Butler = John Talbot 2ⁿᵈ E. of Shrewsbury, d. 1460          James Butler
d. 1473

Anne Talbot = Henry Vernon
d. 1494

Elizabeth Vernon = Robert Corbet          Anne Boleyn          Anne Boleyn
1480-1563          Queen Elizabeth I          Queen Elizabeth I

Dorothy Corbet = Richard Mainwaring
b. 1498?

Arthur Mainwaring = Margaret Mainwaring
1520-1590

Mary Mainwaring = Richard Cotton
1541-1578

Frances Cotton = George Abell
1565-1630

Robert Abell = Joanna ??
1589-1663

Caleb Abell = Margaret Post
1646-1731?

Experience Abell = John Hyde
1674-1763

James Hyde = Sarah Marshall
1706-1793

Abiah Hyde = Aaron Cleveland
1749-1788

William Cleveland = Margaret Falley
1770-1837

Richard Falley Cleveland = Anne Neal
1804-1853

GROVER (STEPHEN) CLEVELAND 1837-1908

22ⁿᵈ and 24ᵗʰ U.S. President

© **Marilyn Roberts 2004**

TABLE XVIII

## The Ancestry of Edith Bolling, wife of Thomas Woodrow Wilson, 28th President of the United States

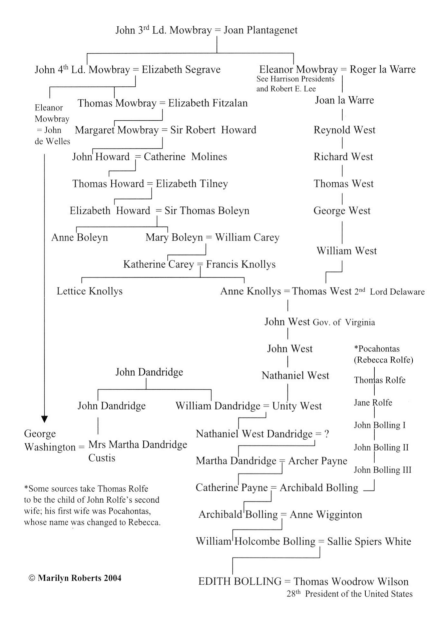

John 3rd Ld. Mowbray = Joan Plantagenet

John 4th Ld. Mowbray = Elizabeth Segrave     Eleanor Mowbray = Roger la Warre
See Harrison Presidents and Robert E. Lee

Eleanor Mowbray = John de Welles

Thomas Mowbray = Elizabeth Fitzalan

Joan la Warre

Margaret Mowbray = Sir Robert Howard

Reynold West

John Howard = Catherine Molines

Richard West

Thomas Howard = Elizabeth Tilney

Thomas West

Elizabeth Howard = Sir Thomas Boleyn

George West

Anne Boleyn    Mary Boleyn = William Carey

William West

Katherine Carey = Francis Knollys

Lettice Knollys    Anne Knollys = Thomas West 2nd Lord Delaware

John West Gov. of Virginia

John West    *Pocahontas (Rebecca Rolfe)

John Dandridge

Nathaniel West    Thomas Rolfe

John Dandridge    William Dandridge = Unity West    Jane Rolfe

George Washington = Mrs Martha Dandridge Custis

Nathaniel West Dandridge = ?    John Bolling I

John Bolling II

Martha Dandridge = Archer Payne

John Bolling III

Catherine Payne = Archibald Bolling

Archibald Bolling = Anne Wigginton

William Holcombe Bolling = Sallie Spiers White

*Some sources take Thomas Rolfe to be the child of John Rolfe's second wife; his first wife was Pocahontas, whose name was changed to Rebecca.

© **Marilyn Roberts 2004**

EDITH BOLLING = Thomas Woodrow Wilson
28th President of the United States

The author wishes to acknowledge *The Royal Descents of 500 Immigrants to the American Colonies or the United States,* by Gary Boyd Roberts, as the starting point for Table XVIII

TABLE XIX

## Presidents James Madison and Zachary Taylor
*descended from Elizabeth Fitzalan and Sir Robert Goushill*

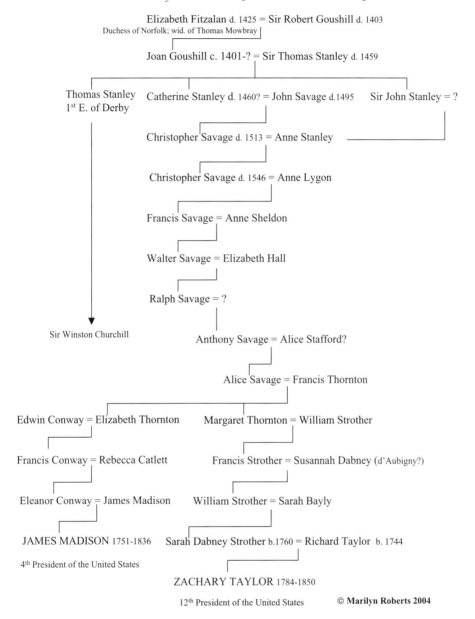

Elizabeth Fitzalan d. 1425 = Sir Robert Goushill d. 1403
Duchess of Norfolk; wid. of Thomas Mowbray

Joan Goushill c. 1401-? = Sir Thomas Stanley d. 1459

Thomas Stanley 1st E. of Derby

Catherine Stanley d. 1460? = John Savage d.1495

Sir John Stanley = ?

Christopher Savage d. 1513 = Anne Stanley

Christopher Savage d. 1546 = Anne Lygon

Francis Savage = Anne Sheldon

Walter Savage = Elizabeth Hall

Ralph Savage = ?

Sir Winston Churchill

Anthony Savage = Alice Stafford?

Alice Savage = Francis Thornton

Edwin Conway = Elizabeth Thornton

Margaret Thornton = William Strother

Francis Conway = Rebecca Catlett

Francis Strother = Susannah Dabney (d'Aubigny?)

Eleanor Conway = James Madison

William Strother = Sarah Bayly

JAMES MADISON 1751-1836

Sarah Dabney Strother b.1760 = Richard Taylor b. 1744

4th President of the United States

ZACHARY TAYLOR 1784-1850

12th President of the United States

© **Marilyn Roberts 2004**

181

TABLE XX
*The Descent of Presidents Franklin Delano Roosevelt,*
*George Herbert Walker Bush & George Walker Bush*
*from Elizabeth Fitzalan, Dowager Duchess of Norfolk,*
*& Her Third Husband, Sir Robert Goushill.*

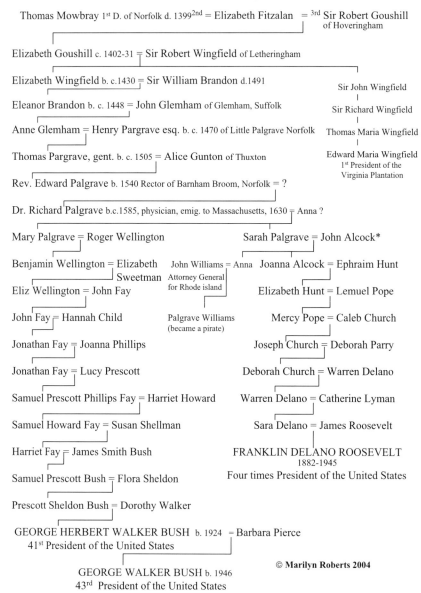

Thomas Mowbray 1st D. of Norfolk d. 1399 2nd = Elizabeth Fitzalan = 3rd Sir Robert Goushill of Hoveringham

Elizabeth Goushill c. 1402-31 = Sir Robert Wingfield of Letheringham

Elizabeth Wingfield b. c.1430 = Sir William Brandon d.1491

Sir John Wingfield
|
Sir Richard Wingfield
|
Thomas Maria Wingfield
|
Edward Maria Wingfield
1st President of the
Virginia Plantation

Eleanor Brandon b. c. 1448 = John Glemham of Glemham, Suffolk

Anne Glemham = Henry Pargrave esq. b. c. 1470 of Little Palgrave Norfolk

Thomas Pargrave, gent. b. c. 1505 = Alice Gunton of Thuxton

Rev. Edward Palgrave b. 1540 Rector of Barnham Broom, Norfolk = ?

Dr. Richard Palgrave b.c.1585, physician, emig. to Massachusetts, 1630 = Anna ?

Mary Palgrave = Roger Wellington

Sarah Palgrave = John Alcock*

Benjamin Wellington = Elizabeth Sweetman

John Williams = Anna  Joanna Alcock = Ephraim Hunt
Attorney General
for Rhode island

Eliz Wellington = John Fay

Elizabeth Hunt = Lemuel Pope

John Fay = Hannah Child

Palgrave Williams
(became a pirate)

Mercy Pope = Caleb Church

Jonathan Fay = Joanna Phillips

Joseph Church = Deborah Parry

Jonathan Fay = Lucy Prescott

Deborah Church = Warren Delano

Samuel Prescott Phillips Fay = Harriet Howard

Warren Delano = Catherine Lyman

Samuel Howard Fay = Susan Shellman

Sara Delano = James Roosevelt

Harriet Fay = James Smith Bush

FRANKLIN DELANO ROOSEVELT
1882-1945
Four times President of the United States

Samuel Prescott Bush = Flora Sheldon

Prescott Sheldon Bush = Dorothy Walker

GEORGE HERBERT WALKER BUSH b. 1924 = Barbara Pierce
41st President of the United States

GEORGE WALKER BUSH b. 1946
43rd President of the United States

© Marilyn Roberts 2004

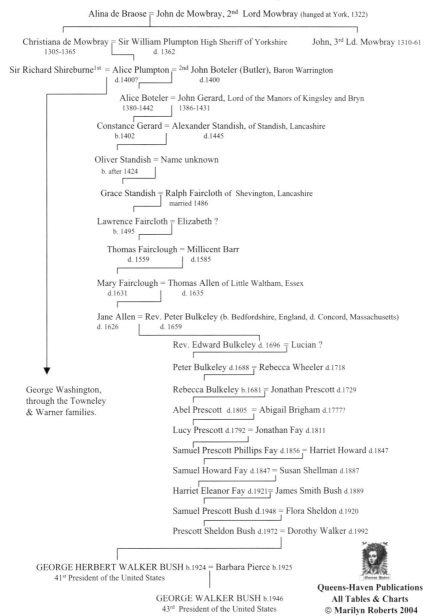

TABLE XXI  *Mowbray Ancestry of George Bush & George Walker Bush, 41ˢᵗ & 43ʳᵈ Presidents of the United States*

Alina de Braose = John de Mowbray, 2ⁿᵈ Lord Mowbray (hanged at York, 1322)

Christiana de Mowbray = Sir William Plumpton High Sheriff of Yorkshire        John, 3ʳᵈ Ld. Mowbray 1310-61
1305-1365                                      d. 1362

Sir Richard Shireburne¹ˢᵗ = Alice Plumpton = 2ⁿᵈ John Boteler (Butler), Baron Warrington
d.1400?                                                       d.1400

Alice Boteler = John Gerard, Lord of the Manors of Kingsley and Bryn
1380-1442      1386-1431

Constance Gerard = Alexander Standish, of Standish, Lancashire
b.1402                              d.1445

Oliver Standish = Name unknown
b. after 1424

Grace Standish = Ralph Faircloth of Shevington, Lancashire
married 1486

Lawrence Faircloth = Elizabeth ?
b. 1495

Thomas Fairclough = Millicent Barr
d. 1559              d.1585

Mary Fairclough = Thomas Allen of Little Waltham, Essex
d.1631                    d. 1635

Jane Allen = Rev. Peter Bulkeley (b. Bedfordshire, England, d. Concord, Massachusetts)
d. 1626              d. 1659

Rev. Edward Bulkeley d. 1696 = Lucian ?

Peter Bulkeley d.1688 = Rebecca Wheeler d.1718

Rebecca Bulkeley b.1681 = Jonathan Prescott d.1729

George Washington,        Abel Prescott d.1805 = Abigail Brigham d.1777?
through the Towneley
& Warner families.        Lucy Prescott d.1792 = Jonathan Fay d.1811

Samuel Prescott Phillips Fay d.1856 = Harriet Howard d.1847

Samuel Howard Fay d.1847 = Susan Shellman d.1887

Harriet Eleanor Fay d.1921 = James Smith Bush d.1889

Samuel Prescott Bush d.1948 = Flora Sheldon d.1920

Prescott Sheldon Bush d.1972 = Dorothy Walker d.1992

GEORGE HERBERT WALKER BUSH b.1924 = Barbara Pierce b.1925
41ˢᵗ President of the United States

GEORGE WALKER BUSH b.1946
43ʳᵈ President of the United States

**Queens-Haven Publications**
**All Tables & Charts**
© **Marilyn Roberts 2004**

# APPENDICES

A    The Twenty-five Known Companions of William the Conqueror at the Battle of Hastings.

B    The Magna Carta Barons.

C    Known Mowbray Residences in the Isle of Axholme.

D    The Struggles Against the Scots.

E    The Model Parliament of 1295.

F    The Mowbray Deed.

G    Thomas Mowbray's Carthusian House at Low Melwood near Epworth in the Isle of Axholme.

H    Rawdon Brown and the 'Mowbray Stone', Venice 1841.

I    The Battles of the Wars of the Roses.

J    Extracts from Certain of the Paston Letters.

K    Elizabeth Fitzalan's Grandsons and the Battle of Bosworth.

L    Palgrave Williams – American Pirate, and Edward Maria Wingfield – First President of the Virginia Plantation, 1607.

M    A Mowbray Connection with the Universities of Oxford and Cambridge.

N    Syria, December 2005 – In Search of Sir Roger de Mowbray

# Appendix A

The Twenty-Five Known Companions of William the Conqueror at Hastings

Robert de Beaumont, cousin of Duke William, later Earl of Leicester
Eustace, Count of Boulogne
William of Evereux, afterwards 3rd Count of Evereux
Geoffrey of Mortagne, afterwards Count of Perche
William Fitzosbern, afterwards Earl of Hereford
Aimery, Vicomte of Thouars
Hugh de Montford, Lord of Montford-sur-Risle
Walter Giffard, Lord of Longueville
Ralf de Toeni, Lord of Conches
Hugh de Grandmesnil, Lord of Grandmesnil
William de Warenne, afterwards Earl of Surrey
William Mallet, Lord of Graville
Odo, bishop of Bayeux, half-brother of the Conqueror
Geoffrey de Monbrai (Mowbray), bishop of Coutances (named by the chronicler William of Poitiers)
Robert, Count of Mortain, afterwards Earl of Cornwall, half-brother of the Conqueror
Wadard
Vital
Turstin Fitzrou, bore the Conqueror's banner
Eugenulf de Laigle, killed in the battle; grandfather of Maud de Laigle
Goubert d'Affray, returned to Normandy after the Conquest
Robert de Vitot, died soon after the Conquest
Roger, son of Turold, died in 1066
Gerelm, died in England
Erchembald, son of Erchembald the Vicomte
Robert Fitzerneis

Based on the list given by L.G. Pine in *They Came With the Conqueror*. This list appeared in a lecture delivered by Geoffrey H. White to the Society of Genealogists in May 1944 in which he drew upon his own researches and also the work of Professor David Douglas of Bristol University. Sources the two men had consulted included the writings of William of Poitiers (not at the battle, but he was a member of Duke William's household), the Norman chronicler Orderic Vitalis, a Latin poem (possibly written by the Bishop of Amiens), and the charters of the Holy Trinity of Rouen. The Roll of Battle Abbey has a very long list of names, but few can be proven beyond doubt; likewise the long list of 'companions' displayed at the Town Hall in Falaise.

# Appendix B

The Magna Carta Barons, 1215

Roger Bigod Earl of Norfolk
Henry de Bohun Earl of Hereford
Richard de Clare Earl of Clare
William de Fortibus Earl of Aumale
Geoffrey de Mandeville Earl of Gloucester
Saher de Quincy Earl of Winchester
Robert de Vere Earl of Oxford
William Marshall the Younger
Robert Fitzwalter of Dunmow
Gilbert de Clare
Eustace de Vesci
William de Hardell
William de Mowbray
Geoffrey de Say
Roger de Mumbezon
William de Huntingfield
Robert de Ros
John de Lacy Constable of Chester
William de Albini (d'Aubigny) of Belvoir
Richard de Percy
William Malet
John Fitzrobert
William de Lanvallei
Hugh Bigod later Earl of Norfolk
Richard de Montfichet

Advisors to King John

Stephen Langton Archbishop of Canterbury
Henry Archbishop of Dublin
William Bishop of London
Peter Bishop of Winchester
Joceline Bishop of Bath and Glastonbury
Hugh Bishop of Lincoln
Walter Bishop of Coventry
Benedict Bishop of Rochester

Pandulphe Pope's Subdeacon (Papal Legate)
Almeric Master of The Knights Templar In England

WILLIAM MARSHAL Earl of Pembroke
WILLIAM LONGSPEE Earl of Salisbury
WILLIAM OF WARENNE and Surrey
ALAN OF GALLOWAY Constable of Scotland
WARIN FITZGERALD
HUBERT DE BURGH
PETER FITZHERBERT
HUGH DE NEVIL
MATTHEW FITZHERBERT
THOMAS BASSET
ALAN BASSET
WILLIAM D'ALBINI (d'Aubigny) Earl of Arundel,
ROBERT DE ROPPEL
JOHN MARSHALL of Hingham
JOHN FITZHUGH

# APPENDIX C

## KNOWN MOWBRAY RESIDENCES IN THE ISLE OF AXHOLME

The Isle of Axholme is in the west of the county of North Lincolnshire. North Lincolnshire itself is of recent creation, coming about in the late 1990's in recognition of the fact that the 1974 Local Government Reorganisation that merged part of the historic county of Lincoln with the historic East Riding of Yorkshire had been over-optimistic. Even the opening of what was then the longest single-span suspension bridge in the world was not enough to unite the Lincolnshire 'Yellowbellies' and Yorkshire 'Tykes' who found themselves living in the new county of Humberside. Throughout this book 'Lincolnshire' is taken to mean the historic county of pre-1974 comprised of Lindsey, Holland and Kesteven.

The Isle of Axholme lies in the north-west of old Lincolnshire and is an 'island' of Mercian Mudstone and Coversands 16 miles maximum length north to south and 6 miles maximum width[1] which, prior to the 17th century draining of the land, was surrounded by boggy ground known as 'carr', but even within the Isle itself there was widespread wetland. Its eastern boundary is the River Trent, while its northwest boundary follows the original course of the River Don; Nottinghamshire lies to the south.

[1] Stephen R. Garner; his book *A Topographical Study of the Wetlands of Axholme* should be consulted for greater detail of the natural features of the Isle.

### KINARD CASTLE.

Information on the Mowbray stronghold at Owston Ferry, formerly Kinard Ferry, is rather sparse, but the ground plan can be easily made out. The motte, or man-made mound, on which the castle keep stood, is still a substantial structure, known locally as 'castle hill'. It seems likely that the church stands in what was once the castle bailey, and parts of the moat can also be easily made out. The Reverend W.B. Stonehouse, writing in 1839, described the castle site as being,

> "A small eminence containing about three acres of ground, which was surrounded completely by the outward wall.
> [There is] A mound, or conical tumulus of raised earth, which measures within the ditch 270 paces and which still retains its ancient form as when the arx or keep of the castle was standing... The moat in one place is as plain to be seen as when it was first made, the sides being quite steep as if newly cut."

It seems possible that the castle was a wooden structure (compare the description of the Mowbray castle at Thirsk, Chapter I), although there would have been ample time to rebuild in stone before Henry II demolished it by way of punishment for Roger de Mowbray's rebellion in the 1170's. It would appear that whatever the nature of its fabric, Kinard Castle was never rebuilt after this.

*THE EPWORTH MANSION ON LAND NOW KNOWN AS 'THE VINEGARTH'.* Marilyn Roberts can take no credit for any original research on the Mowbray residences but would recommend the reader to take a few moments' reflection at this lovely spot nowadays associated with John Wesley, whose father was the Rector of St Andrew's Church which lies alongside the site of the old Mowbray residence. There is no longer any trace of the mansion above ground, but thankfully the area was not fully built-upon as had been threatened in the 1970's. It is a place to allow the imagination free rein and to think of the people who have been there before us, from the banter of the stonemasons carving the Mowbray lion in the porch of the church, to William de Mowbray, the Magna Carta baron, breathing his last in his great house. Picture the mysterious Lady of the Hood returning home, still smiling at the silly antics of the rustics who had been chasing after her bonnet, her face flushed with the biting January air. Then there would be John and his lawyers working out the terms of his famous deed, the long-suffering Elizabeth Fitzalan wondering whatever her husband would do next, and Duchess Katherine dictating her letter to the Pastons...

Local tradition had long held the area known as the *Vinegarth* to be the site of the Mowbrays' Epworth residence, but this was not confirmed until an excavation in the 1970's. Epworth was, and still is, the major settlement in the Isle, with the Vinegarth and the parish church of St Andrew standing on a Marlstone prominence. As far back as 1538, during the reign of Henry VIII, for whom he was conducting a survey, John Leland recorded that there remained, 'a great parte of the maner place of Lord Mulbray of Axholme, chief owner ontyl late dayes of the hole isle'. The house appears to have been increasingly neglected once the Isle of Axholme's link with the Mowbrays ended.

Stonehouse, 1839, refers to a 1749 survey recording 'a capital messuage or manor house' south of the land called the Vinegarth, which is now believed to have referred to newer buildings with no Mowbray connections, and its presence could explain why the Epworth Rectory is some distance from the church. Read, in 1858, reported that tiles bearing the Mowbray arms had recently been found in the field known as the Vinegarth, where large portions of the foundations of buildings believed to be the Mowbrays' house survived, and that eighty years previously a very large cannon had been excavated. Further tiles were found in the late 1960's; in an interview taped on 26ᵗʰ January 1975, the Rev'd W.B. Harvey, then Rector of the parish church, described how the Sexton, Mr. Widdowson, had unearthed what they believed to be fourteenth-century bricks when digging graves. The two men carried out further excavations and requested a professional investigation, but it was not until Boothferry District Council announced plans to put housing on the site that a two-season excavation was undertaken.

The excavation itself was carried out for the Department of the Environment under the direction of R.A.H. Williams and the DoE report gives the following summary,

> "Only the S. wall of the hall remained. This was flanked by a rectangular stone base to an exterior staircase (?), which perhaps explains the absence of a floor. A kitchen was attached to the SW corner of the hall; the centre of its floor was of glazed tiles laid diagonally. Tiles bearing the Mowbray shield were grouped in sets of nine with one row of plain tiles dividing each set. The rest of the floor was of half-baked bricks. S. of the hall and kitchen lay a cloistral walk, 18 metres square. Deep foundations on the W. and other structures farther W. against the S. side of the church would have been service buildings. Documentary evidence suggests that a manor house stood at Epworth in 1266[1]; the part described here probably fell into disuse in the 16th century".

(There is documentary evidence of a Mowbray residence in Epworth long before 1266.)

Details of the excavation, with plans drawn by R.H.A. Williams, may be found in an article by Colin Hayfield entitled Excavations on the Site of the Mowbray Manor House at the Vinegarth, Epworth, Lincolnshire, 1975-1976 in 'Lincolnshire History and Archaeology', Vol. 19,1984. The floor tiles are by far the most interesting find, but other objects included coins, glass, pottery, buckles, a very small bell, possibly of a type worn by a falcon, as well as a bronze candlestick 13.3 cm high. Unfortunately, by the time Colin Hayfield wrote his article many objects had gone missing. The tiles were found in what was a kitchen, but their high quality, many with the Mowbray lion, led Glyn Coppack (who contributed to the Colin Hayfield article) to believe they had been moved to the kitchen from much grander rooms once the Berkeleys or Stanleys were in possession. According to Dr. Coppack, the original pattern could have been groups of nine tiles bearing the figure of a Mowbray lion rampant enclosed by a shield set within borders of plain tiles, but this had only been maintained in the northwestern quadrant of the kitchen floor, the rest of the tiling being haphazard. Five different designs of tile were found in the floor and are believed to have been made in Nottingham and West Cowick:

i) the lion rampant reversed; ii) a rosette within a circle within a square with quarter rosettes in quadrants in the corners; iii) a bell, key and sword within a square; iv) lions' heads and fleurs-de-lis alternate and interlacing; v) a plain border tile with a dark green glaze. The present writer has seen examples of all of these, with the exception of (iii) and (iv), and also a rather dramatic single fleur-de-lis, not mentioned in the report.

Information on the Vinegarth excavation can be found in Sites & Monument Record SMR 2447 at the North Lincolnshire Museum in Scunthorpe.

# APPENDIX D

## THE STRUGGLES AGAINST THE SCOTS

Throughout the period with which we are concerned the English and Scots were involved in cross-border raids and frequently in open warfare. Having lands in Lincolnshire and Yorkshire the Mowbrays were naturally heavily involved in the defence of this part of the realm for generation upon generation.

| | |
|---|---|
| 1058 | Malcolm Canmore, having defeated Macbeth at Dunsinane the year before, becomes Malcolm III (1058-1093), founder of the Canmore dynasty. |
| 1072 | Malcolm's raids into England provoke the Normans to invade Scotland. |
| 1079 | More raids provoke Norman retaliation. |
| 1080 | **Robert de Mowbray (died 1129)** is made Earl of Northumberland. |
| 1091 | Malcolm makes attacks into **Robert's** territory. |
| 1093 | Malcolm III and his son by his first wife are killed by **Robert de Mowbray** at Alnwick. |
| 1138 | David I (1124-1154), third son of Malcolm III by his second wife, is defeated at the Battle of the Standard at Northallerton. Fifteen-year old (?) **Roger de Mowbray (died 1188)** is present. David, however, is allowed effective control over Northumbria and Cumbria. |
| 1157 | Henry II of England forces 16-year-old Malcolm IV (1154-1165) to give up the northern areas. |
| 1174 | William the Lion (1165-1214), King of Scotland, is captured at Alnwick trying to take Northumbria. **Roger de Mowbray** is with him. By the Treaty of Falaise William has to agree to the occupation of major Scottish castles by English garrisons and that the King of Scots will be subordinate to the King of England. |
| 1189 | Richard the Lionheart of England nullifies the treaty in exchange for money to finance his crusading expeditions. |
| 1200 | **Philip de Mowbray, younger brother of the William de Mowbray** (died 1224) of Magna Carta fame, settles in Scotland. |
| 1215 | Alexander II (1214-1249) sees that King John is in a weak position and tries to recover Northumberland. In 1222 he marries the sister of John's son Henry III and a period of peace ensues. |
| 1237 | Alexander II, King of Scots, signs the Treaty of York giving up lands in the north of England. |
| 1258 | **Sir Roger de Mowbray (died 1266)** fights in the Scottish campaigns. |
| 1282 | **Sir Roger de Mowbray (died 1297), later the 1st Lord Mowbray,** begins the first of his periods of service against the Scots. |
| 1286 | Death of Alexander III (1249-1286) in a riding accident; he is predeceased by his wife and sons. His daughter, also dead by now, had married the King of Norway and so Margaret, her three-year-old daughter, is now Queen of Scotland. |
| 1290 | Margaret, the *Maid of Norway* (1286-1290) dies on her way from Bergen to Leith to take up her throne and to marry Prince Edward, son of Edward I of England. Margaret is the last of the Canmore line. |
| 1292 | Thirteen candidates emerge as possible ruler of Scotland. Edward I of England agrees to preside over the selection process as long as he is acknowledged as Lord Superior |

| | |
|---|---|
| | of Scotland. The two finalists are Robert Bruce and John Balliol; Edward chooses the latter and subsequently treats him with such contempt that the ineffectual and intimidated Balliol (1292-1296) is unable to do the job properly. |
| 1295 | The Treaty of Paris between the Scots and French, known now as *The Aulde Alliance*, is seen by Edward I as preparation for war. This is when he summons his famous Model Parliament to deal with the Gascony problem and **Roger de Mowbray becomes the first Lord Mowbray.** |
| 1296 | Edward I massacres three-quarters of the population of Berwick-upon-Tweed. The Scots retaliate with atrocities at Hexham, although the monks at Lanercost Abbey are not harmed. The Scots are defeated at Dunbar and John Balliol resigns his kingdom to Edward, who takes away the precious Stone of Scone to England. |
| 1297 | The Scottish knight Sir William Wallace sacks Lanark, killing the English there. He is defeated by Edward I in 1298 at Falkirk and will be involved in guerrilla warfare until his capture. |
| 1303 | Invasion of Scotland by Edward I. |
| 1304 | Scotland surrenders but the struggles go on. Edward I uses the huge catapult known as the *War Wolf* against Stirling Castle. |
| 1305 | Wallace, captured near Glasgow, is executed at Smithfield in London. |
| 1306 | Robert (the) Bruce, grandson of the Robert Bruce rejected in favour of John Balliol, seizes power as Robert I (1306-1329). Although the family still holds land on both sides of the border and he has spent part of his youth at the English Court, he considers himself to be a Scot. |
| 1307 | Death of Edward I near Hadrian's Wall on his way to face the Scots yet again, 7th July. |
| 1313 | **John Mowbray (1286-1322), 2nd Lord Mowbray** is appointed Warden of the Marches Towards Carlisle. He has been called-up for service against the Scots every August since 1308 and will continue to be so until 1319, becoming Captain and Keeper of Newcastle in 1315. The Scots capture and wreck castles under English control. |
| 1314 | Edward II sees his army decimated at Bannockburn in their amateurish attempt to relieve the besieged Stirling Castle. Stirling's castellan, **Sir Philip Mowbray**, has tried to make Edward understand that an early engagement with the Scots is ill advised, and according to the rules of chivalry is quite unnecessary. |
| 1318 | Bruce captures Berwick Castle. |
| 1327 | Only months after his release from the Tower, sixteen-year-old **John Mowbray (1310-1361), 3rd Lord Mowbray** is called up for his first stint of service against the Scots. |
| 1329 | Death of Robert Bruce. His son and successor, David II (1329-1371), is only five. |
| 1332 | John Balliol's son, Edward Balliol, leads the English who defeat the Scots near Perth. |
| 1333 | Edward III invades in support of Balliol and lays siege to Berwick Castle. The Scots suffer defeat at Halidon Hill as they try to relieve Berwick. The Scots send the boy |

| | |
|---|---|
| | David II to France for his own safety; he will not return until 1341, aged seventeen. |
| 1340 | **John de Mowbray,** appointed Keeper of Berwick Castle, says, "The whole country is in war up to the gates of the town." |
| 1346 | Reeling from the aftermath of the battle of Crécy, and knowing that Edward III has far from finished with them, the French entreat King David to invade Northern England in order to divert Edward's attention and resources. At the battle of Neville's Cross David is captured; **John de Mowbray, 3rd Lord Mowbray,** and his men are praised for their good conduct both during and after the battle. |
| 1356 | By 1356 Edward Balliol gives up his fight and relinquishes his right to the Scottish throne in exchange for a pension from Edward III; **John de Mowbray** is a witness. |
| 1357 | David II is released from the Tower. He dies in 1371 and is succeeded by his nephew Robert Stewart, son of Robert Bruce's daughter Marjorie, as Robert II (1371-1390). |
| 1385 | Robert II's son, ruling because his father is ailing, invades England with the support of a French Army, but is repulsed as far back as Edinburgh. |
| 1388 | The Scots invade into Cumberland and Northumberland and defeat the English at Otterburn. |
| 1389 | **Thomas Mowbray (1366-1399) Earl of Nottingham and later 1st Duke of Norfolk,** becomes keeper of Berwick and Roxburgh. |
| 1406 | The eleven-year-old heir to the Scottish throne is captured by pirates off Flamborough Head in Yorkshire when on his way to France to protect him from the ambitions of the men of his own family. He is sold to Henry IV, and his father, Robert III (1390-1406), dies upon hearing the shocking news. |
| 1437 | **John Mowbray (1415-1461) 3rd Duke of Norfolk,** sometime ambassador to Scotland and Warden of the Eastern March, is made Captain of Berwick and a guardian of the truce concluded with Scotland. |
| 1461 | Henry VI gives Berwick beck to the Scots and offers Carlisle as well if they will help him against the Yorkists. |
| 1464 | A truce is signed with the English. |
| 1481 | **Death of Anne Mowbray (1472-1481), Countess of Norfolk, last of the Mowbrays.** |
| 1482 | English invade in support of the exiled brother of James III (1460-1488). After this Berwick-upon-Tweed will remain in English hands. |
| 1496 | James IV (1488-1513) launches major raids on Northumberland. |
| 1503 | James IV marries Margaret Tudor, daughter of Henry VII of England. |
| 1513 | Queen Margaret's brother, Henry VIII (1509-1547), is invading France; the French seek Scottish help and James IV invades Northumberland. King James and many of his greatest nobles are killed at Flodden near Coldstream and Catherine of Aragon sends his bloodstained coat to his brother-in-law Henry in France. |
| 1542 | The Scots lose the battle of Solway Moss near Carlisle; they had hoped to put a stop to |

| | |
|---|---|
| | the aggression of Henry VIII. Their King, James V (1513-1542), dies two weeks later leaving a six-day-old daughter, Mary, to become the Queen of Scots. |
| 1543 | The Treaty of Greenwich provides for the unification of the two kingdoms through the marriage of Queen Mary to Henry's only son, six-year-old Prince Edward, but the Scottish Parliament has second thoughts and instead pursues an alliance with France. This is followed by what is known as the 'rough wooing' up to 1551 during which time Henry VIII tries to impose the alliance by force. |
| 1547 | The Scots are defeated at Pinkie Cleuch near Edinburgh. |
| 1548 | Mary escapes with the French Fleet and is brought up in France. |
| 1558 | Mary Queen of Scots, aged sixteen, marries the Dauphin of France. Six months later her 25-year-old cousin Elizabeth Tudor becomes Queen of England. Mary does not recognise Henry VIII's divorce from Catherine of Aragon as legal and sees Elizabeth, Anne Boleyn's daughter, as illegitimate and ineligible to rule. **Through her mother Elizabeth I is descended from the Mowbrays.** As a great-grandchild of Henry VII Mary sees the English throne as hers by right. |
| 1561 | Widowed Mary returns to Scotland but is deposed in 1567 in favour of her baby son, her only child by her second husband the dissolute Lord Darnley, her cousin. She flees to England and becomes a focus for the Catholic faction and a huge thorn in Queen Elizabeth's side for over 25 years. |
| 1571 | Elizabeth's nearest male relative of any standing, Thomas Howard, Duke of Norfolk, is executed for plotting to overthrow her in favour of Queen Mary, whom he plans to marry. **Both Howard and Queen Elizabeth are of the ancient Mowbray blood through the marriage of Lady Margaret Mowbray and Sir Robert Howard.** |
| 1587 | Mary Stuart, Queen of Scots, is beheaded for her involvements in plots to assassinate Queen Elizabeth. |
| 1603 | Death of Elizabeth I. It is assumed that she will be succeeded by Mary's only son, James, her nearest eligible male relative, who will thus unite the two crowns as James I of England and VI of Scotland, but she does not actually nominate him until the very last moment, if at all. **Sir Robert Carey, of Mowbray descent through his grandmother, Anne Boleyn's sister Mary,** waits impatiently in the palace courtyard and as soon as Elizabeth dies sets off for Scotland at breakneck speed in order to reap the benefits that will result from being the first person to break the news to King James. |

# APPENDIX E

## THE MODEL PARLIAMENT OF 1295

### *SUMMONS OF THE ARCHBISHOP OF CANTERBURY*
*(This contains the famous declaration of Edward I that what affects all should be approved by all.)*

The King to the venerable father in Christ, Robert, by the same grace Archbishop of Canterbury, primate of all England, greeting. As a most just law, established by the careful providence of sacred princes exhorts and decrees that what affects all, by all should be approved, so also should common danger be met by means provided in common. You know sufficiently well, and it is now, as we believe, divulged through all regions of the world, how the King of France fraudulently and craftily deprives us of our land of Gascony, by withholding it unjustly from us. Now, however, not satisfied with the before-mentioned fraud and injustice, having gathered together for the conquest of the kingdom a very great fleet and an abounding multitude of warriors, with which he had made a hostile attack on our kingdom and the inhabitants of the same kingdom, he now proposes to destroy the English language altogether from the earth…

### *SUMMONS OF A BARON TO THE 1295 PARLIAMENT*
*This particular summons came in October, whereas Roger de Mowbray was amongst the first to be summoned, on 24th June.*
*(In 1953 the Lord Mowbray Segrave and Stourton – see Chapter VIII – did homage to Queen Elizabeth II as Premier Baron.)*

The King to his beloved and faithful relative, Edmund, Earl of Cornwall, greeting. Because we wish to have a consultation and meeting with you and with the rest of the principal men of our kingdom, as to provision for remedies against the dangers which in these days are threatening our whole kingdom, we command you, strictly enjoining you in the fidelity and love in which you are bound to us, that on the Lord's day next after the feast of St Martin, in the approaching winter, you be present in person at Westminster, for considering, ordaining and doing, along with us and our prelates and the rest of the principal men and other inhabitants of our kingdom, as may be necessary for meeting dangers of this kind.

# APPENDIX F

### THE MOWBRAY DEED
AND
### WHICH JOHN DE MOWBRAY?

This translation of the Mowbray Deed from the original French into English by William Ryley (Riley) at the Tower of London in 1652 may be found in the works of both Peck and Tomlinson, see Bibliography.

*A true copy of the ancient deed of JOHN DE MOWBRAY, sometime Lord of the ISLE of AXHOLME, and the Honour of BREMBER\*, made to the Freeholders there after he had made an approvement to himself of some of the Wastes within the manor of EPWORTH in the said Isle: and is now translated out of the French into English by WILLIAM RYLEY, keeper of the records, in the Tower of LONDON. The said MOWBRAY and his predecessors, and also successors, the Dukes of NORFOLK, were a long time lords of the said manor.*
*\*Bramber in Sussex*

This indenture between their thrice honoured lord Sir John de Mowbray, lord of the Isle of Axholme and of the honour of Brember, of the one part; RAWLYN of BRUMHAM, WILLIAM of BRUMHAM, ROGER of BRUMHAM, JOHN of THETILTHORP, THOMAS MELTON, JEOFFREY LUNDELS, VINCENT BAVANT, JOHN GARDNER, JOHN CUTWULF, RICHARD of BELWOOD, and JOHN at HAGH, his tenants of the Isle of Axholme and all the tenants and resiants within the said isle, on the other part, Witnesseth that all the said tenants and resiants have supplicated their said lord Sir John Mowbray, to remedy divers claims touching their rights and divers debates and grievances to them made by the ministers of the said lord Sir John Mowbray upon which supplication it is agreed that the said Sir John, lord aforesaid, hath granted for him and for his heirs, to the said Rawlyn, William, Roger, John, Thomas, Jeoffrey, Vincent, John, John, Richard, and John, tenants aforesaid, and to their heirs, and to all having their estate, or parcel of their estate, and to all the other tenants and resiants, within the Isle of Axholme, and to their heirs and to all that shall hereafter have their estate, all the things underwritten, that is to say: That the said Sir John, nor his heirs, shall not approve any waste, moor, woods, waters, nor make nor shall make any other manner of approvement within the Isle of Axholme. And that the said

Rawlyn, William, Roger, John, Thomas, Jeoffrey, Vincent, John, John, Richard, and John, and their heirs... [etc. etc.] shall have their common which is appendent to their free tenements, according to that which they have used time out of mind.

And also that the aforesaid Rawlyn, William... [etc. etc.] may dig in the moors and marshes, turfs trees and roots found within the soil ...And that one pound containing one half acre, be made at the cost of the said tenants, and maintained hereafter by the said lord and his heirs, in Belton Carr, and one other in Haxey Carr, containing as much, and that they be made in places for the most ease of the said tenants. [Details follow as to the keeping of animals.]

And that the said tenants and their heirs..., may dig and take turf or other earth, for the walls of their houses, and for all other necessaries of the said houses, and for to inclose the walls of their said messuages or mansions. And to dry flags in all the said wastes, for to cover the ridges of their houses and walls, and for bringing the trees to repair the river of Trent, when cause of repairing is, and to make them new.

And that the said Rawlyn, William...[etc. etc.] be not for the future amerced or grieved for default of not appearing to ring their swine. And that they may put hemp to be rated in all the waters of the isle (except for the skires which are severed to the said lord, Sir John Mowbray) and that the said lord, nor his heirs nor his ministers, make no molestations nor grievance to the dogs of the fore-named tenants... and if they do, the tenants shall have their recovery at the common law.

And that the aforesaid Rawlyn, William...[etc. etc.] may fish through all the waters and wastes of the said isle, without impediment of the minister of the said lord Sir John Mowbray, except the skires aforesaid; and also that they may dig turf, and all other manner of earth, in all the wastes aforesaid, to carry and improve their land at pleasure. And that none of the tenants... impeached for trespass of the said lord, be amerced for trespass without answer given in court, and then by their peers to be fined and taxed if they be amerceable.

And the said John granteth, that all the tenants and their heirs... [etc. etc.] which are bound to inclose the woods of the lord, may take underwood and make them new hedges, or to repair them, as much as shall be necessary...without being impeached or grieved by the ministers of the said lord Sir John Mowbray.

And the said John granteth for him and his heirs, that all the things and articles aforesaid be of effect and force in the law, as well to those which are generally named tenants, and their heirs, and those which shall have their estate, or parcel of their estate. And if in the articles aforesaid there be any point which may have divers interpretations or intendments, that it shall be taken to the best advantage of the names, or of the tenants aforesaid, and of their heirs or of those which have their estate, and not otherwise.

In witness thereof the parties aforesaid have interchangeably put their seals. Given at our Mannor of EPWORTH, the First day of May, in the year of the Reign of EDWARD the THIRD, after the Conquest, Thirty-Three.

In the 17th century, when King Charles I allowed the Isle of Axholme to be drained by the Dutch engineer Sir Cornelius Vermuyden, the radical reallocation of land that followed meant an end of the tenants' traditional rights, and the repercussions from these arrangements, including local rioting, went on for years, long after the unfortunate Charles was beheaded and replaced by Oliver Cromwell. The people of the Isle claimed that the 1359 deed granted their rights in perpetuity and that the lord of the manor, no matter who it was, could not alter the status quo. In 1653 and 1654 Daniel Noddel, solicitor for the Freeholders and Commoners of the manor of Epworth, petitioned 'The Parliament of the Commonwealth of England and Every Individual Member Thereof' in an attempt to get some sort of justice for them after the loss of their livelihoods and rights. His evidence against the newcomers reveals that John de Mowbray's wishes had been followed unhindered for 300 years, and it is Noddel who tells us how and where the Mowbray Deed had been kept and when John's portrait was destroyed,

> *"The testimony of ancient witnesses in depositions upon record in the Exchequer, make it clearly appear that all things have gone according to this Deed within the said Mannor till now of late that the projectors [i.e. those who wanted to take away traditional rights] usurped a possession against law...*
>
> *The manner of keeping this Deed hath been in a Chest bound with iron in the parish Church of Haxey, being the greatest town within the Mannor, by some of the chief freeholders, who had the keeping of the keys, which chest stood under a window, wherein was the portraiture of Mowbray set in ancient glass, holding in his hand a writing which was commonly reported to be an emblem of the Deed, till now of late that the glass was broken down; this also appears in the depositions in the Exchequer."*

What happened to the original Mowbray Deed after William Riley translated it from the French remains a mystery. There is no trace of it at The Tower of London, the Lincolnshire Archives or at the National Archive (formerly the Public Record Office) at Kew, although it is just possible that it lies hidden amongst other documents there. It would be good to think that it lies in a dusty attic somewhere waiting to be rediscovered, but it is probably lost to us for all time and may have been deliberately destroyed during the Crown's confrontation with the people of the Isle. (I had wondered if the original Deed and/ or the translation could possibly be with the papers of Sir Cornelius Vermuden who drained the Isle, but so far the search has revealed nothing.)

Reply from Jeremy Ashbee of English Heritage to an enquiry made at the Tower of London, February 2004:

> *Thank you very much for your enquiry about the Mowbray Deed of 1359: I was formerly an assistant curator at the Tower and specialised in the Middle Ages.*
>
> *I am very sorry, but I have no information about this document. I would have to assume that it came to the Tower as part of the private possession of Riley. If the document was held privately by Riley, there is an outside chance that it either remained with his family, or was deposited in some other county record office where his descendants settled. The other possibility would be for the deed to be added to the Chancery records in the Tower Records, which later became the Public Record Office and now National Archive. These documents were brought out of the Tower in the mid-19th century and are now at Kew. However, we know that the records were kept in extreme disorder during periods of the 17th, 18th and 19th centuries, so it comes as little surprise that many of them have been lost.*
>
> *My instinct is that if the document is lying in a corner of the PRO, it will eventually turn up - lots of items are only catalogued in summary form. If it's in the PRO, or in private hands somewhere, it can only be good news that you are now highlighting the problem in your book.*

Stephen O'Connor at the National Archive at Kew had already kindly made a search for the Deed in August 2003:

*"Thank you for your enquiry.*

*I fear that there is no easy answer to your question. As you will appreciate, we have a large collection of ancient deeds here at Kew, but there is no guarantee that the deed you are looking for will be among them... I did a search on PROCAT under both 'Mowbray' and 'Axholme' between the years 1355 and 1365 ... but none of these appears to be the deed you are interested in; nor did the Mowbray search reveal anything obviously significant. There are several enrolments of inspeximus and confirmations of grants by Mowbray in the Patent and Close Rolls, but even if this deed, or a confirmation of it, had been enrolled, it would of course give no clue as to the current whereabouts of the original deed. As you are no doubt aware, a private deed may have ended up in private hands almost anywhere and could prove very difficult to trace. I am sorry not to be more positive.*

*Stephen O'Connor*
*Research and Editorial Services Department"*

September 2011
As yet there is no sign of the original, the only other finds have been:

SHEFFIELD ARCHIVES Bacon Frank Manuscripts ref. BFM/1159 *Copy of Deed confirming rights of the tenants of the Isle of Axeholme (Lincs.) - - date: 5 Feb 1680. Endorsed: Copy of a copy of Sir John Mowbray's Deed. Signed at Sir John's manor of Epworth, 1 May 1359. Certified a true copy by Michael Preston, clerk in Chancery.*

UNIVERSITY OF NOTTINGHAM Special Collections: *Hatfield Chase Corporation 1538-1973.* HCC 9111 is a copy of a copy of the Mowbray Deed of 1359 written by George Stovin, a member of a prominent Isle of Axholme family, c. 1752.
This manuscript was lost for many years and found in a solicitor's office in Doncaster in 1880. This (possibly a copy of the 1680 copy above?) would seem to be a copy of William Riley's 1652 translation of the original of 1359, as it is described as,

*"A true copy of the ancient deed of John de Mowbray....as it is now translated out of the French into English by William Ripley* [Riley?] *Keeper of the Records in the Tower of London."*

## WHICH JOHN DE MOWBRAY?

*WHO WAS THE SIR JOHN OF THE MOWBRAY DEED FAME, AND WHAT IS THE CORRECT DATE OF THAT DEED?*

There are two recurring inconsistencies in references to the Mowbray Deed, namely over the date it was signed and the true identity of the Isle's benefactor.

The date is always given as either 1st May 1359 or 1360, but if William Riley, translating the deed from the French in 1652 was correct in dating it as being granted in the 33rd year of the reign of Edward III, then 1359 would be the year in question, since Edward III acceded on 25th January 1327, making 25th January 1327 to 25th January 1328 year one of the reign, and so forth. This has also been confirmed by Dr. Mike Rogers of Lincolnshire Archives, using *Cheyney's Handbook of Dates for Students of English History*.

As far as the identity of the benefactor is concerned we really do need to know upon whom to heap the praise, as in its day the Mowbray Deed must have represented an exceptionally generous gesture by a great and compassionate lord towards his subjects.

Stonehouse and Read (see bibliography) both attribute the deed to John, 4th Lord Mowbray, husband of Elizabeth Segrave, the John killed near Constantinople in 1368, but since the one relies heavily upon the other it is probably correct to attribute this conclusion to Stonehouse, who went into print first. The quotes from his book that follow below are an attempt to show that if he was mistaken in his assessment of the activities of the father and son at this time, possibly by having relied too much upon Froissart, then Stonehouse could well be mistaken over the identity of the author of the Mowbray Deed. In the paragraph dealing with John 3rd Lord Mowbray (1310-61) he tells us that on the accession of Edward III John and his mother Alina were liberated from the Tower. John's political and military career takes off and,

> *"In ...1340 John was made governor of Berwick-upon-Tweed, He took part in that memorable battle near Durham against David, King of Scotland, who was there taken prisoner. John attended the King in his campaigns abroad..."*

Footnotes in Read tell us that this reference to the father is based on the writings of the chronicler Jean Froissart. The great medieval storyteller was writing after the event and had to depend largely upon hearsay, and his placing of John de Mowbray abroad at this time is known to be incorrect; in this case he has John in two places at once!

Stonehouse/Read do not specifically give a date for John's supposed cross-Channel trips, but the Battle of Crécy was the main event at the time. The Crécy campaign began in the July of 1346, at a time when John de Mowbray was with the garrison at Berwick, arguing with the bishop of Durham and the northern magnates over just who should be paying for their protection from Scottish invaders, and threatening to pack up and go home if some cash was not forthcoming. (The King already owed him a small fortune for expenses already incurred, which John had met out of his own pocket.) Therefore, John was unable to go to France himself but was ordered to send 150 Welshmen from Gower, which his family still held at this point, in time for the Battle of Crécy, fought on 26th August. In September he was unable to free himself from Berwick to attend Parliament and was forced to send a deputy. It was on 17th October that the battle with the Scots took place at Neville's Cross and the Lanercost chronicler praised John for his good grace towards the enemy. So, in the summer and autumn of 1346 John, 3rd Lord Mowbray was far too busy defending the home front to be spared for the French campaign.

> *"He had one son, John, born at Epworth A.D. 1328, by Joan his wife, who was the daughter of Henry, Earl of Lancaster. This John granted the famous deed...."*

Do we take *this John* to be the father or the son? The pedigree chart, again identical in both books, credits the younger John with granting the deed. Were it not for this chart the present writer would have suggested that, due to an ambiguity in the wording of the paragraph, researchers using Stonehouse/Read have misunderstood what they were getting at, namely that when they say *this* John it means the father, the main subject of that particular paragraph. If John the son should have the credit for something as important as the Mowbray Deed one would expect it to be included in the paragraph following, that is devoted entirely to him. However, the statement on the pedigree chart discounts this theory and Stonehouse/Read must indeed have believed the deed to be the work of John the son.

There are several problems with this, not least the status and age of John the son in 1359, the year of the deed. It is now generally accepted that the younger John was born at Epworth on 25th June 1340, and not in 1328, as Stonehouse/Read state; we know his date of birth from the Inquisitions Post Mortem on his father. When he died in 1368 he left behind a brood of small children to his wife Elizabeth Segrave (1338-1368), whom he married between 1349 and 1353. Early marriages between children of great families were not uncommon, as we have seen many times already, and it is likely that a man born in

1328 would have married earlier than 1349 and would have fathered children before the 1360's. There is no evidence that John had been married before.

Then there is the obvious question of why the nineteen-year-old son would be given the responsibility of granting such important and far-reaching rights in 1359 when his forty-eight-year-old father was in good health, and would continue to be so, as far as we know, until the Black Death killed him in 1361. Surely so great a commitment as allocating rights to commoners in perpetuity would be done in the name of the head of the family and not through the heir apparent.

> *"John de Mowbray, [i.e. John, 4th Lord Mowbray] like his father before him, stood high in the favour of the King, whom he attended to the wars in France. ...In the memorable Battle of Crécy, Mowbray is mentioned..."*

Here we are told that John the son was at Crécy, most unlikely if he was born in 1340!

For those who are not so far convinced, there are, however, two very positive pieces of evidence to show that Stonehouse was wrong in attributing the Mowbray Deed to the John who died in 1368. In his 1653 petition to Parliament, Daniel Noddel, mentioned above, includes the following statements in his summary of Mowbray involvement with area,

> *"... John Lord Mowbray, **father of this John that made the Deed**, being in rebellion with those barons that accompanied the Duke [earl] of Lancaster..."*

The rebellious father was John, 2nd Lord Mowbray who was hanged in March 1322; his son *'this John that made the Deed'* was the John who died of the plague in 1361.

> *"...Elizabeth, dowager of Thomas lord Mowbray who was **grandchild to this John that made the Deed**, had her assignation of dower through all the Mannor of Epworth."*

The dowager is Elizabeth Fitzalan whose husband, Thomas Mowbray, 1st Duke of Norfolk, was grandson of the John who died in 1361. So, from the, admittedly somewhat limited, evidence available, this writer concludes it was the Lanercost Chronicler's *'man of grace and bounty'*, John, 3rd Lord Mowbray, (1310-61), not his son John, (1340-68), who was the much-loved and respected mid-14th century benefactor of the people of the Isle of Axholme.

(Several months have passed since I wrote this appendix and last looked at the deed. Having read the translation of the document again and looked at the evidence, I believe there can be no doubt that the date was 1359 and the benefactor was indeed John 3rd Lord Mowbray. Authority for the deed was given at *'our mannor of Epworth'* and I can find no evidence that the manor had been made over to his son John.)

# Appendix G

## Thomas Mowbray's Carthusian House at Low Melwood near Epworth in the Isle of Axholme.

The Carthusian Order was founded by St Bruno in 1094 at Chartreuse near Grenoble. The motherhouse of the order is called the Grande Chartreuse, a name corrupted to *Charterhouse* in England, where only nine such houses were ever founded, the first by Henry II as penance for the death of Becket. Mount Grace Priory in Yorkshire is the best-preserved medieval Carthusian house in Europe. The monks called themselves Christ's Poor Men and lived a silent, solitary and austere life in individual houses with small gardens. The Carthusian Order as a whole suffered badly under the religious reforms of Henry VIII, when the prior of Axholme, Augustine Webster, was sentenced to be hanged, drawn and quartered for refusing to accept Henry as the Supreme Head of the Church. Augustine Webster was canonised in the twentieth century and local Roman Catholics make an annual pilgrimage to Low Melwood to remember him, 4th May being his feast day.

At the Low Melwood site there was already a Premonstratensian chapel founded over a century earlier by followers of St Norbert, dedicated to the Virgin Mary, and known locally as the *Priory of the Wood*. It is believed that a Lincolnshire branch of the Goushill family played a large part in the foundation of the earlier chapel. Thomas Mowbray's Carthusian House of the Visitation of the Blessed Virgin Mary was begun in 1397, when he was at the height of his power, but extra money was still needed for the project, and to preserve the old priory. To this end Pope Boniface IX issued a papal bull proclaiming that should a man visit the shrine on the feast day of the Blessed Virgin, confess, receive absolution *and donate alms*, he would be granted remission of sins from the day of his baptism up to the day of the visit.

In its early years the Axholme Charterhouse had mixed fortunes, but by the mid-fifteenth century it was flourishing, even though lands promised by the 2nd Duke of Norfolk did not come to the priory until the death of his widow, the exceptionally long-lived Duchess Katherine, decades later. The 2nd Duke was buried in the priory and left instructions in his will for his father's remains to be conveyed thither from Venice where he had died in 1399, but this never happened and as late as the 1530's the third Howard Duke of Norfolk was still making enquiries through the Venetian Ambassador. Neither does any trace still exist of the Mowbray alabaster tomb, which, considering the social standing of the occupant, must have been a great work of late medieval art. Today what little remains of the monastery forms part of farm buildings on private land and is not open to the general public.

The North Lincolnshire Museum Sites & Monument Record (SMR) 2471 contains various documents relating to the monastery and includes a description of the site by English Heritage,

> *"The core of the site is a roughly square moated island 148 metres across, surrounded on at least three sides by a 10-metre wide moat ditch. The moated island formed the inner court of the Charterhouse and contains well-preserved earthworks of the priory's cloister, including the cells with their individual small courtyard gardens, which are typical of Carthusian monasteries."*

Foundations of these features, including the monks' cells, show up very clearly on the Royal Commission on the Historical Monuments of England Geophysical Report 95/12 - *Axholme Priory, Humberside*, which is also to be found in SMR 2471, together with the Royal Commission on the Historical Monuments of England Archaeological Report NMR N° SE80 SW3, *Axholme Priory Humberside.*

Following the dissolution in 1539 the estate was granted to John Candysshe of West Butterwick, who used the buildings as a quarry for materials for a fine new house surrounded by gardens and orchards. This was partly rebuilt in the 1680s and the whole rebuilt in the mid 19th century. In the 1960s the remaining building was partly demolished, lowered to single storey and converted to a storehouse for the farm; it was given Grade II Listed Building status in September 1987. The ashlar relief tablet bearing Mowbray arms and mantled helm, was reset in the 1960s. Earlier descriptions of the house, including references to a stone pillar in the cellar, suggest that the house itself was built on the foundations of the priory church, which would be very strong, so it is possible that the second Duke and his wife, Duchess Katherine, lie at rest under what is now a store for farm machinery. There is a local tradition of a tunnel at Low Melwood Farm that links the religious house with the Mowbrays' Epworth mansion, but the distance between them is about three miles, and it would serve no obvious purpose. The author has spoken to residents who recall playing on the farmland as children over 60 years ago and finding an entrance to an arched tunnel: could this have been part of an undercroft or crypt? One lady said that playing there was magical and used to make her feel like a princess.

# APPENDIX H

## RAWDON BROWN AND THE 'MOWBRAY STONE', VENICE 1841

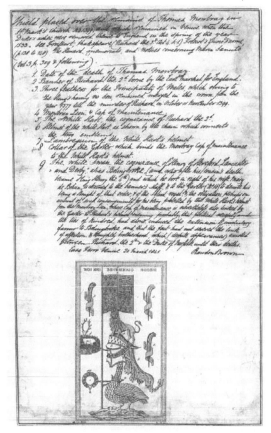

*Shield placed over the remains of Thomas Mowbray in St Mark's Church[a] A.D. 1399 and which remained in Venice when the Duke's ashes were removed thence to England in the spring of the year 1532[b]. See Froissart, Shakespeare (Richard the 2nd Act 4 sc. 1)[c]...*

1 *Date of the death of Thomas Mowbray* - [added to the drawing and the plaster cast by Brown!]

2 *Banner of Richard II borne by the Earl Marshal for England.*

3 *Three feathers for the principality of Wales, which owing to the king's having no son, remained merged in the crown from the year 1377 till the murder of Richard in October or November 1399.*

4 *Mowbray Lion and cap of maintenance.*

5 *The White Hart, the cognisance of Richard II.*

6 *Helmet of the White Hart as shown by the chain which connects the two emblems.*

7 *Lambrequin of the White Hart's helmet.*

8 *Collar of the Garter, which binds the Mowbray cap of maintenance to the White Hart's helmet.*

9 *The White Swan, the cognisance of Henry of Hereford, Lancaster and Derby, alias Bolingbroke (and who after his cousin's death became King Henry IV) and which he bore*

*in right of his wife Mary de Bohun is chained to the banner's staff and to the Garter (10) to denote his being a Knight of that order and of the blood royal, and the obligations perhaps on account of such consanguinity for his being protected by the White Hart's helmet from the Mowbray lion whose cap of maintenance is nevertheless also linked by the Garter to Richard's helmet meaning, probably, that political necessity and the ties of kindred had alone induced the extension of involuntary favour to Bolingbroke and that the fact had not severed the link of affection and knightly brotherhood which (despite appearances) existed between Richard II and the Duke of Norfolk until their deaths.*

*Casa Ferro Venice 20 March 1841 Rawdon Brown*

a  It is generally believed to have been St George's.
b  There is no evidence that the remains were returned.
c  Froissart and Shakespeare are not reliable.

According to the enthusiastic and optimistic Victorian antiquarian Rawdon Brown, writing in the *Preface* to the *Calendar of State Papers Relating to English Affairs in the Archives of Venice,* of which he was the editor, there was evidence that in 1682 a monumental achievement was to be seen in the external gallery of the Ducal Palace, where it had long been embedded in the wall opposite to St Georgio Maggiore, a church dedicated to the patron saint of England. In 1810, during the French occupation of Venice, this stone, bearing the arms of England, was ordered to be defaced, but the workman, instead of destroying the fine carving, incorporated it into a pavement face downwards. Brown claims to have found the man in 1839, one Domenico Spiera, who helped him recover it; he then sent it to Mowbray descendants at Corby Castle near Carlisle, where it is still located. He admitted the theft and presented the Venetians with a plaster cast - to which he added Thomas Mowbray's date of death - and they exhibited it in the *Palazzo Ducale*! At some stage this strange copy found its way back to England and now lives in all its gilded and painted glory at Madingley Hall, Cambridge University.

There were doubts in England over this interpretation from the start, and it was thought possible that the so-called 'Mowbray Stone' was more correctly associated with a visit Henry Bolingbroke had made to Venice in the early 1390's.

*Reproduced by kind permission of the Society of Genealogists, London.*

# APPENDIX I

## THE BATTLES OF THE WARS OF THE ROSES

| | |
|---|---|
| 1455 (2 May) | First Battle of St Albans; the Duke of Somerset killed. The 3rd Duke of Norfolk arrives too late for the battle. |
| 1459 (23 September) | Blore Heath |
| 1460 (10 July) | Northampton. |
| 1460 (30 December) | Wakefield; Richard of York and his second son killed. |
| 1461 (2 February) | Mortimers Cross; Owen Tudor captured and beheaded. |
| 1461 (17 February) | Second Battle of St Albans; Elizabeth Woodville's first husband killed. |
| 1461 (29 March) | Towton; the worst casualty figures for any British battle, before or since. The Duke of Norfolk arrives late again but with his 5,000 men turns the tide in favour of the Yorkists. |
| 1464 (25 April) | Hedgeley Moor |
| 1464 (15 May) | Hexham |
| 1464 (14 June) | Bamburgh Castle |
| 1469 (26 July) | Edgecote |
| 1470 (12 March) | Empingham |
| 1471 (14 April) | Barnet; Warwick the Kingmaker killed. |
| 1471 (12 May) | Tewkesbury; the young Prince of Wales killed. |
| 1485 (22 August) | Bosworth; Henry Tudor victorious. John Howard and Richard III killed. |
| 1487 (16 June) | Stoke Field; Tudor defeats supporters of the pretender Lambert Simnel, whom the Earl of Lincoln is passing off as Edward, Earl of Warwick, son of Richard's brother the Duke of Clarence. Henry Tudor already has the real Edward imprisoned in the Tower. |

# Appendix J

### Extracts from Certain of the Paston Letters

William Paston, 2nd Earl of Yarmouth, sold the famous Paston Letters and other significant documents to the antiquary Peter le Neve in the eighteenth century. Neve's widow married Thomas Martin of Pargrave in Norfolk and the documents changed hands then went missing for a time and were assumed to have been forgeries. They are now scattered amongst the British Library, Orwell Park Ipswich, the Bodleian Library Oxford, Magdalen College Oxford and Pembroke College Cambridge.
(Additional comments – Marilyn Roberts, 2004)

## Volume I
### Letter 44
### After 1444(?)

Katherine, Dowager Duchess of Norfolk to John Paston

(Duchess Katherine has arranged to stay at the Pastons' London house on Fleet Street. Furniture and furnishings travelled with their owners in medieval times and the 'stuff' she is about to send on will be her own beds, bedding, linen, wall hangings, and possibly other pieces of furniture. She is writing from the Vinegarth in Epworth.)

*To our right trusty and hertily wellbeloved John Paston, Squier.*

*Kateryn Duchesse*
*of Norff.*

*Right trusty and entirely wellbeloved, we grete you well hertily as we kan. And for as moche as we purpose with grace of Jesu to be at London within bryff tyme, we pray you that your place ther be redy for us, for we wole sende our stuff thedir to for [before] our comying; and siche agreement as we toke with you for the same, we shall duely perform yt with the might of Jesu, who haff you in his blessed keping.*

*Wryten at Eppeworth 2nd day of Octobre.*

## INTRODUCTORY VOLUME
### LETTER XIV
### 10ᵀᴴ JULY 1449 (?)

SIR JOHN FASTOLF TO JOHN PASTON

(Fastolf did not reside at Caister castle, which he built for his retirement, until 1454 and it would appear that for some reason the date of 1449 was added later. Fastolf wants Paston to put pressure on the Prior to pay the back rent for lands in Hellesdon manor. Calling someone *'cosen'* does not necessarily mean the two are related, but it seems likely that in this case they were. The spelling of the word Parlement reminds us that in French *'parley ment'* originally meant a talking place.)

*To the worshypful, and my right well beloved cosen, John Paston.*
*WORSHYPFULL and right welbelovyd cosyn, I comaund me to you. Plese you to here that the Pryore and Convent of Norwyche have wythalden certeyn rent for the landes that they have halden of me wythinne my maner of Haylysdon,* [goes on to grumble about money owing for wax candles, etc.]…..*Praying you to speak with the Pryore…that ye lyke to move hym to make me payment of his dewtee is, so y have no cause to give further, and to do as justic requyreth…. More over y pray you, cosen, that y may speke with you or* [before] *y ride, and that on Thursday by the ferthest; and then y shall tell you tydyng of the Parlement, and that ye fayle not as my trust ys yn you. I pray God have you in Hys guidance.*

*Wreten at Castor, the x day of Julie 1449.*
*Your cosen*

*John Fastolfe.*

❦

## VOLUME I
### LETTER 121
### 22ᴺᴰ OCTOBER 1450 (?)

('*Right trusti and right welbelovid*' is a common form of greeting.)

THE DUKE OF NORFOLK TO JOHN PASTON.

*Oure right trusty and welbeloved servaunt, John Paston, Squier,*

*The Duc of Norffolk*

*Right trusti and right welbelovid, we grete yo hertily well, praying you specially that ye will make you ready to awayte upon us at Yippiswich toward the Parlement the 8ᵗʰ day of Novembre in your best array, with as many clenly people as ye may gete for our worship at this tyme; for we will be ther like oure estate in oure best wise without any delay. Yeven under our signet in our Castell of Framlyingham, the 22ⁿᵈ of Octobre.*

# INTRODUCTORY VOLUME
## LETTER LXXII
### 18ᵀᴴ MAY 1467

THE DUKE OF NORFOLK TO SIR JOHN HOWARD.

(This is the last Mowbray duke, father of the Lady Anne, and with his death the dukedom became extinct; Sir John Howard, son of Mowbray's great-aunt Margaret Mowbray, became Duke of Norfolk in a new creation under Richard III in 1483.

The tournament referred to was between Lord Scales (Anthony Woodville, later Lord Rivers, brother-in-law of Edward IV) and the Bastard of Burgundy (Count la Roche, half-brother of Charles the Bold, making him the brother-in-law of Edward IV's sister Margaret), at Smithfield, 11-12 June 1467, when Mowbray would have been expected to be responsible for the arrangements and be in attendance as Earl Marshal. This was a major social event as both were greatly accomplished knights; the contest was fought on horse and foot over two days and was declared a draw. Whether the *'great infirmity and disease'* that God had inflicted upon John Mowbray was of a serious nature is not known, but obviously he was expecting to be indisposed for some time; he died nine years later at the age of 31.)

*The Duke of Norfolk*

*RYGTH trusty and enteerly beloved Cousyn I comaunde me to you with all myn herte. And lyke it you to wete that God hath vyset me with grete infirmite and disease, wherthurgh I neyther can nor may at this season and comynge of the Bastard of Burgoyne attend to th'execucion of myn office, as my wyll and duete were to, in myne*

216

*owne persone. Wherefor of verray necessite I must depute suche a person in all goodly hast to occupye as my deputee and to have my full power undere me at that season as is both of birth honorable and in all other wyse lykly.*

(He goes on to tell Howard what a very good sort of chap he is, etc. Howard himself acted as deputy to the Earl Marshal on this occasion.)

*Wryten under my signet the 18ᵗʰ day of May.*

◈

## VOLUME III
### LETTER 715
### 1472??

JOHN PASTON TO THE DUKE OF NORFOLK

(The younger John Paston (III) is tactfully asking for the restoration of Caister Castle to his brother, Sir John Paston (II). Although the language is very proper and suitably grovelling, Paston tries to shame the Duke by appealing to the better side of his nature through references to charity, the law and good conscience.)

The letter ends:

*Wherfor as I have ofte tymes befor thys, I beseech your good grace at the reverence of God, and in the waye of charyte, that my sed brodyr may by your hyghness be agan restoryed in to the possession of the sey maner, according to the lawe and good conscyence; and wee shall prey to God for the preservacion of your most nobyll estate.*

◈

## VOLUME III
### LETTER 768
### 17ᵀᴴ JANUARY 1476

LETTER FROM SIR JOHN PASTON TO HIS BROTHER JOHN, OR PERHAPS EVEN TO HIS MOTHER, MARGARET PASTON.

(Sir John is thought to have gone to Framlingham Castle in an attempt to reason with the 4<sup>th</sup> Duke of Norfolk over the latter's continued occupation of Caister Castle. John Mowbray, who had no son, has died suddenly in the early hours of the morning and the dukedom will become extinct. By sending home for the cloth of tissue he had purchased for his own father's tomb, John Paston (II) is trying to ingratiate himself with the newly widowed Duchess, Elizabeth Talbot, in order to get her support over his claim to Caister. Like his mother, John Paston is not impressed with the local shops and suppliers, '*thys contre is nott well purveyd...*' The hearse was an ornamental cage over a tomb often covered with expensive material, only a handful of which survive, the most famous being that of Richard Beauchamp, Earl of Warwick in the Collegiate Church of St Mary, Warwick. Paston has already told the late Duke's Council that he can get the material and promises his mother it will be returned safely to her. It needed to be sent as soon as possible, either with 'Sym' or 'Mother Brown'.)

> *Lyke it you to weete, that not in the most happy season ffor me, it is so ffortuned, that wher as my Lorde of Norffolke, yisterdaye beying in goode heele, this nyght dyed abowte mydnyghte ...And it is soo, that thys contre is nott well purveyd off clothe off golde for the covering of hys bodye and herse.... Wherffore please it yow to sende me worde iff it be so, that ye have, or kan kom by the clothe off tyssywe that I bought for our ffadre's tombe....and I undertake it shal be saved again for yow at my peril...I deem hereby to get great thanks and great assistance in time to come... Within 4 dayes I hope to see yowe.*
>
> *Wreten of Wednysdaye 17<sup>th</sup> daye of Janyver.*
>
> *John Paston K.*

## VOLUME III
### LETTER 771
### 27<sup>TH</sup> JANUARY 1476

SIR JOHN PASTON (II) TO HIS BROTHER JOHN PASTON (III)

(Sir John reports that he is facing criticism from the Mowbray household for bringing up the subject of Caister Castle with Duchess Elizabeth so soon after her husband's death. The letter contains other references to the property but then, after sending greetings to his mother, the writer expresses his worries about the thought of Edward IV marrying off his younger son to the little Lady Anne Mowbray, now Countess of Norfolk; possibly he expects the King to claim Caister Castle for the boy. There is some speculation that the Duchess could be carrying her late husband's son, but, if a baby was born, it did not survive. Edward restored the castle to the Pastons within months, even though, as John had predicted, the two young children did marry and Edward used Parliament to secure the little girl's money and property for his son. )

> .....*I praye you recomande me to my mooder, and latte us alle prey God sende my Lady off Norffolk a soone ...for if the Kynge's soone mary my lord's dowghter, the Kynge wolde that hys soone sholde have a ffayr place in Norffolk.*

## VOLUME III
### LETTER 884
### AUGUST 1485

THE DUKE OF NORFOLK TO JOHN PASTON

(Written after John Howard, Duke of Norfolk, received news that Henry Tudor had landed at Milford Haven with an army of about 2,000 French mercenaries and an assortment of both Lancastrian and Yorkist exiles on the evening of 7th August and was meeting little resistance in Wales and the West Country. Howard, known as 'Jockey', or 'Jack', of Norfolk, and who by now could have been in his early to mid-sixties, was the son of Lady Margaret Mowbray and Sir Robert Howard. He was a loyal supporter of Richard III who had conferred the dukedom of Norfolk upon him after the late Anne Mowbray's husband Prince Richard of York and his brother Edward V had been declared illegitimate. The tone of his letter makes one feel he was a great friend to the Pastons but he had, in the past, supported his bullying Mowbray cousins in the struggles against them.

It is possible that the King did not learn of Tudor's landing for 4 days, so it is small wonder that Howard's letter had to be delivered to Paston in haste if the company of tall men had to be assembled, kitted out and made ready for action before his meeting with Norfolk at Bury St Edmunds, Suffolk. Deference to Our Lady made King Richard set out later than was wise, but he would have done well to set forth upon the Day of the Assumption of Our Lady on 15th August, for he arrived at Bosworth ill-prepared. The Pastons were Lancastrian by sympathy and it is not absolutely certain that the contingent of tall men ever materialised.

This is one of Howard's last letters, as he was killed at Bosworth on 22nd August 1485.)

*To my welbelovyd frend, John Paston, be thyss byll delyveryd in hast.*

*WELBELOVYD frend, I cummaunde me to yow, letyng yow to undyrstond that the Kyngs enmysse be a land, and that the Kynge wold hafe set forthe as uppon Monday but only for Howre Lady Day; but for serten he gothe forward as upon Tewsday, for a servant of myne browt to me the sertente.*

*Wherfor, I pray yow that ye met with me at Bery* [Burry St Edmunds], *for by the grace of God, I purposse to lye at Bery as upon Tewsday nyght, and that ye brynge with yow seche company of tall men as ye may goodly make at my cost and charge, be seyd that ye have promysyd the Kyng; and I pray yow ordeyne them jackets of my levery, and I shall contente yow at your metyng with me.*

*Yower lover*
*J. Norffolk*

Taken from *The Paston Letters, 1422-1509 A.D.* Edited by James Gairdner of the Public Record Office and published in Edinburgh 1910.

# Appendix K

## Elizabeth Fitzalan's Grandsons
## and the Battle of Bosworth

An Elizabeth Fitzalan/Thomas Mowbray grandson, John Howard, Duke of Norfolk, fought against Elizabeth Fitzalan/Robert Goushill grandsons, Lord Thomas and Sir William Stanley, at the Battle of Bosworth, 22nd August 1485.

The date of birth of the Lady Margaret Mowbray, daughter of Thomas Mowbray and Elizabeth Fitzalan is not known for certain but was probably around 1388; her husband, Sir Robert Howard of Stoke Neyland, was born around 1383. Their son John became Duke of Norfolk under Richard III, whom he served loyally, and for whose cause he perished at the Battle of Bosworth in 1485.

Thomas Mowbray died in exile in 1399, and in 1401 his widow Elizabeth married Sir Robert Goushill of Hoveringham, by whom she had the daughters Joan and Elizabeth, but the new family's happiness was short-lived, for Sir Robert was killed in 1403 at the Battle of Shrewsbury. Joan Goushill married Sir Thomas Stanley, later Lord Stanley of Lathom, who was born around 1405 and died in 1459. Lord Stanley was Lord Lieutenant of Ireland in 1430, Justice of Chester, Flintshire and North Wales in 1448, Warden of Calais in 1451 and a Knight of the Shire in 1455-56. Joan Goushill was the mother of Lord Thomas Stanley, later Earl of Derby, and of Sir William Stanley, who was beheaded in the 1490's.

The younger Thomas Stanley took as his second wife the Lady Margaret Beaufort, Countess of Richmond, widow of Edmund Tudor and a descendant of John of Gaunt, Duke of Lancaster. These were the years of the Wars of the Roses, but the Lady Margaret managed to stay at Court through the rule of both the Lancastrian Henry VI and the Yorkists Edward IV and Richard III, although latterly she worked covertly with Edward's widow, Queen Elizabeth Woodville, towards the overthrow of King Richard. The two mothers planned the marriage of their children Henry Tudor, Earl of Richmond, and Princess Elizabeth Plantagenet, Elizabeth of York being the heiress of Edward IV once his two sons were assumed murdered. The accession of Richard III was the death-knell for the ambitious Woodvilles. Elizabeth, to whom Richard disparagingly referred as, *'Dame Elizabeth Grey, lately calling herself Queen of England'*, had to bear not only the death of her husband and the disappearance of her young sons, but also the execution of her brother Anthony and of Mowbray descendant

## Chart 14: *The Stanley Connection*

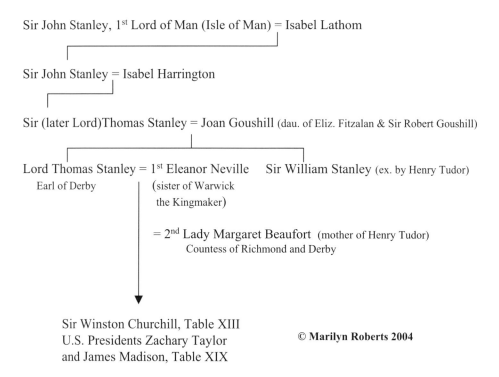

Sir John Stanley, 1ˢᵗ Lord of Man (Isle of Man) = Isabel Lathom

Sir John Stanley = Isabel Harrington

Sir (later Lord)Thomas Stanley = Joan Goushill (dau. of Eliz. Fitzalan & Sir Robert Goushill)

Lord Thomas Stanley = 1ˢᵗ Eleanor Neville     Sir William Stanley (ex. by Henry Tudor)
    Earl of Derby       (sister of Warwick
           the Kingmaker)

= 2ⁿᵈ Lady Margaret Beaufort (mother of Henry Tudor)
     Countess of Richmond and Derby

Sir Winston Churchill, Table XIII
U.S. Presidents Zachary Taylor
and James Madison, Table XIX

**© Marilyn Roberts 2004**

Richard Grey, one of her sons by her first marriage to Sir John Grey, who was charged with 'estranging' Edward V from his uncle, then imprisoned in Pontefract Castle and beheaded.

Henry Tudor, aged twenty-eight in 1485, had spent much of his life in exile in France but in the mid 1480's, he found himself the leader of the Lancastrians through the lineage of his mother. Margaret Beaufort, exceptionally intelligent and well-read, was wise enough to realise that a woman could not hope to succeed as a ruler in those troubled times, and fully supported her beloved only child; what a pity she never knew that her great-granddaughter, Queen Elizabeth I, would be one of the greatest rulers, and certainly the best-educated monarch, Britain has ever had.

Thomas Stanley was put in a very awkward position when it became apparent that Henry Tudor would invade and claim the throne by right of his mother, for although the would-be usurper was his own stepson, Stanley had sworn allegiance to King Richard. He made an excuse to go to his northern estates, and in July, when a suspicious Richard commanded that he return to Court, he pleaded he was a victim of the dreaded and frequently fatal sweating sickness and not well enough to travel. Richard, based at the time at Nottingham Castle, then demanded he send to him his eldest son, Lord Strange, as hostage against his father's possible defection. Strange attempted to escape and in the subsequent questioning implicated his uncle, Sir William, in treasonable activities, but not his father.

On 7th August Henry Tudor landed at Milford Haven with 2,000 mercenaries and various disaffected English, both Lancastrians and Yorkists, and met with hardly any resistance as he made his way through Wales, even though Sir William Stanley was Chamberlain of North Wales and could have made more effort to stop him. Arriving in the Midlands almost unopposed, and gathering more men every day, Henry knew his numbers were still far short of those of his enemy and must have been aching to see what the Stanleys were planning to do, for although they were on the march with a force of between 3,000-4,000 men between them, their intentions were clear to nobody, and even after he managed a meeting with them at Atherstone on 20th August, Henry was still not sure of them. On 21st August King Richard made his way from Nottingham to Leicester, wearing around his helmet the famous circlet of gold later found upon the field of battle.

Meanwhile, John Howard, that other grandson of Elizabeth Fitzalan, was preparing to serve as a leading man in the army of Richard III. John Howard, Duke of Norfolk, was placed at the centre of the action, on Ambion Hill, but the Stanleys were on the periphery, ideally placed to sit it out and wait to see which way the battle was going to go before finally committing themselves to one side or the other. Richard knew what was going on and sent a message to Thomas Stanley that if he didn't immediately declare himself for the King his son would be beheaded, but even though the chilling response from Stanley was that he had other sons, Lord Strange survived Bosworth.

The Stanleys stood idly by until they could see Richard was in serious trouble as he took the decision to break free from the thick of the action and make for Tudor to try to kill him off, thus depriving the Lancastrians of their reason for being there. It was only as Richard was being hacked to death that Lord Thomas and his brother came down on the side of Henry Tudor. Supposed eyewitness accounts tell us that it was Thomas Stanley himself who placed the King's fallen golden circlet on his stepson Henry Tudor's head at a place ever since called Crown Hill.

John Howard was killed early in the battle. His kinsmen, the Stanley brothers, went on to achieve great things, Lord Thomas becoming Earl of Derby, while his younger brother was made Lord Chamberlain and given large grants of land, making him one of the richest commoners in the realm. However, in the 1490's Sir William was implicated in the Perkin Warbeck conspiracy against Henry Tudor, now King Henry VII, who agonised over the decision but concluded that he had no option but to behead his stepfather's brother. Perkin Warbeck was claiming to be Anne Mowbray's husband, Richard Duke of York.

# APPENDIX L

PALGRAVE WILLIAMS – AMERICAN PIRATE,
AND
EDWARD MARIA WINGFIELD – FIRST PRESIDENT OF THE VIRGINIA PLANTATION, 1607.

Descendants of Elizabeth Fitzalan and Sir Robert Goushill through the Wingfield family. (Both appear on TABLE XX)

## PALGRAVE WILLIAMS

The Palgrave sisters, Mary and Sarah, were born in Norfolk where their father, Dr. Richard Palgrave, a descendant of Elizabeth Fitzalan and Sir Robert Goushill's granddaughter Elizabeth Wingfield, was rector of Barnham Broom, and travelled to America with their parents on the Winthrop Fleet of 1630. Mary, born about 1618, married Roger Wellington, a planter of Watertown, Massachusetts, in about 1637, and by him had six children, one of whom, Benjamin Wellington, was an ancestor of George Bush and George W. Bush, Presidents of the United States. Sarah Palgrave was born in about 1621 and in 1648 married Dr. John Alcock, son of George Alcock, who had also sailed with the Winthrop Fleet. They had nine children including Joanna, who married Ephraim Hunt and was an ancestor of President Franklin Delano Roosevelt.

Every family has its black sheep, however, and the Palgraves were no exception. Sarah's daughter Anna Alcock married John Williams, Attorney General of Rhode Island, and it is their son, Palgrave Williams, who brought disgrace on the family by having a mid-life crisis at thirty-nine and abandoning his very respectable wife and children to become a pirate. He became quartermaster to the notorious Captain Samuel 'Black Sam' Bellamy and participated in a raid on the New England coast when three men were kidnapped and forced into service under him. Following the wreck of Captain Bellamy and his fleet in 1717, Palgrave Williams, whose vessel remained undamaged, is alleged to have sailed to the Bahamas where he set up a supply base for pirates.

Based on an Extract from *History & Lineage of the Palgraves*, Palgrave Society 1978. (Thanks to Derek Palgrave for this information.)

## EDWARD MARIA WINGFIELD

Elizabeth Wingfield's brother, Sir John, sheriff of Norfolk and Suffolk who died in 1481, was one of seven sons Elizabeth Goushill bore Sir Robert Wingfield. John's son, Sir Richard Wingfield of Kimbolton Castle, was Ambassador to Spain, and died in Toledo in 1525. Sir Richard's son, Thomas Maria Wingfield, M.P. for Huntingdon, was the father of Edward Maria Wingfield, who became the first President of the Virginia Plantation in 1607.

# APPENDIX M

## A MOWBRAY CONNECTION WITH THE UNIVERSITIES OF OXFORD AND CAMBRIDGE[1]

This line of enquiry is in its very early stages and so far has revealed only one candidate, whose identity does not sit easily with the rest of the main branch of the family, but who is probably connected with the Kirklington branch.

JOHN MOWBRAY (MOMBRAY, MOUBRAY)

| | |
|---|---|
| Born 1350 | Yorkshire. |
| | Father, Sir John Mowbray, knight. |
| 1369 | awarded BA degree. |
| 1369 (3rd May) | granted a papal dispensation to hold a benefice with cure of souls on attaining his 20th year. |
| 1369 | rector of Ripley, Yorks. |
| | Held various religious appointments but never achieved the ecclesiastical greatness of that first Mowbray to set foot in England, namely bishop Geoffrey of Coutances. |
| 1379 | one of the committee of 12 appointed by the Chancellor of Oxford University to examine Wycliffe's writings.[2] |
| | As an envoy of Richard II he was granted safe conduct to pass through the Duchy of Milan. |
| October 1389 | died in Rome. |

[1] *Biographical Register of the University of Oxford to A.D. 1500,* Volume II.

[2] John Wycliffe, who was Master of Balliol College Oxford, believed that the established Church was corrupt, all men were equal in the sight of God, and that not even the Pope could be sure of salvation. His followers, because of their habit of quiet prayer, were nicknamed *Lollards*, a Dutch word meaning a 'mumbler'. He was lucky to live, since what he preached was regarded as heresy. At his trial of 1377 John of Gaunt spoke on his behalf, and the following year Joan

Plantagenet, the Black Prince's widow, spoke up for him. In 1380 he translated the Bible into English, but possession of a copy was illegal. In 1401 the Act of Parliament *De Heretico Comburendo* [On the Burning of Heretics] was introduced and many Lollards, including Sir John Oldcastle, possibly in his youth a page to Thomas 1st Duke of Norfolk, were consigned to the flames and died a most noble death. In 1429 a priest named John Waddon was in the custody of the 2nd Duke of Norfolk at Framlingham Castle before being burnt to death as a Lollard.

# Appendix N

## Syria, December 2005 - In search of Sir Roger de Mowbray

It was recently my very good fortune to take a short holiday in Syria, a journey that proved to be one of the most rewarding I have ever undertaken. Yes, convoluted politics and exotic-sounding allegiances that confound and confuse many westerners can make this an anxious part of the world in which to find oneself, and with the Iraq debacle showing little sign of sorting itself, we did wonder what sort of reception a small party of Britons (17) could expect. We need not have worried: the Syrian people were invariably courteous, helpful and welcoming, and theft and muggings appear to be almost unheard of. At one very pleasant traditional restaurant where we had lunch the wrought iron stair banisters had been draped with Christmas greenery and *Jingle bells* was playing in the background 'so that you can feel at home'. Tourists are still a bit of a novelty and I shall never forget the droves of excited schoolchildren in Aleppo Museum who wanted to practise their English on real westerners.

Syria is a beautiful country with vast ancient sites like Ugarit, Ebla, Palmyra and Apamea, many of them World Heritage Sites we in Europe hear little or nothing about, and on a scale that cannot possibly be comprehended from photographs. There is also the string of mighty fortresses associated with the Crusaders, and what an outrageous and daunting adventure it must have been in the twelfth century when knights such as Sir Roger de Mowbray set off for the Holy Land. The hardships endured by long-distance travellers in the days before seasickness tablets, bottled water and diarrhoea remedies must have been unmentionable, quite apart from the toll on the general health; and that's before the fighting had even started!

Roger took part in the Second Crusade, and I found myself thinking about him often, and not just when we visited the great castle Le Krak des Chevaliers ('the Castle of the Knights' that Lawrence of Arabia declared to be the finest castle in the world), the Saladin Citadel near Latakia, also one of the greatest of the Crusader castles, or the great Citadel of Aleppo. Close to the 1½-mile long remains of the colonnaded main street of the vast Roman city of Apamea, Qalaat al-Mudiq Citadel is still occupied by local people who resolutely refuse to leave their village within the castle's all-embracing walls, where huddled rooftops now bristle with satellite dishes so that they can follow the fortunes of Manchester United. Was Sir Roger de Mowbray ever here, in these exotic and majestic places?

I thought about him as we made our way through the narrow streets of Old Damascus, barricaded in July 1148 by terrified citizens who thought they were facing a protracted siege. Roger was a religious man so would he, I wondered, have ventured down the Street Called Straight to the house of Ananias where the blind St. Paul was taken to have his sight restored after the incident on the road to Damascus? Walking down that street, I from North Lincolnshire, ancient Mowbray territory, was as far removed in time from Sir Roger as he was from St Paul, and yet he would not go very far from my thoughts.

One has, however, to be realistic: yes, I was retracing his steps across Syria in general, but the only time Roger was likely to be inside the city's defences was if he had been taken there as an old man in 1187 with other of Saladin's prisoners waiting to be ransomed after the horrific battle of Hittîn near the Sea of Galilee to the south.

Eight hundred years on and Syria appears to tolerate a rich and varied brew of religious beliefs. We saw that several Christian households and businesses were already putting up Christmas decorations, including the occasional inflatable Father Christmas complete with red-nosed reindeer, something one suspects would not appeal too much to Sir Roger and his companions, if by some miraculous intervention they could be here with us today.

November 2011
Sadly, six years on from the visit, Syria is in the throes of revolution and almost daily the television news is bringing images of the sufferings. Let us hope that this volatile, yet beautiful, part of the world will soon be granted the calm and peace its people deserve.

# Places to Visit.

*Epworth:* the grassy area where the Mowbray mansion or fortified manor house once stood is adjacent to St Andrew's Church on a piece of land known locally as the 'Vinegarth'; a floor tile excavated from the site and bearing the Mowbray lion is to be found a few hundred yards away on display at The Old Rectory, once the home of the Wesleys. Also St Andrew's Church with its Mowbray lion in the porch.

*Haxey Church:* 'the cathedral of the Isle' is of majestic proportions for a country church. A Mowbray lion is to be found in one of the windows of otherwise plain glass; could this have been the location of the stained-glass portrait of John, 3rd Lord Mowbray holding the famous Mowbray Deed? There is a marvellous kneeler worked by Miss Charlotte Leggott between 1956-58, which includes her idea of what the image of John might have been like.

*The Haxey Hood Game – Haxey & Westwoodside Villages:* a good natured rough-and-tumble of a game rather like a gigantic rugby scrum played in muddy fields and village streets with the object of pushing Lady Mowbray's hood, now a tough rope in a leather cylinder, to one of the pubs in the villages of Haxey or Westwoodside. Held annually on 6th January. The Mowbray lion badge, argent (silver) on gules (red), fixed to an ancient post on Green Hill is believed to have associations with Elizabeth Fitzalan and Thomas Mowbray.

*The Carthusian monastery at Low Melwood:* between Epworth and Owston Ferry: the few remains are part of a working farm and are not accessible to the public. However, local company Gordon Video Services has produced *Epworth and the Wesleys*, which not only features the monastery, but also Epworth and the surrounding Mowbray territory and explains the family's importance to the area and their links with the historic practice of strip farming.

*Owston Ferry:* this Trentside village is the 'Kinard Ferry' of Mowbray times; of Roger de Mowbray's supposedly impregnable castle only the earthworks remain in a tranquil little corner of England adjacent to the beautiful church.

*LINCOLNSHIRE*

*Lincoln:*
It was here in Lincoln that Roger de Mowbray found himself on the losing side in the Stephen and Matilda conflict and his grandson William de Mowbray, the Magna Carta baron, was captured in 1217, when many of the city's women and children drowned in the River Witham.

**Lincoln Castle:** has one of only four remaining copies of Magna Carta signed by King John. This medieval city with its great cathedral towering above on the ridge also has associations with John of Gaunt and Katherine Swynford. Katherine lived near Lincoln Cathedral after John's death and was buried there with their daughter Joan Beaufort, the mother of Katherine Neville, Duchess of Norfolk.

## YORKSHIRE

The Mowbrays had huge holdings throughout the county and some connections remain.

**The city of York** is a mass of connections with the medieval Mowbrays.

### York Minster

*Stone shields:*

The nave: west of the Tower – colourful stone shields representing many of the great nobles who fought in the Scottish campaigns of Edwards I and II; the silver Mowbray lion on its red background is on the south side, third from the great West Door, in illustrious company including Percy, Warenne, Edward I, Margaret of France, de Bohun. East of the tower Mowbray is represented on the sixth shield on the south side, again in the company of the greatest names in the land, including Edward III and the Black Prince.

In the South Choir transept the Mowbray shield is surmounted by a female head, from its date it is very possibly that of Elizabeth Fitzalan.

*Stained glass:*

Clerestory north side of the nave – two Mowbray lions; choir clerestory south side, Mowbray lion facing Arundel and Fitzalan opposite. The Peter de Dene window north side of the nave was donated by a Minster canon between 1304 and 1320; images include Edward I, Margaret of France, Eleanor of Castile, and some smaller figures, including the John de Mowbray hanged in at York in 1322. The St William window, north choir transept, thought to have been given by Margaret, Lady Roos in memory of her sons killed in France in 1421; scenes include her son John with his wife Marjory Despenser on whose gown are the arms of Despenser quartering Goushill.

*St Stephen's Chapel*, the tomb of Richard Scrope, Archbishop of York, beheaded at York with Thomas Mowbray in 1405. Henry IV, disturbed because he had sanctioned the prelate's death, allowed Scrope to be buried in the Minster in a plain tomb but it was not until 1972 that the Scrope family was granted permission to decorate it.

**The Holy Trinity Church** on Goodramgate: here can be found the stained glass Mowbray lion with its remarkable set of teeth.

*Clifford's Tower:* Sir Roger de Clifford's body was hung in chains over the castle keep in 1322 after the Battle of Boroughbridge.

*St George's Fields:* given to the Templars by the Mowbrays, the fields are now a public car park.

A walk on or beside the city walls is essential and will include:

*Bootham Bar* (i.e. gate) which could be where the head of 19-year-old Thomas Mowbray, Earl of Nottingham was displayed on a spike, while Nunnery Lane reminds us of his place of execution.

*Micklegate Bar* is where the heads of Richard of York and his young son were impaled after the Battle of Wakefield.

*Bishopthorpe Palace*, two miles outside the city: the official residence of the Archbishop of York. More the size of a manageable mansion than a palace, it is very attractive and very much a home. Included in the tour is the room where Thomas Mowbray, Earl of Nottingham, and Archbishop Scrope were tried and condemned. The palace is open to groups by appointment only.

The Yorkshire religious houses founded or aided by the Mowbrays include*Byland, Fountains, Rievaulx, and Newburgh Abbeys* and *St Mary's Abbey* in York.
*Mount Grace Priory:* has the best remains of any medieval Carthusian House in Europe as well as a reconstruction of a monk's cell and, although not associated with the Mowbrays, it does give some idea of what the priory at Low Melwood was like before the Dissolution.

*Harewood House* near Leeds has within its grounds All Saints Church which houses the Gascoigne tombs, including that of Sir William Gascoigne and his wife Elizabeth Mowbray of the Kirklington branch of the Mowbray family. Gascoigne tried the younger Thomas Mowbray in 1404 and purportedly refused to sign the death warrant of archbishop Scrope,

*Kirklington's* St Michael's church has a fine tomb of Sir Alexander de Mowbray holding a shield bearing a superb Mowbray lion.

*Pontefract and Tickhill:* there are still substantial ruins of the royal castles in these towns.

### NORFOLK

*Thetford Priory:* when the priory became a victim of the Dissolution the then Duke of Norfolk (Howard) moved and reburied his father and grandfather but this was a very expensive undertaking and the Mowbrays, including the 3$^{rd}$ Duke and his wife Eleanor, were left behind; the superstructures of their tombs are gone but their remains could still lie buried in the priory ruins.

*Drayton & Hellesdon:* the two manors left to John Paston by Sir John Fastolf are now suburbs of the city of Norwich.

*Caister Castle:* ruins of the retirement castle built by Sir John Fastolf that caused so much bad blood between the Mowbrays and the Pastons.

## SUFFOLK

*Framlingham Castle:* the castle, which came to the Mowbray family through Elizabeth Segrave, is a magnificent sight from the outside with its 13 towers and gives the impression of being complete; sadly it is no more than a shell, but nevertheless still worth a visit. There are some magnificent Howard tombs in the nearby St Michael's Church, some moved from Thetford at the Dissolution, as well as that of Henry Fitzroy, illegitimate son of Henry VIII and Elizabeth Blount, who before his untimely death was married briefly to a Howard daughter. Unfortunately, the Howard dukes did not go to the trouble and expense of removing the remains of their various Mowbray ancestors from abbeys and monasteries throughout the land before the buildings were sold off.

*Letheringham Church:* tombs and other associations with the Wingfield family, including fine brasses.

*Long Melford Church:* has a beautiful stained glass window featuring a Mowbray lion and the Duchess of Norfolk Elizabeth Talbot, mother of Anne Mowbray, and Elizabeth Tilney, Countess of Surrey, grandmother of Anne Boleyn and Kathryn Howard, and great-grandmother of Queen Elizabeth I.

## NOTTINGHAMSHIRE

*Hoveringham,* near Southwell: the Church of Saint Michael and All Angels houses the tomb of Elizabeth Fitzalan and Sir Robert Goushill. Unfortunately, the medieval church was demolished and rebuilt by the Victorians and, although the new church is very pleasant and beautifully kept, the Victorian architects could have afforded the tomb greater consideration instead of squashing Elizabeth against a wall and under a brick arch. Having said that, it was very touching to see their last resting place still more or less intact when the rest of the Mowbray tombs have been lost.
Sir Robert's effigy has the face and figure of an older man, while his wife, who outlived him by more than twenty years, is represented as being more youthful and slender. Both effigies are badly damaged but it is fortunate that so much

remains. A visit is recommended and the field behind the church where Sir Robert's home once stood is a lovely unspoilt corner of England – and long may it remain so. The church has to be kept locked, so an appointment with the Churchwarden is necessary.

## NORTHUMBERLAND

**Tynemouth Priory and Castle:** Robert de Mowbray's castle on the coast guarded the mouth of the River Tyne in the days when he was the haughty and mighty Earl of Northumberland. He founded the priory, located within his castle walls for protection against the Scots, as a dependency of St Albans in 1085, much to the annoyance of the bishop of Durham. The forces of William II dragged him injured out of the priory, where he had sought sanctuary, and took him to Bamburgh.

**Bamburgh Castle:** majestically perched on the volcanic outcrop called the Great Whin Sill and looking out across the North Sea, Bamburgh Castle on the Northumbrian coast has to be one of the world's most spectacular buildings, at least from the outside. Although no doubt changed since Robert de Mowbray was threatened with blinding outside its great walls unless his young wife surrendered the castle, Bamburgh in its incredible setting is always a memorable sight at any time of year, especially from the beach.(Of the two northern castles particularly associated with various Mowbrays during their service against the Scots, the keep at *Carlisle* in Cumbria is in good condition and has carvings on the walls probably done by members of the garrisons trying to while away the boredom of long hours of inactivity. *Berwick Castle,* on the other hand, is no more and its site has given way to a railway station built with some of its stones.)

## LONDON

**The British Library:** hundreds of documents associated with the Mowbrays and their contemporaries including accounts of grants to religious foundations, and household accounts of various Mowbrays and their acquaintances such as Sir John Fastolf. Also of enormous interest is the account book of John Howard (later Duke of Norfolk) from 1462-1469, with his own jottings in the margins, found in a little room in Framlingham Castle, May 1724; a delight to hold.

*Magna Carta:* two of the four remaining originals of 1215 are to be found here.

*The Bible of Thomas of Woodstock:* the earliest datable manuscript (London pre-1397) of the first complete translation of the bible into English, it is an early version of the Wycliffe Bible, John Wycliffe being the founder of the Lollard movement. It was a risky thing to own at the time.

*Thomas Hoccleve, The Regimen of Princes,* c. 1413: a long poem offering advice to the young Prince of Wales (Henry V), who is shown with a young man variously said to be Hoccleve himself or John Mowbray, 2nd Duke of Norfolk, for whom it was made. Inside an illuminated letter underneath the picture there is the Mowbray lion.

*Jean Froissart, Chronicles:* Wonderful accounts and illustrations, but Froissart needs to be taken with a large pinch of salt. There are depictions of Thomas Mowbray and Bolingbroke, sometimes wearing the fashions that so scandalised Peter Idley for being 'cutted on the buttock' to incite the ladies to lecherous desires. (The Bibliotheque Nationale in Paris has a superb copy of Froissart executed by a very skilled artist and includes a lively scene of Thomas of Woodstock being strangled while in Mowbray's custody.)

*The Hastings Hours:* beautiful illuminated book that belonged to the Lord Hastings beheaded without trial by Richard III at about the same time that the young Princes were in the Tower.

*Some of the Paston Letters.*

**The British Museum Medieval Galleries:** everything from the Dunstable swan, reminiscent of the bird on the Mowbray Stone, to fragments of wall paintings from St Stephen's Chapel in the old Palace of Westminster, where five-year-old Lady Anne Mowbray and four-year-old Prince Richard were married in 1478.

*National Archives:* the Historic Manuscripts Commission has now relocated to Kew where, together with the former Public Record Office, it forms the National Archives.

**The Tower of London:** William the Conqueror's awe-inspiring keep still stands proud surrounded by walls and other buildings erected by his descendants, but sadly the whole complex is smothered by some rather unlovely 20th century concoctions nearby. John of Mowbray Deed fame and his mother Alina were imprisoned here by Edward II.

*Tower Hill:* plaques on the site of the scaffold record that Sir Simon Burley, Richard Fitzalan, and some of the Howards bade the world farewell at this spot. Although the Dissolution of the Monasteries in the 1530's and the Great Fire of 1666 destroyed many of the old religious buildings, some of the old street names remain, such as Bread Street off Cheapside, where Richard Fitzalan was buried in the church of the Augustine Friars.

*Smithfield:* a plaque on the side of Bart's Hospital reminds us that Sir William Wallace, the Scottish rebel, was put to death on a piece of land adjoining a hospital and a church.

***The Palace of Westminster:*** the present Houses of Parliament, erected on the site of the old palace where the earliest Parliaments met, was built in the 19th century Victorian Gothic style after fire destroyed what was left of the original. Of the St Stephen's Chapel where the Lady Anne married the little Duke of York, only the crypt remains, which is still used as a church.

***Westminster Abbey:*** Edward the confessor's Abbey of St Peter has been altered beyond all recognition over the centuries and is now only a shadow of is former self, most of the domestic buildings having been destroyed at the Dissolution or in the Reformation. However, the Abbey church itself was spared by Henry VIII, who could hardly allow wholesale desecration of the tombs of his ancestors, including that of his parents Henry Tudor and Elizabeth of York, so we have here the burial place of some of the monarchs whom the Mowbrays served. It is ironic that for all their striving none of the Mowbray males achieved a position worthy of interment in this last resting place of kings; instead, their once-great name is represented here by the lowly remains of a child, the Lady Anne, Duchess of York and Norfolk.

***Victoria and Albert Museum,*** Cast Courts: casts of the tombs of the Angevins Henry II and Eleanor of Aquitaine and their son Richard I from the French abbey of Fontevrault. King John was buried at Worcester but there is a cast of his tomb effigy here.

***Broken Wharf:*** close to the Millennium Bridge lie Lep House, an office block, and Norfolk House a small block of flats overlooking the Thames, both constructed in the 1980's. Bigod House at Broken Wharf dated from the late 12th century and came to the Mowbrays through Margaret of Brotherton; it was here her great-grandson John Mowbray convalesced after being invalided home from France in 1415. The Broken Wharf itself survived as a barge dock until 1974 and the lane on the east side of the site of the old Mowbray property still goes by that name, but the house itself was razed to the ground by the Great Fire of September 1666; Norfolk House and part of Lep House now occupy the site.

***St Clare Street*** off the Minories, Tower Hamlets: nothing remains of the convent of St Clare where Anne Mowbray's mother ended her life in relative poverty and where Anne's remains were found in 1964. It is a true concrete jungle and one has to hope that if the remains of Elizabeth Talbot and Anne Boleyn's grandmother Elizabeth Tilney are still in the vicinity, they lie beneath one of the very few remaining patches of grass.

### SUSSEX

***Arundel Castle:*** the keep was begun by William d'Albini (d'Aubigny) *Stronghand*, husband of Adeliza of Louvain. In time it became the childhood home of Elizabeth Fitzalan, who married Thomas Mowbray there in 1384; it is now the principal residence of the Fitzalan-Howard Dukes of Norfolk.

*Bramber Castle:* a few miles from Arundel, this castle, now in ruins, was brought into the Mowbray family by Alina de Braose, daughter of the Lord of Bramber and Gower.

*WALES*

*Chepstow Castle:* spectacular ruins of a great castle that came to the Mowbrays through the marriage with Thomas de Brotherton's granddaughter, Elizabeth Segrave.

*Swansea Museum* (Archaeology Gallery, case 22): a carving of a female head thought to be that of Alina de Braose, mother of John, 3rd Lord Mowbray; part of a mullion window of about 1330 from St Mary's Church.

There are some substantial and picturesque ruins of the Braose family castles in Gower that came into Mowbray possession through marriage but that fell into decay through absenteeism:

*Oystermouth Castle*, Mumbles.

*Pennard Castle.*

*Swansea Castle:* now incorporated into modern buildings and surrounded by high-rise developments.

# Sources And Bibliography

ANONYMOUS, (possibly by John Hamilton, Congregational minister at Crowle in the Isle of Axholme, from 1870 to 1878), *The Manuscript in a Red Box*; originally published by the Bodley Head in 1903 and more recently by the Isle of Axholme Family History Society, 1999. Engaging romantic novel about the drainage of the Isle of Axholme in the seventeenth century and the loss of the Commoners' rights they cherished under the Mowbray Deed. The manuscript appeared on the Bodley Head's London doorstep and the identity of the author remains a mystery.

ARCHER, Rowena E., 'Rich Old Ladies: the problem of the late Medieval Dowager'; in *Property and Politics: Essays in Later Medieval History*, ed. Tony Pollard, Alan Sutton 1984.

ARUNDEL CASTLE ARCHIVES
Arundel Castle Library; A.C. MSS. MD 1499; contemporary copy of the pre-nuptial settlement (specifies the estates) on the marriage of Anne Mowbray and the Duke of York. Separate pages stitched together as 1 roll. Many other Mowbray references and documents and copies of wills, including that of Thomas Fitzalan who died in 1415.

ARVANIGIAN, Mark & LEOPOLD, Antony, *Illustrative Documents* (essay in *The Battle of Neville's Cross 1346*) Shaun Tyas 1998.

BANKS, Charles Edward, *The Winthrop Fleet of 1630 – An Account of the Vessels, the Voyage, the Passengers and Their English Homes, from Original Authorities*; first published 1930, reprinted 2003 Genealogical Publishing Company Inc., Baltimore. List of and information on the 700 passengers believed to have sailed from England with John Winthrop in 1630.

BARKER, Juliet, *Agincourt: the king, the campaign, the battle*; Little, Brown, 2005.

BERKELEY CASTLE MUNIMENTS AND THE GLOUCESTER RECORDS OFFICE. Information on the Mowbray affairs in general. They are also available for search Online through the National Archives, see below.

BLACK, WH, ed. *Illustrations of Ancient State and Chivalry from manuscripts Preserved in the Ashmolean Museum* (Roxburgh Club, 1840) printed in London by Wm. Nichol, (describes Anne Mowbray's wedding).

*Biographical Register of the University of Oxford to A.D. 1500, Volume II*, Oxford, at the Clarendon Press, 1958.

BOARDMAN, A.W., *The Battle of Towton*, Alan Sutton 1994.

BRITISH LIBRARY, Account Books of Robert Southwell Receiver – general to John Mowbray Earl Marshal (2nd Duke of Norfolk). BL Add. Charts 16555 and 17209.

BRYANT, Arthur, *Makers of the Realm*, Collins 1953.

BRYANT, Arthur, *The Age of Chivalry*, Collins 1963.

BURKE, Sir Bernard, *A Genealogical History of the Dormant, Abeyant, Forfeited and Extinct Peerages of the British Empire*, 1883 (reprinted 1962).

BURKE'S GENEALOGY PUBLICATIONS, *Burke's Peerage &*

*Baronetage*, 106th edn. 1999, Vol. II.

BURTON, Janet, 'Fundator Noster: Roger de Mowbray as Founder and Patron of Monasteries', in *Religious and Laity in Western Europe 1000 -1400,* Brepols publishers, 2007.

*Case on Behalf of the Right Honourable Charles Joseph Botolph Stourton, Lord Mowbray, senior co-heir to the earldom of Norfolk in the peerage of England*, Billing & Sons 1901.

*Revised Case on Behalf of the Most Noble Henry, Duke of Norfolk, in Opposition to the Petition of Charles Joseph Botolph Stourton, Lord Mowbray*, Few & Co. 1903.

CASTLEDEAN, Rodney, *Harrap's Book of British Dates*, Harrap 1991. Very useful for putting people and events into context at a glance.

CHEYNEY, C.R. (ed.), *Cheyney's Handbook of Dates for Students of English History*, Cambridge University Press 1995.

CHRONICLES, see individually below:
Henry of Huntingdon
John of Hexham:  see Stevenson
Jordan  Fantosme
Jean Froissart
'The Monk of Malmesbury', see Denholm-Young
Roger of Hoveden (or Howden)
Roger of Wendover
Simeon of Durham
Orderic Vitalis , see Douglas
William of Newburgh, see Gillingham
William of Tyre

CLARKE, Sir George (ed.), *Oxford History of England.*

CLAY, John William FSA, Vice President of the Yorkshire Archaeological Society, *The Extinct and Dormant Peerages of the Northern Counties of England*, pub.1913 James Nisbet & Co. Ltd.

COKAYNE, G.E., *Complete Peerage of England, Scotland, Ireland, Great Britain and the United Kingdom,* 13 volumes published between 1910 - 59, revised by Vicary Gibbs, H.A. Doubleday, Duncan Warrand and Lord Howard de Walden. Copious references. Most volumes have been used at some stage, but in particular:

Vol. I
Preface to Vol. I for details of the 1283 Assembly at Salisbury
pp. 230-260 – *Arundel* (d'Aubigny, or d'Albini, and later Fitzalan)
Vol. II
pp. 118-149 – *Berkeley*
pp. 364-373 – *Buccleuch*
Vol. V
pp. 309-363 – *Ferrers*
pp. 391-392 – *Fitzalan* (barony of Oswestry)
Vol. VI
p. 42 – *Goushill*
pp. 151-188 – *Grey*

pp.457-477 – *Hereford (de Bohun)*
pp. 583-593 – *Howard*
Vol. VII
pp. 378 - 398 – *Lancaster*
Vol. IX
pp. 366-387 – *Mowbray* (includes some of the d'Aubigny family)
pp. 600-615 – *Norfolk* (the Mowbray & Howard dukes)
pp. 701-706 – *Northumberland* (Robert de Mowbray)
Vol. XII, Part I,
pp. 515-520 – *Sussex*
Vol. XII
pp. *436-488 – de Welles*
pp. 739 – *Wiltshire* (i.e. Boleyn, see also Ormonde, Vol. X)
Various *Complete Peerage* appendices:
Vol. II
C/ *The Battle of Boroughbridge*
D/ *The Great Offices of State*
Vol.III
A/ *The Surrender of Peerages in England*
Vol. IV
H/ *Earldoms and Baronies in History and in Law, and the Doctrine of Abeyance*
Vol. V
F/ *Peerage Titles Assumed By Peers*
Vol.VI
A/ *The Use of 'De' in Titles*
E/ *The Claim to the Earldom of Norfolk*
Vol. VII
C/ *The Barony of Berkeley*
Vol IX
G/ *Some observations on the Mowbray and Segrave Case of 1877*
Vol. X
G/ *The Rise of the Marshal*
Vol. XI
B/ *The Battle of Bannock Burn*
Vol. XII Part I
A/ *Baronies By Writ*
(*The Complete Peerage* is an invaluable resource with exhaustive footnotes and further references; family members are dealt with in chronological order; a good starting point for research.)

COPPACK, Glyn, *Mount Grace Priory*, English Heritage.

CRAWFORD, A., 'The Mowbray Inheritance', in *The Ricardian* (journal of the Richard III Society), June 1981.

DENHOLM-YOUNG, Noel, trans., '*The Monk of Malmesbury', The Life of Edward II*, Thomas Nelson & Sons 1957.

*Dictionary of National Biography (DNB),* and references therein. Detailed, but confusing for someone just beginning research as the entries within a family are in alphabetical order of forename and not in chronological order. Revised 2004 as ODNB (Oxford), with different format.

DIXON, Marie C,. *John de Coupland – Hero to Villain* (essay in *The Battle of Neville's Cross 1346*) Shaun Tyas 1998.

DOUGLAS, David C., ed., *English Historical Documents*, Vols. 2-4, Eyre & Spottiswoode, revised 1968. Includes extracts from the great medieval chroniclers; the Hastings account by Orderic Vitalis from his *Historia Ecclesiastica* appears in chapter 7 and there is information about translations of Orderic's work.

DRAKE, Francis, *Eboracum, or the History and Antiquities of the City of York*, originally printed in London for the author in 1736; reprinted EP Publishing, Wakefield 1978.

DUGDALE, Sir William: *Monasticon Anglicanum*, revised 1717. A beautiful old book worth reading for its own sake; details of Byland Abbey and of the Carthusian House founded by Thomas Mowbray in 1397.

EVANS, Joan ed., *The Flowering of the Middle Ages*, Thames and Hudson 1998.

FOX-DAVIES, Arthur Charles, *A Complete Guide to Heraldry*, T.C & E.C. Jack, London 1909

FROISSART, Jean, *Chronicles*, ed. and translated by Geoffrey Brereton, Penguin Books 1968.

FUNK & WAGNALL (publishers), *The Presidents*, New York, 1999. This is used by Brian Tompsett of Hull University on his *Royal Genealogy* website, see below, and helps, in some cases, to bridge the gap between the Mowbrays and later eminent persons via the Howard and Berkeley families.

GAIRDNER, James, ed., *The Paston Letters, 1422-1509 A.D. (A reprint of the edition of 1872-75 which contained upwards of Five Hundred letters, etc., till then unpublished, to which are now added others in a Supplement after the Introduction.)* pub. in Edinburgh by John Grant 1910.

GARNER, Stephen R., *A Topographical Study of the Wetlands of Axholme*, 1997.

GILLINGHAM, John, 'Two Yorkshire Historians Compared: Roger of Howden & William of Newburgh', *Haskins Society Journal 12*, 2003

GILYARD-BEER, R, 'Byland Abbey and the Grave of Roger de Mowbray', in *Yorkshire Archaeological Journal 55*, 1983

GREEN, R., *The History, Topography and Antiquities of Framlingham and Saxted*, 1834.

GREENWAY, Diana, *Charters of the Honour of Mowbray*, Oxford University Press 1972. Exhaustive research into the holdings and charters of Nigel d'Aubigny and his son, the first Roger de Mowbray.

HALLAM, Elizabeth, ed., *Chronicles of the Wars of the Roses*, Weidenfeld & Nicholson 1988.

HALLAM, Elizabeth, ed., The *Plantagenet Encyclopedia*, Crescent Books 1996.

HAWES, R. & LODDER, R., *History of Framlingham*, 1798.

HAYFIELD, Colin, 'Excavations on the Site of the Mowbray Manor House at the Vinegarth, Epworth, Lincolnshire, 1975-1976', *Lincolnshire History and Archaeology, Vol. 19*, 1984.

HENRY of HUNTINGDON, *Chronicle*, ed. & tr. Thomas Forester, London 1853

HICKLING, Douglas, *Which John de Mowbray was the Brother of Christiana de Plumpton?* At www.medievalgenealogy.org.uk

HILLS, Peter J., *The Priory of the Wood. An outline history of the Carthusian priory of the Blessed Virgin Mary, situated at Melwood, within the parish of St Martin, Owston Ferry, within the Isle of Axholme*; pub. 1961. Informative booklet giving the background to the founding of the Carthusian House by Thomas Mowbray, 1st Duke of Norfolk.

HMSO (Aspects of Britain series) *Honours and Titles,* 1992. A handy little book; concise and very readable.

HOPKINS, Andrea, *Most Wise and Valiant Ladies*, Collins & Brown 1997. Has a chapter on the Paston family and how Margaret Paston tried to defend their properties against the Mowbrays.

HUNTING, PENELOPE, *St Paul's Vista – A history commissioned by Lep Group plc to mark the redevelopment of the Sunlight Wharf site*, 1988.

JORDAN FANTOSME, *Chronicle of the War between the English and the Scots in 1173 and 1174*: with translations, etc. by Francisque Michel, 1840.

KIRBY, John L, 'An Account of Robert Southwell , receiver-general of John Mowbray, earl marshal, 1422-3', in *Bulletin of the Institute of Historical Research, 27,* 1954.

KNIGHT, Charles Brunton, *History of the City of York*, 1st edition 1944.

LANGLAND, William, *Piers Plowman* (translated by A.V.C. Schmidt) Oxford University Press, 1992.

Le PATOUREL, John, Geoffrey of Montbray, Bishop of Coutances, in *English Historical Review*, May 1944, pp 129-161.

MECHANICS' INSTITUTE, EPWORTH, library full of local interest including the classic reference books Peck, Stonehouse, etc.; also archive of the local newspapers *Epworth Bells* and *The Axholme Herald.*

MOLLESON, Theya, Anne Mowbray and the Princes in the Tower: a Study in Identity, in *The London Archaeologist,* Vol. 5 no. 10, 1987.

MOYE, Lucy Ellen, *The Estates and Finances of the Mowbray Family, Earls Marshal and Dukes of Norfolk, 1401-1476*, Ph.D thesis, Duke University 1985; can be found in Norwich Library.

MUSEUM OF LONDON Archaeological Archive and Research Centre (LAARC), Anne Mowbray Archive (ref: AMS 64)

NATIONAL ARCHIVES
References to the Mowbrays scattered throughout:
*Calendars of Close Rolls*
*Calendars of Fine Rolls*
*Calendars of Inquisitions Post Mortem*
*Calendars of Patent Rolls*
*Calendar of State papers Relating to English Affairs in the Archives of Venice*

The National Archives Online Catalogue also itemises the contents of the records of the Berkeley Castle Muniments; of especial interest:

The Mowbray Inheritance – ref.BCM/D/1
The Beauchamp Inheritance - ref.BCM/D/2
The Breouse (Braose) Inheritance - ref.BCM/D/3
The Arundel Inheritance - ref.BCM/D/4
The Segrave Inheritance -ref.BCM/D/5
The Chaucombe Inheritance -ref.BCM/D/6
The Brotherton Inheritance -ref.BCM/D/7

NORTH LINCOLNSHIRE MUSEUM, Scunthorpe, Sites & Monument Record (SMR) 2471 which contains various documents relating to Thomas Mowbray's Carthusian monastery; also SMR 2447, relating to the excavations and history of the Vinegarth at Epworth.

OBSERVER COLOUR MAGAZINE 23 May 1965, *The World of Anne Mowbray*; also *The Observer* for 2 January 1966 has a report giving photographs and information on the examination of the remains.

ORDNANCE SURVEY MAP of 1824 shows the village now known as Owston Ferry was still called Kinard's Ferry.

OWEN, Dorothy M, *Church and Society in Medieval Lincolnshire;* Lincoln Local History Society, 1971. Refers to religious foundations associated with the Mowbrays.

PECK, W. *Topographical Account of the Isle of Axholme Being in the Western Division of the Wapentake of Manley in the County of Lincoln*, 1815; has a copy of William Riley's 1652 translation of the Mowbray Deed.

PLANCHÉ, J.R., (Somerset Herald at the College of Arms) *The Conqueror and His Companions*, London, Tinsley Brothers, 1874.

PRYME, Abraham de la, *The Diary of Abraham de la Pryme*, ed. Charles Jackson, Surtees Society, Durham 1870. Pryme gives a description of the mansion built from the stones of the Carthusian monastery at Low Melwood as he remembered it had been in his youth.

PUREY CUST, Very Revd A.P., Dean of York, *The Heraldry of York Minster*, Vol. 1, 1890.

READ (FLETCHER, Thomas C. ed.), *History of the Isle of Axholme, its Manors and Parishes, with biographical notes of Eminent Men*, Epworth 1858. Some caution is necessary as this volume relies heavily on its predecessor, see Stonehouse, below.

REEVES, Compton, *Pleasures and Pastimes in Medieval England*, Alan Sutton, 1995.

ROBERTS, Gary Boyd, *The Royal Descents of 500 Immigrants to the American Colonies or the United States*, Genealogical Publishing Company, Baltimore 1993. The *Royal Descents* is a useful reference book in that it contains a list of over 500 named colonists and their relatives. Probably best used in conjunction with *Complete Peerage* and the books of F.L. Weis (see below), both of which enable a reader to begin building up information on a family.

ROBERTS, Marilyn, *The Bare Bones of British Royal Family Trees*, Queens-Haven Publications, revised 2012. Shows how descendants of some of the great medieval families are still prominent today.

ROBERTS, Marilyn, *The High and Excellent Princess*, Queens-Haven Publications 2012.

ROBERTS, Marilyn, *Trouble in Paradise: Queen Katherine Howard, the Dowager Duchess and Norfolk House, Lambeth.* Queens-Haven Publications 2012.

ROBINSON, John Martin, 'As Old as the Hills', article in *Country Life* 22nd April 2004. A survey showing the Berkeleys to be the oldest landed family; also refers to descent through the female line and gives examples of husbands legally changing their names in order to save a great family's name from becoming extinct.

ROGER DE HOVEDEN, *The Annals of Roger de Hoveden,* tr. H.T. Riley, London 1853 vol. II

ROGER OF WENDOVER, *Flowers of History,* tr. G.A. Giles, London, 1849

ROLLASON, David, & PRESTWICH, Michael (eds.), *The Battle of Neville's Cross 1346,* Shaun Tyas 1998.

ROUND, J. Horace, M.A., Ll.D, *Peerage & Pedigree: Studies in Peerage Law and Family History,* Vol. One, James Nesbit & Co. Ltd. at the St Catherine Press, London 1910. Useful for the Mowbray/Segrave Case of 1877 and for Fitzalan family information.

ROWSE, A.L., *Bosworth Field and the Wars of the Roses*, Macmillan, 1966.

SANFORD, J. and TOWNSEND, M., *Great Governing Families of England*, Vol. II, 1865.

SAYER, Michael, Norfolk Involvement in Dynastic conflict 1469-1471 and 1483-1487, *Norfolk Archaeology*, Vol. 36 Part IV.

SETON, Anya, *Katherine,* Hodder & Stoughton 1954. Now recognised as a classic of its type, this great romantic novel tells the story of Katherine Swynford and John of Gaunt and includes many of the fourteenth-century figures featured in this book, although the Mowbrays themselves are mentioned only fleetingly.

SEYMOUR, William, *Battles in Britain 1066-1746*, Wordsworth Military Library 1997. Includes plans of battlefields and photographs of what the sites are like today.

SHAKESPEARE BIRTHPLACE TRUST RECORDS OFFICE, Stratford-upon-Avon: the library holds documents relating to the Mowbrays holdings in Warwickshire, including some bearing well-preserved seals of the first Roger de Mowbray (deeds deposited by Colonel A. Gregory-Hood).

SHAKESPEARE, William, *King Richard the Second;* includes the feud between Thomas Mowbray, Duke of Norfolk, and Henry Bolingbroke.

SHAKESPEARE, William, *The Second Part of King Henry the Fourth;* features Thomas Mowbray, Earl of Nottingham and Archbishop Scrope in their rebellion against the King.

SHAKESPEARE, William, *King Richard the Third.*

SLOCOMBE, George, *Sons of the Conqueror*, Hutchinson, 1960

STEVENSON, Joseph, *The Church Historians of England: Chronicles of John and Richard of Hexham; Chronicle of Holyrood; Chronicle of Melrose*

STONEHOUSE, Rev. W. B., *History and Topography of the Isle of Axholme, being that Part of*

*Lincolnshire which is West of Trent*, London 1839. Invaluable, but has errors concerning the Mowbray Deed, and the Mowbray pedigree chart. The date of the Deed was 1359, the time of the 3rd Lord Mowbray, but Stonehouse on his pedigree chart and in the text attributes it to the 4th Lord. Also an error of a hundred years in the date of the letter sent from Epworth by Duchess Katherine to John Paston.

SUNDAY TIMES, *Richest of the Rich – The Wealthiest 200 in Britain Since 1066,* March 2000 supplement, Times Newspapers.

*THE TIMES* of January 4th 1928 ran an article on the Haxey Hood game, and linked the Mowbray lion in Haxey village to Elizabeth Fitzalan.

*TESTAMENTA VETUSTA*: being illustrations from wills, of manners, customs, &c. as well as of the descents and possessions of many distinguished families. From the reign of Henry the Second to the accession of Queen Elizabeth, Volume I (available as Google eBook. Includes the wills of some of the Mowbray dukes and duchesses and their contemporaries.)

TOMLINSON, Edward Murray MA, *A History of The Minories, London,* Smith, Elder & Co, London, 1907.

TOMLINSON, John, *The Level of Hatfield Chace and Parts Adjacent*, first published in 1882; limited edition (100 copies) published by Epworth Mechanics' Institute, 1980. A very good quality publication with several useful appendices, including the Mowbray Deed and the legal documents drawn up between Charles I and Sir Cornelius Vermuden with regard to the draining of the Isle of Axholme, and also the Declarations of Daniel Noddel, solicitor for the tenants.

UNIVERSITY OF NOTTINGHAM Special Collections: Hatfield Chase Corporation 1538-1973. The Stovin MS (HCC 9111) is an eighteenth century copy of an earlier copy of the Mowbray Deed of 1359.

VAN LENMAN, Hans, *Medieval Tiles*, Shire Books 2000

WARREN, W.L., *King John*, Eyre & Spottiswode 1961.

WARWICK, Roger, Anne Mowbray: skeletal remains of a medieval child, *in The London Archaeologist* Vol. 5, No. 7, Summer 1986.

WEA, East Midlands District, & Louth Literary Society, 1996, *The Lincolnshire Rising 1536*. The local reaction to the Dissolution of the Monasteries and the fate of the Prior of Axholme Augustine Webster, and of the Dymoke family, who, through marriage with the Mowbrays, were ancestors of George Washington.

WEIR, Alison, *The Princes in the Tower*, Random House 1992.

WEIR, Yvonne E., *A Guide to the Heraldry in York Minster*, Dean and Chapter of York 1986.

WEIS, Frederick Lewis, *The Magna Charta Sureties, 1215*; *The Barons Named in the Magna Charta, 1215 and Some of Their Descendants Who Settled in America in the Early Colonial Years*, 5th edition 1999; Genealogical Publishing Co., Baltimore. At first glance I thought this fairly slim volume consisting of lists of generations would not be very helpful; happily, I was wrong. Excellent thumbnail sketches & very liberal with dates, which helps considerably in cross-referencing, but only as far as the eighteenth century. Contains 50 years of research and revision.

WILLIAM OF TYRE, *A History of Deeds Done Beyond the Sea*, tr. Emily A. Babcock and A.C. Krey, (New York: Columbia University Press, 1943).


INTERNET:
Although a wonderful tool for research, the utmost care is necessary when using the Internet, and facts and figures should always be checked against an established source such as *Complete Peerage*. There is an awful lot of careless and misleading rubbish online as far as royal and noble genealogy is concerned. However, some academic and other reputable sites are very useful and can provide a lead into further document-based research.

Brian Tompsett's website *Royal Genealogical Data* at Hull University Department of Computer Science is well-respected and very useful for checking information against, although Brian freely admits there could be some errors.

www.medievalgenealogy.org.uk run by Chris Phillips; through this site all manner of information can be accessed.

Further information on the Mowbrays, including photographs, may be found at the author's own site www.queens-haven.co.uk

# Queens-Haven Publications
### Two new Mowbray/Howard titles

The original purpose of the latest research was to trace the Mowbray/ Howard London properties – Broken Wharf near St Paul's and Norfolk House in Lambeth – of which nothing now remains above ground, but, as is often the case, things did not go quite to plan, and it was the people who had been associated with them that came to the fore instead.

## *The High and Excellent Princess*
### Lady Anne Mowbray, the five-year-old bride
### of a Prince in the Tower

Lady Anne Mowbray married the younger son of Edward IV when she was five and he four years old. Neither child was destined to make old bones – although for very different reasons. On Friday 11th December 1964, at about 2.40 in the afternoon, in Stepney, an area of the East End of London situated north of the Tower, contractors clearing a building site behind St Clare Street broke through a wall and discovered an underground chamber. There, in a brick-lined vault 11 feet below street level, they discovered what curious office workers running downstairs into the street for a better view were soon dubbing 'the mummy'. It was no such thing of course: they had come upon the body of a very special little girl, encased in lead, which had lain undisturbed for over 450 years two miles away from its original interment in Westminster Abbey.

## *Trouble in Paradise*
### Queen Katherine Howard, the Dowager Duchess
### and Norfolk House, Lambeth

Norfolk House was situated on what is now busy Lambeth Road, south of the Thames and almost opposite Westminster Palace. Obviously it has been built-over for hundreds of years, but excavations carried out in 1988 and 1990 have given us at least some idea of what Katherine Howard's step-grandmother's home was like when, in the spring of 1540, the besotted Henry VIII came to call on the 'rose without a thorn'. Nowadays Lambeth in general is not the most tranquil of places, and it is difficult to imagine that there was once a grand Tudor mansion here where the carefree young Katherine strolled with her paramours in its acres of gardens and orchards, now home to blocks of flats, a Novotel Hotel, the headquarters of the Royal Pharmaceutical Society of Great Britain, a multi-storey car park and Costa Coffee's roasting works.

Queens-Haven Publications
info@queens-haven.co.uk
www.queens-haven.co.uk